Teaching Science in Secondary Schools

The Open University *Flexible* Postgraduate Certificate in Education

The readers and the companion volumes in the *flexible* PGCE series are:

Aspects of Teaching and Learning in Secondary Schools: Perspectives on practice

Teaching, Learning and the Curriculum in Secondary Schools: A reader

Aspects of Teaching Secondary Mathematics: Perspectives on practice

Teaching Mathematics in Secondary Schools: A reader

Aspects of Teaching Secondary Science: Perspectives on practice

Teaching Science in Secondary Schools: A reader

Aspects of Teaching Secondary Modern Foreign Languages: Perspectives on practice

Teaching Modern Foreign Languages in Secondary Schools: A reader

Aspects of Teaching Secondary Geography: Perspectives on practice

Teaching Geography in Secondary Schools: A reader

Aspects of Teaching Secondary Design and Technology: Perspectives on practice

Teaching Design and Technology in Secondary Schools: A reader

Aspects of Teaching Secondary Music: Perspectives on practice

Teaching Music in Secondary Schools: A reader

All of these subjects are part of the Open University's initial teacher education course, the *flexible* PGCE, and constitute part of an integrated course designed to develop critical understanding. The set books, reflecting a wide range of perspectives, and discussing the complex issues that surround teaching and learning in the twenty-first century, will appeal to both beginning and experienced teachers, to mentors, tutors, advisers and other teacher educators.

If you would like to receive a *flexible* PGCE prospectus please write to the Course Reservations Centre at The Call Centre, The Open University, Milton Keynes MK7 6ZS. Other information about programmes of professional development in education is available from the same address.

D0682856

Teaching Science in Secondary Schools
A reader

Teaching Science in Secondary Schools: A reader introduces and explores a broad range of contemporary issues and key ideas and will provide a useful background for those teaching and training to teach this core subject.

The book is concerned with exploring the bigger picture of science education. Divided into five sections to help structure reading, it covers:

- The changing nature of science education
- A re-appraisal of practical work
- Science education and research
- Theories of learning, principles of teaching and classroom practice
- The gender perspective
- Children's ideas and understanding
- Vocational approaches
- Multi-cultural and anti-racist science education

The *Teaching in Secondary Schools* series brings together collections of articles by highly experienced educators that focus on the issues surrounding the teaching of National Curriculum subjects. They are invaluable resources for those studying to become teachers, and for newly qualified teachers and more experienced practitioners, particularly those mentoring students and NQTs. The companion volume to this book is *Aspects of Teaching Secondary Science: Perspectives on practice.*

Sandra Amos and **Richard Boohan** are Lecturers in Education at The Open University and have responsibility for the Open University *flexible* PGCE, Science course.

Set book for the Open University *flexible* PGCE, Science course EXS880.

Teaching Science in Secondary Schools
A reader

Sandra Amos and Richard Boohan

London and New York

First published 2002
by RoutledgeFalmer
11 New Fetter Lane, London EC4P 4EE

Simultaneously published in the USA and Canada
by RoutledgeFalmer
29 West 35th Street, New York, NY 10001

RoutledgeFalmer is an imprint of the Taylor & Francis Group

© 2002 Compilation, original and editorial matter,
The Open University

Typeset in Goudy by Bookcraft Ltd, Stroud, Gloucestershire
Printed and bound in Great Britain by Bell & Bain Ltd, Glasgow

British Library Cataloguing in Publication Data
A catalogue record for this book is available from the British Library

Library of Congress Cataloging in Publication Data
A catalog record has been requested

ISBN 0–415–26071–X (pbk)
ISBN 0–415–260–701 (hbk)

Contents

Figures

Tables

Abbreviations

$(SI)^2$	Students' Intuitions and Science Instruction
4S	Society for Social Studies of Science
ASEP	Australian Science Education Project
ATL	Association of Teachers and Lecturers
BCCS	British Columbia Science Surveys
BSCS	Biological Sciences Curriculum Study
CASE	Cognitive Acceleration through Science Education
CBA	Chemical Bond Approach
CHEM	Chemical Education Material
CIA	Chemical Industries Association
CSE	Certificate of Secondary Education
CSTI	The Consortium of Science and Technology Institutes
DES	Department for Education and Science
EASST	European Association for the Study of Science and Technology
EOC	Equal Opportunities Commission
ESG	Education Support Grants
GRIST	Grant-Related In-Service Training
IEA	International Association for the Evaluation of Education Achievement
INSET	In-Service Training
IRR	Institute of Race Relations
NACCCE	National Advisory Committee on Creative and Cultural Education
NAEP	USA National Assessment and Educational Progress
NFER	National Foundation for Educational Research
NGO	Non-governmental organization
PAVOT	Perspective And Voice Of the Teacher
PEEL	Project for Enhancing Effective Learning
PLAN	Projekt for Lärande under eget Ansvar
PSSC	Physical Science Study Committee
SATIS	Science and Technology in Society
SATs	Standard Attainment Tasks
SCISP	Schools' Council Integrated Science Project
SEAC	Schools' Examinations and Assessment Council
SISCON	Science In a Social CONtext

SLIP	Supported Learning in Physics
SMILES	School–Museum Integrated Learning Experiences in Science
SPACE	Science Processes And Concept Exploration
SSCR	School Science Curriculum Review
TGAT	Task Group on Assessment and Testing
UN	United Nations
UNESCO	United Nations Educational, Scientific, and Cultural Organization

Sources

Where a chapter in this book is based on or is a reprint or revision of material previously published elsewhere, details are given below, with grateful acknowledgement to the original publishers. In some cases chapter titles are different to the original title of publication; in such cases the original title is given below.

Chapter 2 This is an edited version of a chapter originally published in Hodson, D. *Teaching and Learning Science*, Open University Press, Buckingham (1998).

Chapter 3 This is an edited version of a chapter originally published in Reiss, M. *Science Education for a Pluralist Society*, Open University Press, Buckingham (1993).

Chapter 4 This is an edited version of a chapter originally published in Wellington, J. (ed.) (1998) *Practical Work in School Science: Which Way Now?*, Routledge, London.

Chapter 5 This is an edited version of a chapter originally published in Peacock, A. *Opportunities for Science in the Primary School*, Trentham Books, Stoke on Trent (1997).

Chapter 6 This is an edited version of an article originally published in *School Science Review* 79(286), Association for Science Education, Hatfield (1997).

Chapter 7 This is an edited version of a chapter originally published in Fensham, P. (ed.) (1988) *Development and Dilemmas in Science Education*, The Falmer Press, Lewes, with additional material.

Chapter 8 This is an edited version of an article originally published in *School Science Review* 73(264), Association for Science Education, Hatfield (1992).

Chapter 9 This was originally published in *School Science Review* 77(280), Association for Science Education, Hatfield (1996).

Chapter 10 This was originally published in Driver, R. *Pupil as Scientist?*, Open University Press, Milton Keynes (1983).

Chapter 11 This was originally published in *School Science Review* 76(277), Association for Science Education, Hatfield (1995).

Chapter 12 This was originally published in Ratcliffe, M. (ed.) (1998) *ASE Guide to Secondary Science Education*, Stanley Thornes Publishers Ltd, Cheltenham.

Chapter 13 This is a substantially abridged version of a chapter originally published as

'Children learning science' in Jennison, B. and Ogborn, J. (eds) (1994) *Wonder and Delight*, Institute of Physics Publishing, Bristol.

Chapter 14 This was originally published in Sutton, C. *Words, Science and Learning*, Open University Press, Milton Keynes (1992).

Chapter 15 This is an edited version of an article originally published as 'Learning science through practical experiences in museums' in the *International Journal of Science Education* 20(6), Carfax Publishing, Taylor & Francis Ltd, London (1998).

Chapter 16 This was originally published in Sear, J. and Sorenson, P. (eds) (2001) *Issues in Science Teaching*, RoutledgeFalmer, London.

Chapter 17 This was originally published in *School Science Review* 80(291), Association for Science Education, Hatfield (1998).

Chapter 18 This is an edited version of an article originally published as 'On the significance of journals in science education: the case of IJSE' in the *International Journal of Science Education* 16(4), Carfax Publishing, Taylor & Francis Ltd, London (1994).

Chapter 19 This is an edited version of an article originally published in the *European Journal of Science Education* 6(2), Taylor & Francis Ltd, London (1984).

Chapter 20 This is an edited version of an article originally published in the *International Journal of Science Education* 20(4), Carfax Publishing, Taylor & Francis Ltd, London (1998).

Chapter 21 This was originally published in the *International Journal of Science Education* 17(6), Carfax Publishing, Taylor & Francis Ltd, London (1995).

Chapter 22 This was originally published in *Studies in Science Education* 31, Studies in Education, Nafferton (1998).

The Editors and Publishers would like to thank the following copyright holders for permission to reproduce these figures.

Figure 2.1 Taken from Hodson, D. (1998) *Teaching and Learning Science: Towards a Personalized Approach*, Buckingham: Open University Press. Originally published as Porter, P.B. (1954) 'Another puzzle picture' in the *American Journal of Psychology*, 67, 550–1, University of Illinois Press.

Figure 3.1 Taken from Reiss, M.J. (1993) *Science Education for a Pluralist Society*, Buckingham: Open University Press. Reproduced by permission of Royal Mail and Giant Limited.

Figure 3.2 Taken from Reiss, M.J. (1993) *Science Education for a Pluralist Society*, Buckingham: Open University Press. Reproduced by permission of Caroline Allen.

Figure 3.3 Taken from Reiss, M.J. (1993) *Science Education for a Pluralist Society*, Buckingham: Open University Press. Reproduced by permission of Chris Madden.

Figure 3.4 Taken from Reiss, M.J. (1993) *Science Education for a Pluralist Society*, Buckingham: Open University Press. Copyrght British Museum.

Foreword

The nature and form of initial teacher education and training are issues that lie at the heart of the teaching profession. They are inextricably linked to the standing and identity that society attributes to teachers and are seen as being one of the main planks in the push to raise standards in schools and to improve the quality of education in them. The initial teacher education curriculum therefore requires careful definition. How can it best contribute to the development of the range of skills, knowledge and understanding that makes up the complex, multi-faceted, multi-skilled and people-centred process of teaching?

There are, of course, external, government-defined requirements for initial teacher training courses. These specify, amongst other things, the length of time a student spends in school, the subject knowledge requirements beginning teachers are expected to demonstrate or the ICT skills that are needed. These requirements, however, do not in themselves constitute the initial training curriculum. They are only one of the many, if sometimes competing, components that make up the broad spectrum of a teacher's professional knowledge that underpin initial teacher education courses.

Certainly today's teachers need to be highly skilled in literacy, numeracy and ICT, in classroom methods and management. In addition, however, they also need to be well grounded in the critical dialogue of teaching. They need to be encouraged to be creative and innovative and to appreciate that teaching is a complex and problematic activity. This is a view of teaching that is shared with partner schools within the Open University Training Schools Network. As such it has informed the planning and development of the Open University's initial teacher training programme and the *flexible* PGCE.

All of the *flexible* PGCE courses have a series of connected and complementary readers. The *Teaching in Secondary Schools* series pulls together a range of new thinking about teaching and learning in particular subjects. Key debates and differing perspectives are presented, and evidence from research and practice is explored, inviting the reader to question the accepted orthodoxy, suggesting ways of enriching the present curriculum and offering new thoughts on classroom learning. These readers are accompanied by the series *Perspectives on practice*. Here, the focus is on the application of these developments to educational/subject policy and the classroom, and on the illustration of teaching skills, knowledge and understanding in a variety of school contexts. Both series include newly commissioned work.

This series from RoutledgeFalmer, in supporting the Open University's *flexible* PGCE, also includes two key texts that explore the wider educational background. These companion publications, *Teaching, Learning and the Curriculum in Secondary Schools: A reader* and *Aspects of Teaching and Learning in Secondary Schools: Perspectives on practice*, explore a contemporary view of developments in secondary education with the aim of providing analysis and insights for those participating in initial teacher training education courses.

Hilary Bourdillon – Director ITT Strategy
Steven Hutchinson – Director ITT Secondary
The Open University
September 2001

Introduction

Over the last few decades, science education has undergone many changes. Much has been done to make science more accessible to a wider range of pupils, to broaden the focus of the curriculum and to develop a more diverse and effective repertoire of teaching strategies. Despite these successes, there is concern that the changes have not gone far enough, and that the science on offer in schools is not appropriate to the needs of pupils today. In selecting the chapters for this book, we have attempted to reflect key issues and ideas in these debates. Questions that are addressed include:

- What are the purposes of studying science?
- What is science itself like and how is it portrayed in the curriculum?
- How has the science curriculum changed and where might it be going?
- What do we know about the way pupils learn science?
- What are the implications that this has for teaching and assessment?
- What kind of research in science education is undertaken?
- How can research be used to inform teaching?

We explore each of these issues briefly in the first chapter of the book, and refer to later chapters in the book where the ideas are discussed more fully. In addition to the introductory chapter, we have also included an introduction to each of the sections which address the nature of science and its place in the curriculum, curriculum innovation, learning science and research in science education. In essence, the book is about what is taught, who is taught, and how research can contribute.

The section 'Science in the curriculum' considers how science is currently reflected in the curriculum. It discusses a widespread concern that the science curriculum is too restricted, depersonalized and insufficiently motivating. It is still dominated by a traditional content which has changed little for decades, and is not serving the needs of pupils in today's society. Having said that, however, science education has changed in many ways. In the section 'Curriculum innovation', some examples of these changes are discussed – primary science, vocational science, social and technological issues, anti-racist and multi-cultural science – as well as some possibilities about where science education may be heading in the future. The section 'Learners' turns its attention from what is taught to who is taught. It emphasizes that pupils are active learners in the classroom, making sense of their experiences and constructing their own meanings. Paying attention to learners as individuals has important consequences for teaching and assessment, and these are explored in this section. Finally, the section 'Research' includes some examples of studies into children's understanding of scientific concepts, a major focus of research in science education, and it considers the significance of research for science teachers.

This book complements the companion volume *Aspects of Teaching Secondary Science: Perspectives on practice*, in which the focus is more directly on teaching in the classroom. In one sense, the issues discussed in this book are more removed from these day-to-day realities; however, teachers' actions in the classroom are greatly influenced by their views on the role of science in the curriculum, by how they think that children learn, and by what they value in education. A critical understanding of these issues is essential if teachers are to be active professionals, able to shape their own practice and contribute to the debate.

We should like to thank the authors for their permission to use their work, and for all their efforts in adapting and abridging existing text and in writing new material.

Sandra Amos
Richard Boohan
The Open University
February 2001

Section 1

Introduction

1 The changing nature of science education

Sandra Amos and Richard Boohan

The development of science has been an extraordinary human achievement. It has given us remarkable insights into ourselves as human beings and into the universe around us, and at a practical level, it has transformed our lives. What science does, it does rather well. At the same time, the questions it can address deal with only a limited part of our experience. So, while science captures the imagination of many pupils (and adults too), others are indifferent or even hostile. It is in this context that we need to think about the place of science in the school curriculum.

In this chapter, we explore what the study of science can contribute to a learner's education, how the science curriculum has evolved and how learners come to learn about science. The chapter loosely follows the structure of the book as a whole, so as well as telling its own story, it is intended that it should provide an overview of the themes in the book. We shall refer to the later chapters in the book where relevant, as well as to other references that we consider to be useful further reading.

The rest of the book has been grouped into four sections, concerned with the place of science in the curriculum, curriculum innovation, learning in science, and science education research. The chapters, however, cannot be so neatly categorized, and inevitably many issues will appear in different guises throughout the book. Clearly, the science curriculum cannot be considered in isolation from the pupils as learners, and both are informed by research.

The science curriculum

We begin this section by considering the fundamental question about why young people should study science. We go on to look at the place of science in the current curriculum, how we got here and where we might be heading in the future.

Why study science?

It is perhaps surprising that no statement about the purposes of science education was given in any of the successive versions of the National Curriculum for England and Wales until 2000. (The Northern Ireland curriculum has for some time included a statement of purposes.) In a brief introductory paragraph in the latest version for England (DfEE/QCA 1999) on 'The importance of science' a number of themes can be discerned. Examples include exciting and satisfying pupils' curiosity in the world around them, engaging learners through direct practical experience, understanding how science contributes to technological change, recognizing the cultural significance of science, and questioning and discussing science-based issues. Thinking seriously about the purposes of science education should be a fundamental part of teachers' work. It is not just for curriculum developers to address these issues, since what teachers value will influence their day-to-day choices in their planning and teaching of that curriculum.

Black (1993) suggests four main purposes of a science education that would be appropriate for all pupils:

- Through their science education, pupils should be given a basis for understanding and coping with their lives, and for understanding the applications and effects of science in society. Science can contribute to their understanding of personal issues, such as health and sexuality, and social issues such as pollution and global warming. Here, pupils are learning *from* science.
- Pupils should learn *about* science. This involves learning about the concepts and methods that are combined in scientific enquiry and should give pupils insights into what science, seen as a human activity, is really like. They should appreciate that imagination and creativity have been central in the way in which science has progressed.
- Science should contribute to pupils' personal and intellectual development. It can also contribute to the development of their practical capability and decision-making, as well as helping them to learn to work with others.
- Finally, it is necessary for the science curriculum to address the needs of future specialists. It should provide pupils with a basis for making choices about whether to continue with their study of science, and to provide motivation to do this.

In the science education literature at present, there is a broad consensus that these are the kinds of purposes that need to be addressed by science education at the start of the twenty-first century. The extent to which these purposes are being met in the current curriculum and how they might better be achieved will be explored later in this chapter, and in many of the subsequent chapters in this book.

Any discussion of purposes relates, of course, to a particular time and a particular culture. The concern for a 'science for all' in Britain dates from the 1980s; before that time science education provision was marked by its fragmentation. Solomon (1993) discusses the purposes of science education from an international perspective, arguing that as well as differences in broad institutional factors between countries, there are differences in the 'regulative principles of thought' which affect purposes. These are deeply rooted within the culture. For example, she contrasts the humanist tradition of Sweden to the rationalist tradition of France. In many respects, Britain is closer to Sweden in its concern for the education of the whole child. Rationalism emphasizes the intellect, and the content of the science curriculum in France is more abstract with little discussion of social issues and a focus on rigorous assessment.

Our views about science education are influenced not only by the purposes of education but by our views about the nature of science itself. It is arguable that the philosophy of science has had little effect on the practice of science; philosophers may try to characterize the nature of science, but science carries on its own business regardless. But the same cannot be said about science education. Of central importance are questions such as: What is the status of scientific knowledge?, What is a 'fact'?, What is a 'theory'?, Is scientific knowledge 'true'?, What makes science different from other disciplines?, Is there such a thing as 'the scientific method'? In one sense, these are very deep questions – about the nature of the universe and about the way that we, as human beings, make sense of and construct knowledge of the world around us. In another sense though, these issues are the day-to-day stuff of every classroom. Every activity, every piece of text, every discussion reveals something about the assumptions, the beliefs and the values of everyone concerned.

Though there is no consensus amongst philosophers and sociologists about what science *is*, it is clear what it is *not*. Science is *not* a body of absolutely true knowledge that progresses by the accumulation of new knowledge; and there is no unique mechanistic scientific method that collects objective facts about the world and turns them into scientific theory. Chalmers (1999) gives a readable introduction to the nature of science. There is also a widespread concern that something like this is the view that many people have, and one that is presented in the school curriculum (for example, Hodson 1998a; 1998b). Section 2 of this book explores how science is reflected in the current science curriculum, focusing on the nature of science (Hodson Chapter 2), the cultures within which science is undertaken (Reiss Chapter 3) and practical work (Wellington Chapter 4).

Where are we now?

Many of the chapters in this book raise concerns about the difficulties faced in science education. While it is important to look critically at the current state of science education, it is also important to recognize what has been achieved. As we are writing this chapter, in January 2001, the Association for Science Education (ASE) is celebrating its centenary at its annual conference. Though teacher morale has suffered over recent years with increased workloads and pressures, there are many achievements to celebrate (Nott, forthcoming). The move in the 1980s towards a 'science for all' has led to a broadening of the student population, of the teaching of science and of the conception of science itself.

Science teaching has broadened to encompass a wider range of students. Science is now a core subject in the curriculum, and is compulsory up to the age of 16. There has been a major expansion in the amount and nature of science education in the primary school (Peacock Chapter 5), and an increase in the quality of teaching. In the secondary school, the majority of pupils now take a double GSCE examination in science; science is no longer for an academic elite. Gender differences in the sciences studied have lessened, with boys and girls studying physical and biological sciences within a common curriculum. Post-16 education has seen the development of science-related vocational courses (Coles Chapter 6).

Approaches to the teaching of science have also broadened, partly as a result of the broadening of the student population, and partly due to factors in the wider context of education. There is less emphasis on recall of factual scientific information, and an increased emphasis on scientific processes and on active learning approaches. Students are required to undertake their own investigative work and to undertake extended project work. Assessment practices have changed to reflect these new ways of working.

There have also been moves to broaden the nature of science in the curriculum. Though the effects of this are limited at present, its influence in school science can nevertheless be seen. The Science, Technology and Society (STS) movement has resulted in the development of curriculum materials, and has influenced the National Curriculum (Solomon Chapter 7). Students are expected to know about how knowledge is constructed by the science community and to know about how scientists work. They need to consider how science is related to issues in the wider social context and to the ethical issues involved. There is an increased awareness of the contribution of many cultures and peoples to scientific progress. Dennick discusses multi-cultural and anti-racist science education in Chapter 8.

Despite all these efforts, there is much unease about the state of science education. One area of concern arises from the results of research into what pupils understand of science. Over the past twenty years or more, research journals in science education have been filled with dozens of papers which have shown that there is an enormous gulf between what pupils and students understand about scientific concepts, and what it is intended that they should have learned. These studies have spanned across the sciences, and from primary school pupils to undergraduates. It really does seem that science *is* difficult – at least, the science which is currently taught. A useful review of the literature can be found in Driver *et al.* (1994). Some work has also been undertaken into pupils' understanding of the nature and methods of science, and the results have been disappointingly similar (Driver *et al.* 1996).

A second concern is that while young children are enthusiastic and curious about the scientific world, their interest declines as they grow older. Motivation is not sustained from primary to secondary school. This used to be reflected in the number of students who dropped science at age 14. Since it has become compulsory to study at least a single science up to the age of 16, take-up of examination courses in science has become less of an issue, but the issue of motivation remains (Osborne *et al.* 1998). While there has not been a decline in the proportion of students taking up post-16 science courses, the numbers have not shown the marked growth that other subjects have over the last ten or fifteen years.

Unease about the low level of pupils' understanding of science and the widespread disaffection towards it have naturally led science educators to doubt whether what is being offered to them in the science curriculum is right. Many aspects of it are now being questioned. But before we consider where science education might be heading in the future, it is helpful to trace some of its recent history in order to see what has shaped its development.

Where have we come from?

The current curriculum has been shaped by a number of forces – by debates about fundamental issues in science education, by evidence about what has worked and what has not, and by compromises in successive changes so that the 'new' never departs too radically from the 'old'. Being aware of these issues allows teachers to take part in the debate, or at the very least, not to feel subject to forces outside their understanding. Here we offer not a history, but some thumbnail sketches tracing the ideas which have influenced the current position. An account of the development of the science curriculum, and its causes and effects, can be found in Turner and Turner (2000), with more extended discussions in Jenkins (1979) and Donnelly and Jenkins (2001).

In the first part of the twentieth century, science education might be broadly characterized as 'science for the few'. It was academic and elitist, with an emphasis on the learning of content; it was dominated by the independent sector and determined by higher education. In the second part of twentieth century, there was increasing concern to make science accessible to all. There has been a shift from 'content' to 'process', or from 'science as knowledge' to 'science as a way of finding out'. The debate about content and process has been central to science education over the last few decades, and the debate continues. How can we characterize the content of scientific knowledge and the processes by which this knowledge is constructed and used? How are they related and what constitutes an appropriate balance between them?

The 1950s and 1960s saw the start of major science curriculum reforms in the UK and elsewhere in the world. Here, the main driving force for this change came from the Nuffield projects, as well as from the Schools Council's curriculum projects. There were Nuffield projects in each of the sciences at different levels, and though they were distinct and independent initiatives, they did share some common approaches. The emphasis was not just on understanding the content of science but on how science is discovered. The slogan of being a 'scientist for a day' captured the spirit of this thinking. Children would learn by 'guided discovery'; instead of practical work being done to 'prove theory', through their experiments children would generalize and come to an understanding of scientific laws. A supposed Chinese proverb was much quoted: 'I listen and I forget, I see and I remember, I do and I understand'.

The approach, however, is problematic. Science is not like this and scientific theory does not emerge directly from observation. It ignores the creative and social dimension, and we cannot expect children to make these imaginative leaps. In any case, even if science were like this, it is not obvious that being a scientist for a day is a good way of learning. The Nuffield projects were developed mainly in independent and selective schools, and in the 1970s, when science became an important part of the curriculum for pupils in the developing comprehensive sector, the projects were perceived as too difficult and too academic. Further curriculum development, including more Nuffield projects, took place aimed at a broader range of pupils.

The Nuffield innovations did not change substantially the content of what was to be learned. However, the limitations, the major achievement of these projects was to shift the emphasis from a passive transmission model of learning to the pupil as an *active learner*. This shift is the lasting legacy of the curriculum developments from this period.

A different model of scientific process developed out of the work of the Assessment of Performance Unit (APU). This was established in 1975 to monitor pupils' performance in a range of curriculum areas including science, and is discussed later in this chapter. Although the APU was concerned with assessment, its work on characterizing both the processes as well as the content of science influenced the specification of the investigative components of the later GCSE syllabuses and the National Curriculum.

In an extreme form, it led to the 'process science' movement that achieved some popularity in the 1980s (see Wellington 1989, for a critical discussion). Rather than focusing on content, pupils would learn to be 'scientific' by developing skills such as observation, prediction, hypothesizing, and so on. Since these are skills that are used in everyday life, pupils would be learning 'transferable skills' that could be used in other contexts. A fundamental problem with this approach is that there is no such thing as a single scientific method which can be characterized by a set of processes that can be applied in a formulaic way. Furthermore, problems with the transferability of skills from one context to another are well known even when the skills are well-defined. 'Skills' such as predicting and hypothesizing are very general, and children from an early age are rather good at these in their everyday life. Learning science is not about learning new processes, but in learning to do them *in a scientific context*. Processes are important in science, but divorced from content they make no sense (Millar and Driver 1987).

In 1985, the Department for Education and Science (DES) published a document that set out a policy on a 'science for all', detailing the principles which should guide the development of a broad and balanced science curriculum for all pupils from ages 5 to 16 (DES 1985). The ASE welcomed these proposals, which indeed reflected the thinking in its own previous discussion document (ASE 1981), though it did raise serious concerns about the apparent lack of commitment towards resources for its implementation (ASE 1985). The document from the DES set the stage for the development of the new GCSE courses starting in 1988 and the National Curriculum, first introduced in 1989. Throughout the many consultative and statutory versions of the Science National Curriculum, the process/content debate has always been to the fore.

In the version first proposed, there were twenty-two attainment targets, numbers one to sixteen being largely about traditional content, while the remaining six were rather innovatory; they concerned areas such as investigative science, working in groups, communicating, social and technological aspects, and the nature of science. These proposals were successively simplified in the three subsequent versions that came into force in 1989, 1991 and 1995 (for a summary, see Laws 1996). By 1995, the original attainment targets one to sixteen had been reduced to three (Sc2, Sc3 and Sc4), while little remained of the other six attainment targets except the investigative aspect (Sc1). The demands of complex curriculum and assessments arrangements, made worse by this succession of rapid changes, led to a five-year 'moratorium', before a new National Curriculum was introduced in 2000. The main change was the broadening of Sc1 to include a wider range of scientific enquiry, since the previous versions had been much criticized for offering too restricted and artificial a view of the nature of scientific investigation.

The most significant innovation that has been brought about by the National Curriculum in science and by the GCSE has been the introduction of investigations; this kind of work hardly existed before. In discussing the design of the APU monitoring instruments of practical work, Black (1990) uses the analogy of 'mirror or torch'; should the assessment reflect existing practice or should it try to move ahead of current practice? He argues that it was important that they chose to do the latter. With regard to the National Curriculum, Sc1 built on the work of the APU and had a similar aim. Its implementation, however, has been a painful process for teachers. Donnelly (1995) argues that, while apparently being a progressive development, its effect has been to 'de-skill' teachers and to undermine their professionalism by not recognizing and valuing their existing practices. When the assessment of practical investigations was introduced as part of the new GCSE examination courses in 1988, the needs of assessment meant much time needed to be given to measuring pupils' competence at the expense of developing it (Buchan 1993). Teachers were expected to complete countless 'tick-boxes' matching pupils' performance against very specific criteria, reflecting a 'process' approach to practical work based on assessing discrete skills, thus undervaluing teachers' professionalism. The situation has now improved, with assessments being less atomistic. But the problem of how to bring about significant curriculum change while at the same time not moving too far ahead of existing practice remains critical.

After over a decade of the National Curriculum, what have been the gains? In a survey commissioned by the Qualifications and Curriculum Authority (QCA), Nott and Wellington (1999) report that though there have been successes, there are concerns in a number of areas, for example, investigative work, KS2/KS3 continuity and the teaching of the nature of science. A curriculum imposed by legislation may not necessarily translate into classroom practice as intended:

> Teachers, students and pupils have constructed their own critique of the science National Curriculum.... Policymakers need to realise that the participants mediating a codified curriculum topped with a layer of performance indicators will learn to play the game in ways that contradict the often good intentions.
>
> (Nott and Wellington 1999)

Where might we be going?

It would be foolish to try to predict how the science curriculum will change over the next ten or twenty years, but what is certain is that it will change. Amongst the pressures that will make this happen are the changing nature of society and its expectations of education, the advances in science and technology and of what is to be studied, and the changes in pedagogy, brought about, not least, by the impact of new technologies. What is also certain is that curriculum change will be subject to the influence of many interested parties. The situation today is very different from the Nuffield projects in the 1960s, when the new approaches being developed were largely determined by practitioners themselves. In Chapter 9, Millar takes a critical look at the reasons why pupils should study science and the extent to which these are currently being met. He proposes the basic features of a curriculum that would serve better in developing public understanding of science.

As we outlined earlier, the last forty years have seen an enormous variety of curriculum initiatives in science, but underlying all of this, the *content* of the curriculum has changed only a little. The current National Curriculum still strongly reflects its roots in the O level syllabuses of the 1950s, and this has provided a major obstacle to radical curriculum innovation. Though new teaching approaches may have helped to increase pupils' motivation, they appear to have done little to raise their levels of understanding. Gott and Johnson (1999) argue that science educators are collectively responsible for the generally poor level of understanding of science, not from our personal lack of ability to teach, but from our not having looked carefully at what to teach in the first place. They argue that in the present curriculum, progression is achieved by the increasing complexity of information recall, with insufficient attention paid to the development of understanding. They suggest that by reducing the curriculum drastically to a few key areas, what is required for real understanding at each level could be specified in more detail.

Fundamental curriculum change, however, has costs. The first few years of the National Curriculum saw frequent changes and understandable resentment and disorientation of teachers, and in recent years the changes have been slower and more modest. There is clearly a tension between the need for the curriculum to change and the need of teachers for stability. Slow-moving and piecemeal change might be palatable, but it is inadequate for the needs of the next generation of pupils.

In 1997 and 1998, the Nuffield Foundation funded a series of meetings amongst science educators to formulate a vision of what a new science curriculum might look like and how it might be achieved, and these led to the report *Beyond 2000: Science Education for the Future* (Millar and Osborne 1998); a summary of the report can be found in Millar, Osborne and Nott (1998). It proposed a number of recommendations for a curriculum aimed at general 'scientific literacy', which is not distorted by the requirements of the minority of pupils who will become specialists in science. Amongst the recommendations is the proposal that scientific knowledge should be presented through a set of 'explanatory stories' which would emphasize the central ideas of science, and how they are inter-related, without being obscured by the current weight of detail. More emphasis should be put on the relationship between science and technology, on the ways in which scientific knowledge is obtained, and on a wider variety of teaching approaches, including case studies of historical and current issues. New and broader approaches to assessment would need to be developed in order to encourage pupils and teachers to focus on the more important aspects of learning. Finally, the report recommends that a formal procedure should be established for trialling innovations before incorporation into the National Curriculum. Changes to the National Curriculum in the past have been characterized by hasty consultations about untrialled proposals, with insufficient time for teachers to prepare for their introduction on a national scale.

There is a widespread misconception that although doing science requires dedication and systematic thought, it does not require imagination; to put it crudely, 'science is for people who are clever but dull'. But science is about the imaginative exploration of the world and about creating new ideas to interpret it; creativity is the very essence of science. An important recent report by the National Advisory Committee on Creative and Cultural Education (NACCCE 1999) emphasized that creativity applies to all human activity and, moreover, that it can be taught and developed. This report has received a positive response from the government which has acted on a number of its recommendations, though as yet these have focused on the 'creative arts'.

In a recent survey, students with good GCSE science grades were asked why they chose, or did not choose, to study A level physics. One girl, who chose humanities A levels, remarked that she did not pursue her study of physics because, as she said 'I'm interested in people and ideas'. That she felt that science has little to do with people is sad, but perhaps unsurprising. That she thought it has nothing to offer about 'ideas' is nothing less than tragic. The apparent failure of GCSE science for this pupil, and no doubt for many others, to portray science as a human, creative and imaginative enterprise is damning indeed.

Children as learners

The 'delivery of the curriculum' is a phrase that seems to have slipped into common usage, though it does not take much experience of teaching to realize that knowledge cannot be simply 'delivered' to pupils. Teaching and learning require an interaction between teachers and learners. It is not a one-way process. We now turn our attention, therefore, from 'what' is taught to 'who' is taught. Theories about how children learn have had an important influence both on the curriculum and on how to teach. In Chapter 10, Driver explores how pupils bring their own experiences and beliefs to lessons, and how these affect the meanings that they construct. Teaching pupils is not about 'filling empty vessels', and the evidence that such approaches are not effective is overwhelming.

What do we know about children's learning in science?

It may be difficult to teach children an understanding of science, but it is surprisingly easy to teach a pigeon to play ping-pong. But are they the same kind of thing? Pigeons can be trained to perform apparently remarkable tasks by rewarding small units of desirable behaviour. This is a *behaviourist* approach to learning. What would this imply if applied to the learning of science, for example, the concept of force? Here is a possible way. First, the knowledge that is required to be learned would need to be broken into a number of small discrete units and sequenced in an appropriate way. Each of these units of knowledge would be presented to the learner (perhaps in a few sentences) and a question asked. If the learner answers correctly they proceed; if not, they repeat until a correct response is given. This programmed learning approach achieved some popularity in the 1950s and 1960s, even being applied in the design of mechanical teaching machines, but there are serious problems in applying the approach to science education.

The first is the assumption it makes about the nature of scientific knowledge. In a formal sense, one can think of scientific concepts as being related in a hierarchical structure by definition, they must be in a programmed learning approach. Force is defined in terms of mass and acceleration; work and energy can be defined in terms of force. But scientific knowledge is more complex and inter-related than this; learning scientific concepts is more like coming to know the characters in a novel than building a wall from bricks.

The second is concerned with the learner. Behaviourism pays no attention to what is going on in the learner's head. Indeed, this is part of its essence since only *observable* stimuli and responses can be admitted into the theory; the learner is treated as a 'black-box'. What has emerged from extensive research is that it is of central importance to pay attention to *cognitive* aspects of learning – what a learner already knows and is able to do, and what happens during learning. Two examples are discussed below of research and development projects which have been influential in the UK and which have developed teaching approaches based on cognitive theories of learning.

The CASE project (Cognitive Acceleration through Science Education) is a continuation of the work done in the 1970s into the cognitive demands of various science courses (Shayer and Adey 1981). This work was based on Piagetian stage theory, the focus being on *context-free scientific processes* (for example, proportionality or control of variables). The research attempted to measure the match between the stages of development of pupils (determined empirically through testing) against the cognitive demand of various topics of the curriculum. At the time, there were widespread concerns about the difficulties of some aspects of science courses, and the results from the research suggested where the demands of the curriculum could be reduced. The CASE project (Adey and Shayer 1994), which is being used in a significant number of schools, looks at the other aspect of the possible mismatch, and attempts to increase the level of the pupil's thinking. The aim here, then, is to improve pupils' understanding of science by increasing their ability to process information.

In contrast, the focus of the Children's Learning in Science Project (CLISP) was on *specific scientific concepts* (see for example, Driver and Oldham 1986). From the work of this project, as well as from a very large number of studies worldwide, it became clear that, despite teaching, many children held ideas different from the accepted scientific ideas, for example that plants obtain their food from the ground or that something travels out from the eye in order for us to see. In the teaching approaches developed by CLISP, the importance of children's own ideas is stressed, and the way in which the learner must restructure these in order to accommodate new ideas. Such a view of learning has been termed 'constructivist', since knowledge is not simply passed on, but each learner needs to construct their own knowledge. However, the notion of constructivism is open to naive interpretations. Saying that a learner needs to construct their own knowledge should certainly not be taken to mean that this could be done by an isolated *individual* simply from their personal experience with the *physical world*.

These two projects illustrate approaches which pay attention to content and to processes. In Chapter 11, Leach and Scott discuss conceptual learning and the differences between everyday and scientific ways of knowing, and in Chapter 12, Adey considers the theoretical ideas behind the CASE project and some practical examples. A critical perspective on different theories of learning is given by Bliss in Chapter 13.

What are the implications for teaching?

In understanding the complexities of pupil learning, it is important to hold on to two simple truths. *Telling* pupils does not mean that they learn; *not telling* pupils does not mean that they learn better! In constructing their knowledge of science, pupils need, of course, to gain experiences of the physical world. But on their own, these experiences are not sufficient for them to construct, for example, ideas about genetic inheritance, atomic theory or the laws of motion. They need to know about how scientists have made sense of the world. In Chapter 14, Sutton argues the importance of 'telling and puzzling' in coming to understand science – of pupils being presented with scientific ideas as expressions of people's thoughts about the world, and being given the opportunity to interpret them for themselves. This theme is developed more fully in Sutton (1992; 1998).

A teacher may face thirty individuals in a class. Each of those individuals will have constructed their own unique set of understandings, resulting in thirty pupils with individual needs. However, the variation in children's ideas is not infinite, and commonly held ideas have been detected by researchers worldwide. This research has been usefully summarized by Driver *et al.* (1994) and provides teachers with a starting point when considering the ideas that may be held by their pupils. Though much research has been done to probe these ideas, there has been less success in working out how to use the findings in teaching. Harlen (1999) points out that there is little consensus on how the scientific view should be introduced to pupils, and various teaching approaches have been put forward; examples are presenting the learner with experiences that generate evidence conflicting with their ideas, or eliciting pupils' ideas and giving them the opportunity to test them and reflect on their validity. However, there are no easy answers, and there is no firm evidence of the effectiveness of different approaches. What *is* known is that conceptual change is often difficult, as learners hang on tightly to some of their ideas. For example, a group of students were investigating the swing of a pendulum and predicted that the weight on the end of the pendulum would be a key factor affecting the time period. Despite carefully collecting data, which showed conclusively that the weight did not affect the time taken to swing, the group could not reject their hypothesis. Instead, they rejected the reliability of their work and decided to repeat the exercise. Children, especially, will find ways to explain or dismiss results that do not corroborate their existing ideas. To move the learner on, teachers need to be able to challenge these ideas. But before pupils put forward and explore their ideas, they need to feel safe and supported, and trust that their ideas will not be ridiculed or dismissed. Teachers have to work at achieving such an environment.

It may be tempting to draw a parallel between the way children learn and the way that science itself has developed, and even to use this as a model of teaching science. Scientific theories attempt to propose explanations for what is known about the world; these theories survive so long as they are found to be useful. If new, conflicting evidence is found, the theory is not immediately abandoned, but if another theory emerges that better accounts for the evidence, then the new may replace the old. However, the development of theories by communities of scientists over periods of many years is very different from the individual learner constructing knowledge in the social setting of the classroom. The metaphor of a 'pupil as a scientist' is very misleading; pupils do not hold the same criteria about consistency and evidence as scientists.

There are, however, some interesting parallels between some of the ideas held by children and theories that can be found in the history of science. Children try to create their own theories to help them make sense of their experiences. Even though these ideas are incorrect, some people have preferred to use the term 'alternative frameworks' to describe them rather than terms such as 'misconceptions', to reflect their role in the child's understanding of the world. It is true that science is a human construction, but from this it does not follow that theory choice is a matter of personal preference. Some ways of looking at the world work better than others. It is because children's 'alternative frameworks' are incorrect that teachers need to change them, but it is because they mean something in the child's world that this must be done with sensitivity.

Teachers have the difficult task of managing large groups of pupils, but also of seeing those pupils as individuals. Here, we have touched on just one aspect of that individuality – the variety of children's scientific ideas. But there are many others – there are girls and boys, differences in cultural and ethnic backgrounds, different preferred learning styles, and so on. In Chapter 15, Griffin argues about the importance of treating pupils as individuals in an informal learning setting, and in Chapter 16, Murphy looks at the influence of gender on attainment and attitudes in science.

How do we find out what children understand?

'Ways of finding out what children understand and can do' is really just another way of saying 'assessment'. However, the term 'assessment' often evokes a more restricted meaning. Examinations and end-of-topic tests are important, but are just part of what assessment means. In lessons, teachers are constantly making judgements about their pupils from their observations of them, discussions with them, reading what they have written, and so on. Formal tests often give limited information about the development of pupils' understanding; it is through *formative assessment* that real understanding can be assessed in order to improve pupil learning.

The Assessment of Performance Unit (APU) was set up in 1975 by the Department for Education and Science, and between 1980 and 1984 it undertook a national study into children's performance in science. One of the significant features of this study was the wide range of tools used by the researchers to build up a picture of pupils' performance. The assessment framework adopted enabled questions to explore three dimensions (processes, conceptual understanding and context), and in analysing pupils' responses, attention was paid not simply to identifying correct answers, but categorizing incorrect or incomplete answers. The APU has been influential in a number of ways, for example, in providing the starting point of the CLISP project, and in providing a framework for the design of Sc1 in the National Curriculum. In reviewing its achievements, Black (1990) notes that an important lesson from the APU was that teachers could build up, over time, far more reliable assessment records than external tests; despite this evidence, when the National Curriculum was introduced, it was the latter which seemed to command far more political and public confidence. Since then, there has been no large-scale national monitoring of performance in the same way. The assessments undertaken by all pupils at the end of each Key Stage do not provide the detailed insights into pupils' understandings that could be obtained through the sampling methods and range of tasks used by the APU.

A phrase used by White and Gunstone (1992) as the title of their book neatly describes the elicitation of an individual's ideas as *probing understanding*. They argue that the nature of understanding is too complex to be assessed by any single style of test and cannot be represented by a single numerical score. How to probe real understanding requires more careful consideration; it may need to use a variety of methods and may be done on several occasions. The probes that White and Gunstone describe go beyond simple tests and questions. They present a range of activities that can be used to reveal conceptual understanding, including concept mapping, 'predict–observe–explain', relational diagrams, drawings, question generating and interviews about instances. Probes are more complex than traditional tests, and there is no simple, easy score. Children's responses have to be looked at carefully, and not taken at face value. They may need to be followed up with a discussion before an interpretation can be made.

In school, much time is often given to tests designed to assess the recall of scientific knowledge. It is easy to fall into a trap of testing to find out whether pupils can describe phenomena or remember technical language, without revealing the understanding of the concepts that lie beneath. Despite a general acceptance of the impact that pupils' prior ideas have on learning, little more than lip-service is paid to probing these understandings. At the start of a topic, teachers often use 'question-and-answer' about the ideas the children already hold. Teachers may have a variety of reasons for doing this, but it yields very little or no information about individuals that can inform their planning. More systematic strategies are needed. An example of a published curriculum scheme that provides these is

Nuffield Primary Science (1997). This is based on research evidence into children's ideas and includes probes that teachers can use with pupils at the start of each topic so that action can be planned to take account of the findings.

However, probing learners' underlying understanding is a threatening business. It can reveal that despite the carefully orchestrated teaching, their existing ideas may remain and the new ideas they have been taught may have been modified in order to be accommodated into their existing frameworks. It is much easier to give them the end-of-topic test and move on! In Chapter 17, Black reviews the evidence about the effectiveness of formative assessment and argues that it has the potential to lead to major gains in achievement and attitudes. But it does require a shift in the outlook on learning, and a move away from the notions of 'delivery' and 'coverage' of the curriculum.

Research

There is no shortage of research in science education. At issue is whether this research is useful to science teachers, and if so, how it can be used. In the Hillage Report, a picture is portrayed of a fragmented educational research community which lacks co-ordination among funders, lacks the involvement of teachers, has a varied quality of output and lacks effective dissemination of its research (Hillage *et al.* 1998). In Chapter 18 of this book, Gilbert sets out the challenges facing science education and what it needs to do to meet these. White (Chapter 22) explores the current state of research in science education and why teachers largely ignore it. He notes that there is much research of relevance and that it is widely disseminated through science teacher conferences and journals, so these factors cannot be blamed. More likely explanations for this lack of engagement by teachers are the conditions under which they work and the widely held perception that research is not relevant to them as individual practitioners in the classroom. Increasingly, there is talk of teaching as an 'evidence-based profession' and a movement towards research that will support this; on the other hand, Ball (1990) warns of 'the discourse of derision', which rejects views that seek to use critically-informed opinions as the basis for decision taking. Educational research has become a political football.

What kind of research in science education is done?

In science, we are familiar with the approach to experimentation which is characterized in the National Curriculum as 'fair testing'. Having controlled all the other variables we can think of, the effect of changing the independent variable on the dependent variable is measured. In the past, such an approach has been common in educational research, deriving from the tradition of experimentation in behavioural psychology. Thus, by using a control group and an experimental group, the effects of an 'intervention', such as a different method of teaching, could be measured by a comparison of, for example, the improvement in the scores on tests. The difficulty of this approach is that it is not possible to separate and control variables, and so the findings are of limited applicability. Context is an important element of practice, as are the values of teachers, the school and the community. Findings may conflict with other studies, and the research does not suggest the reasons *why* different approaches may work or not. Teachers are left with very little to take from such studies.

Educational research has moved on, and by broadening its range of methods, it can provide insights into what is happening and why. The theoretical frameworks it provides can help to interpret observations, and can complement and enhance the detailed practical understanding teachers have about their own classrooms and learners. Because contexts vary widely, research cannot prescribe solutions, but it can provide possibilities for action when seeking to improve practice and its outcomes. Research in science education increasingly aims to develop approaches to science teaching that can be used in real classrooms. A critical discussion of science education and research can be found in Ogborn (1996).

Science education research has been dominated over the last two decades by studies of pupils' conceptual understanding. As discussed earlier, in many curriculum areas it has been found that pupils hold ideas, even after teaching, that are very different from the scientific view. Some research has also been done on how teaching can address these findings, and on looking more fundamentally at the structure and origin of these ideas. More recently, attention has turned to pupils' understandings of the processes of scientific enquiry, the nature of scientific knowledge and science in society, which reflect the increasing importance placed on these aspects in the curriculum. Researching pupils' *attitudes* presents more difficulties than researching their understanding, but significant work has been done in this area, particularly in regard to gender differences. Though most research has been focused on learners as individuals, attention is turning to the social contexts of learning, to the role of language, explanation, argumentation, group work, and so on. A huge body of research evidence was generated by the APU related to assessment; less is done in this area now, but some work still continues on diagnostic and formative assessment. Not all learning of science takes place in the classroom. 'Informal learning' takes place in a variety of ways and this has been an active area of research, particularly into museums and interactive science centres. Finally, not all research into science education is empirical; important work is done, for example, in thinking about the purposes of science education, or the nature of science and its place in the science curriculum.

Two books have recently been published (Harlen 1999; Monk and Osborne 2000) which draw together the findings of science education research in a way that is accessible to teachers. Monk and Osborne argue that research has the potential to build a better understanding of teaching, learning and classrooms, to support teachers in their improvement of practice, and to improve pupil achievement and attitudes to science. Investment in research is investment in belief. While some research leads to major shifts in thinking, other research may not, and it is not possible to predict what will result in these leaps forward. But that is the nature of research.

How is research carried out?

Most research in science education is conducted as part of the work of university departments of education, whose main teaching responsibilities include the initial training of teachers, and higher degrees and doctorates in education. The research represented in Chapters 19, 20 and 21 of this book illustrate some typical examples. One was done by an academic, another by a teacher undertaking research and who subsequently became an academic, and the third by a group of academics carrying out a funded research project. Currently, the direction of science education research is determined largely by the academic community, though it is also influenced by targeted programmes of the research funding councils. Another influence on the direction of research is the commissioning of research by government agencies which may be carried out by universities or by independent organizations. Recently, however, National Educational Research Forum has been established. Its remit is to provide strategic direction for educational research nationally and to raise the quality and profile and impact of educational research. Its key objective is to develop a national framework for a coherent and relevant research programme in education.

In the past, research has had little or no impact on teachers, often being disregarded by them as irrelevant. There has been a tendency for teachers to perceive it as something done by those in university departments, and something which has very little to do with them, their classroom, or their practice. A significant proportion of teachers, though, do undertake educational research themselves, through part-time study in higher education. Often this research may not relate directly to the teachers' own practice, its approach reflecting the kind of research of the university community within which their own research is located. A different tradition is the 'action research' or 'teacher as researcher' movement. Action research is about developing a critical and reflective view about one's practice, and formulating and testing hypotheses in order to improve that practice (Hopkins 1993). Through this, teachers gain increased responsibility for their actions, and professional development comes about by teacher involvement in curriculum development and evaluation. In the action research tradition, classroom research is increasingly seen as being set within the context of the whole school. Individual change is difficult to achieve, and teachers need to break out of isolated classrooms and to collaborate with others.

How is research disseminated?

There are a number of science education journals through which research is disseminated. The research papers which we have selected for Section 5 of this book are taken from the *International Journal for Science Education*. This is a UK publication, but has contributions from many countries; it is now published monthly with over sixty research papers per year. Other research journals include *Research in Science and Technological Education* (UK), *Journal of Research in Science Teaching* (USA), *Science Education* (USA), and *Research in Science Education*

(Australia). An annual publication, *Studies in Science Education*, contains reviews of research in particular areas of science education, drawing out the key issues and providing an overview of the literature.

There are also professional journals aimed directly at science teachers. Of particular importance is the *School Science Review*, the main journal of the Association for Science Education (ASE). The ASE also publishes a number of other journals, organizes regional events and holds an annual conference which is attended by a very large number of science teachers. Each of the three professional scientific associations publishes an educational journal – *Journal of Biological Education* (Institute of Biology), *Education in Chemistry* (Royal Society of Chemistry) and *Physics Education* (Institute of Physics). A very accessible source of information is the *Times Educational Supplement*, which periodically includes a 'curriculum special' on science and technology education.

Teaching as a research-based profession

The climate in which teachers work has changed considerably over the past few decades. Successive governments have made education a target for reform. Teachers have had to cope with initiative after initiative. In terms of professional development, these include stricter induction procedures for new entrants, threshold, appraisal and performance management. The phrase 'teaching as a research-based profession' is increasingly being heard, drawing parallels with a similar movement in the medical profession. A key feature of a profession is that there is an associated body of knowledge derived from research, undertaken by some members of that profession for the advancement of knowledge. The endeavour to know and understand more is a central part of being a professional. In this respect, the educational community is a professional one. There is an active educational research community, and a huge research base that teachers can draw upon.

How do teachers learn? Monk and Osborne (2000) argue that research can inform science teaching, and point out that teachers do not *only* learn from each other. Nor should they learn from trial and error practice. If this was the way our doctors gained their professional knowledge there would be a public outcry! Teachers are being urged to become researchers of their own practice through action research and partnerships with HEIs, and through initiatives such as the DfEE Best Practice research scholarships. Though there are so many administrative pressures on teachers that they lack time to research their practice, some teachers are doing some worthwhile small scale research activity, and published accounts can be found, for example, in *School Science Review*. Research projects are beginning which are focusing on evidence-based practice in science education, and there is growing international recognition of the need to pay attention to how research can bring about improvement in practice (Millar *et al.* 2000).

Society asks teachers to do a serious and important task. The vast majority of teachers respond to that challenge with enthusiasm and dedication. They do it because of their desire to be involved with the intellectual and social growth of young people – put more simply, they love teaching. Few teachers are attracted to the profession because of money or status. What is expected of teachers? There is much craft knowledge to be learned in teaching. It is an essential thing to have and its value should not be underestimated. But to see teaching simply as a craft diminishes it. Encouraging enthusiasm and dedication cannot be done by turning teaching into a set of techniques for delivering a prescribed curriculum. Teachers need to be able to work within the conditions and culture that enable them to be critical, reflective practitioners who have something to contribute to teaching and science education.

References

Adey, P. and Shayer, M. (1994) *Really Raising Standards: Cognitive Intervention and Academic Achievement*, London and New York: Routledge.

ASE (1981) *Education through Science*, Hatfield: Association for Science Education.

ASE (1985) 'Science 5–16: a response from the ASE', *Education in Science* 114: 13.

Ball, S. (1990) *Politics and Policy Making in Education*, London: Routledge.

Black, P. (1990) 'APU Science – the past and the future', *School Science Review* 72(258): 13–28.

Black, P. (1993) *The Purposes of Science Education*, in R. Hull (ed.) *ASE Secondary Science Teachers' Handbook*, Hemel Hempstead: Simon and Shuster Education.

Buchan, A. S. (1993) 'Policy into practice: the operation of practical assessment in the GCSE', *School Science Review* 75(270): 7–15.

Chalmers, A. F. (1999) *What is this Thing Called Science?*, Buckingham: Open University Press.

DES (1985) *Science 5–16: A Statement of Policy*, London: HMSO.

DfEE/QCA (1999) *The National Curriculum: Handbook for Secondary Teachers in England (Key Stages 3 and 4)*, London: HMSO.

Donnelly, J. (1995) 'Curriculum development in science: the lessons of Sc1', *School Science Review* 76(277): 95–103.

Donnelly, J. F. and Jenkins, E. W. (2001) *Science Education: Policy, Professionalism and Change*, London: Paul Chapman Publishing.

Driver, R. and Oldham, V. (1986) 'A constructivist approach to curriculum development in science', *Studies in Science Education* 13: 105–22.

Driver, R., Leach, J., Millar, R. and Scott, P. (1996) *Young People's Images of Science*, Buckingham: Open University Press.

Driver, R., Squires, A., Rushworth, P. and Wood-Robinson, V. (1994) *Making Sense of Secondary Science: Research into Children's Ideas*, London and New York: Routledge.

Gott, R. and Johnson, P. (1999) 'Science in schools: time to pause for thought?', *School Science Review* 81(295): 21–8.

Harlen, W. (1999) *Effective Teaching of Science: A Review of Research*, Edinburgh: The Scottish Council for Research in Education.

Hillage, J., Pearson, R., Anderson, A., and Tamkin, P. (1998) *Excellence in Research on Schools*, London: Department for Education and Employment.

Hodson, D. (1998a) *Teaching and Learning Science: Towards a Personalised Approach*, Buckingham: Open University Press.

Hodson, D. (1998b) 'Is this what scientists really do? Seeking a more authentic science in and beyond the school laboratory', in J. Wellington (ed.) *Practical Work in School Science: Which Way Now?*, London and New York: Routledge.

Hopkins, D. (1993) *A Teacher's Guide to Classroom Research,* Buckingham: Open University Press.

Jenkins, E. W. (1979) *From Armstrong to Nuffield: Studies in Twentieth Century Science Education in England and Wales,* London: John Murray.

Laws, P. M. (1996) 'Investigative work in the Science National Curriculum', *School Science Review* 77(281): 17–25.

Millar, R. and Driver, R. (1987) 'Beyond processes', *Studies in Science Education* 14: 33–62.

Millar, R. and Osborne, J. (1998) *Beyond 2000: Science Education for the Future,* London: King's College London, School of Education.

Millar, R., Leach, J. and Osborne, J. (2000) *Improving Science Education: The Contribution of Research,* Buckingham: Open University Press.

Millar, R., Osborne, J. and Nott, M. (1998) 'Science education for the future', *School Science Review* 80(291): 19–24.

Monk, M. and Osborne, J. (2000) *Good Practice in Science Teaching: What Research has to Say,* Buckingham: Open University Press.

NACCCE (1999) *All our Futures: Creativity, Culture and Education,* Sudbury, Suffolk: National Advisory Committee on Creative and Cultural Education.

Nott, M. (ed.) (forthcoming) *Celebrating the Teaching of Science,* Hatfield: Association for Science Education.

Nott, M. and Wellington, J. (1999) 'The state we're in: issues in Key Stage 3 and 4 science', *School Science Review* 81(294): 13–18.

Nuffield Primary Science (1997) *A Guide for Primary Teachers,* London: Collins Educational.

Ogborn, J. (1996) 'Science', in P. Gordon (ed.) *A Guide to Educational Research,* London: Woburn Press.

Osborne, J., Driver, R. and Simon, S. (1998) 'Attitudes to science: issues and concerns', *School Science Review* 79(288): 27–33.

Shayer, M. and Adey, P. S. (1981) *Towards a Science of Science Teaching,* London: Heinemann Educational.

Solomon, J. (1993) 'Science education from a European perspective', in M. Ratcliffe (ed.) *ASE Guide to Secondary Science Education,* Cheltenham: Stanley Thornes.

Sutton, C. (1992) *Words, Science and Learning,* Buckingham: Open University Press.

Sutton, C. (1998) 'Science as conversation: come and see my air pump', in J. Wellington (ed.) *Practical Work in School Science: Which Way Now?,* London and New York: Routledge.

Turner, S. and Turner, T. (2000) 'Science teaching in an era of change', in A. Kent (ed.) *School Subject Teaching: The History and Future of the Curriculum,* London: Kogan Page.

Wellington, J. (ed.) (1989) *Skills and Processes in Science Education,* London and New York: Routledge.

White, R. and Gunstone, R. (1992) *Probing Understanding,* London: Falmer Press.

Section 2

Science in the curriculum

Introduction

This section explores the nature of science itself and how it is reflected in the current science curriculum. There are many concerns that are shared by the authors. The image of science presented in schools is often too restricted. There is a tendency for it to reinforce the naive and mistaken view that science is a body of 'true' knowledge, generated unproblematically by the application of a prescriptive 'scientific method'. It does not seem to suggest that science requires creativity and personal involvement, or that it is constructed by a community of people. Theories are not 'out there' simply waiting to be discovered by observing nature; they are human constructions and shape the way in which we observe the world. The point here is not just that school science may be presenting a *misleading* view of science; it may be presenting a view of science that is *alienating* and *demotivating* for many pupils. 'Putting people back into science' means that pupils may come to see science not as 'knowledge found in books', but as a creative and imaginative human activity in which they can participate.

While there are common themes, each of the chapters has its own particular emphasis. In Derek Hodson's chapter, a key issue is the discussion of epistemology (how we know what we know). He points out the untenability of an inductivist view of science, in which laws and theories are derived by generalizing from objective observational data. He argues that there are other philosophical positions about the way in which knowledge is constructed which give pupils a more balanced view of science and scientists. Michael Reiss focuses on broadening the conception of who does science. Science is often seen stereotypically as a male, white, individualistic activity, and he demonstrates how science is a social activity which has been undertaken by people in many different cultures. He also broadens the notion of what should be seen as 'science'; physical science should not be held up as the paradigm against which other sciences are judged. By moving away from the idea that science is exclusively about 'experiments to test hypotheses in the laboratory', pupils will gain a better understanding of the real nature of scientific enquiry. Much time in science lessons is spent doing practical work, and Jerry Wellington considers the value of this and how it relates to 'real' science. He examines different approaches to practical work and how they can present misleading images of the nature of science. Often, justifications put forward for practical work are problematic, and it may be done in an unthinking and ritualistic way. In this way, its role becomes self-perpetuating (like many other practices). With greater clarity about purposes, practical work can make a better contribution to conveying the nature of science to pupils.

2   Towards a personalized science

Derek Hodson

In many school curriculums, science is presented as the meticulous, orderly and exhaustive application of a powerful, all-purpose, objective and reliable method for ascertaining factual knowledge about the universe. Scientists are portrayed as rational, logical, open-minded and intellectually honest individuals who are required to adopt a disinterested, value-free and analytical stance, and who readily share their procedures and findings with each other. In Cawthron and Rowell's (1978: 32) memorable words, the scientist is regarded as 'a depersonalized and idealized seeker after truth, painstakingly pushing back the curtains which obscure objective reality, and abstracting order from the flux, an order which is directly revealable to him through a distinctive scientific method.'

There are several reasons why such a depersonalized image of science and scientists is to be deplored. First, it seriously misrepresents the nature of science and scientific practice. Second, it is immensely off-putting for large numbers of students and so discourages them from pursuing science further. Third, by presenting scientific knowledge as a collection of fixed, non-negotiable, authoritative pronouncements by 'experts', it dissuades students from critical scrutiny of the justification for scientific belief. Thus, it contributes to continued intellectual dependence on others and to the disempowerment that results from scientific illiteracy. What I am arguing here is that critical scientific literacy depends on a clear understanding of the epistemological foundations of science and recognition that scientific practice is a human endeavour that influences, and is influenced by, the socio-cultural context in which it is located. The first step in developing a more personalized view of science is to consider the ways in which the knowledge, experience, beliefs, values and aspirations of people influence the kind of science they choose to do and, to an extent, the ways in which they do it.

The theory dependence of observation

The traditional school curriculum description of science says two things about observation. First, nothing enters the mind of the scientist except by way of the senses – that is, the mind is a tabula rasa on which the senses inscribe a true and faithful record of the world. Second, the validity and reliability of observation statements are independent of the opinions and expectations of the observer and

Figure 2.1 Find the hidden man

can be readily confirmed by other observers. Neither is true. In reality, we interpret the sense data that enters our consciousness in terms of our prior knowledge, beliefs, expectations and experiences. As Barlex and Carre (1985: 4) say, 'We do not see things as they are, we see them as *we* are' (emphasis added).

Consequently, a change in mental constructs brings about a change in perception. For years, I was unable to see a face in the snowy landscape of Figure 2.1. It remained for me a series of blotches, despite the insistence of colleagues that it reveals the face of Jesus of Nazareth. Earlier this year, confronted by a giant reproduction of the picture at the Ontario Science Centre and urged by my wife to squint, stare hard, and think of the familiar picture of Che Guevara, I finally saw the face. Now I can't look at the picture without seeing the face. Similarly, once you have seen the faces hidden among the foliage in those puzzle pictures often found in children's comics, you can no longer see the trees without the faces. However, it is not the image falling on the retina that has changed. Rather, it is the observer that has changed. The observer now has a different perspective, a different view of the world.

Scientific inquiry, and the experimentation and observation that accompany it, is a selective process and requires a focus of attention and a purpose. A scientist needs an incentive to make one observation rather than another. As Peter Medawar (1969: 29) says, 'We cannot browse over the field of nature like cows at pasture'. The traditional view of science as beginning with the open-minded assembly of observational data does not provide that incentive. In practice, making a scientific observation presupposes a view of the world that suggests that particular observations can be made, and are worth making. In other words, it is not innocent and unbiased, it is theory-dependent. Doing science (choosing a focus, designing and conducting an inquiry, and communicating findings) depends on who we are, what we know, and what we have experienced. Some view of the world, some theoretical perspective, precedes observation. It is simply not possible to observe things that you don't expect, don't know how to look for, and are not conceptually prepared for – a position admirably summed up by David Theobald (1968: 26): 'If we confront the world with an empty head, then our experience will be ... meaningless. Experience does not give concepts meaning; if anything concepts give experience meaning.'

Also, observation statements are expressed in the language of some theory, and such statements are as vague or as precise as the underlying theoretical and conceptual framework allows. Thus, the quality and usefulness of observations depend crucially on the observational language available to the observer. Without an adequate conceptual framework, perceptions cannot be given meaning; without an adequate observational language, they cannot be recorded, criticized and communicated. Even an apparently simple, objective statement such as 'Anhydrous copper sulphate has a solubility of 205 grams per litre at 20 °C' can only be made in the light of a prior theoretical framework involving concepts such as dissolving, temperature, hydration and volume.

Because the collection and interpretation of observational data can only take place within a theoretical framework, it follows that prior knowledge determines the observations that scientists (and students in school science) can make and the meanings they can ascribe to them. Also, because sense data may be interpreted in a variety of ways, it is necessary to learn how to observe 'correctly' – that is, in accordance with the currently accepted paradigm. Thus, the key to good observation in science is a sound theoretical frame of reference. As Medawar (1967: 133) says, what a person sees 'conveys no information until he knows beforehand the kind of thing he is expected to see'. This is in stark contrast to the view usually promoted through the science curriculum, that observation precedes theory. In emphasizing and promoting 'open-eyed' and 'open-minded' observation, many contemporary science curriculums miss the essential point that good scientific observation depends crucially on education and training. Without an appropriate theoretical framework, there can be no guarantee that students will observe 'correctly' even the readily observable. They may fail to see the phenomenon under investigation or, indeed, may see something else entirely.

Scientific method

Textbook accounts of science often assert that science proceeds inductively (Figure 2.2) and that inductive generalizations can be relied upon, provided that certain conditions are met.

1 The number of observation statements must be large.
2 The observations must be repeated under a wide variety of conditions.
3 No accepted observation statement should conflict with the derived generalization or universal law.

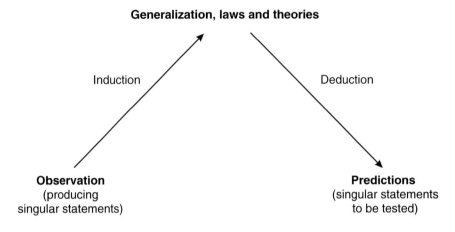

Figure 2.2   Science as induction

This model of science has enormous appeal and is seen to lend authority and predictive capability to the knowledge it generates. Observations can be made by anyone, by careful use of their senses. No personal, subjective element is involved. The validity of observation statements, when correctly acquired, is not dependent on the opinions and expectations of the observer. Provided that the three conditions for inductive inferences are met, the generalization will be valid. If the generalization is true, any predictions derived from it are bound to be true.

Quite apart from the matters already discussed, there are several problems with this model of science. One concerns the three conditions for drawing inductive generalizations. What, for example, constitutes a 'large' number of observations? How does one know which variables are significant in attempting to provide a 'wide variety of conditions'? How does one know whether a conflicting observation is merely an erroneous reading or a potential falsifier? The answer in each case is, of course, theoretical understanding, but this has been ruled out from the start by insistence that scientific inquiry is objective, value-free and unprejudiced by theory.

It is important for students to be brought to the realization that objectivity in science does not consist of placing equal weight on all observations (something that children consider to be 'fair' and which the traditional view of science seems to emphasize). Rather, they should be led to an awareness that they need to select relevant and appropriate observations and discard irrelevant and incorrect ones (Hodson 1986). Observations often have to be checked for acceptability by recourse to theory. This is the reverse of what we usually tell children. The usual message is that scientists test their theories for acceptability against reliable observations. In reality, we often reject sense data on theoretical grounds: the earth is not flat, a stick partially immersed in water is not bent, distant stars are not red. A secure and well-understood theoretical perspective is essential if students are to make these decisions. Of course, observations will also be misleading when the theory underpinning them is mistaken, or is insufficiently sophisticated for the task-in-hand (see later).

There is an interesting paradox with which students can be confronted: unless they know what to look for, they may not see anything; yet if they concentrate only on what they expect, they may miss or seriously misinterpret the unexpected. Students can begin to appreciate this point by considering how they might design an apparatus to detect particular entities. Unless they speculate about their proper-ties, they cannot design instruments to detect them. Moreover, the instruments will fail to detect them if their properties deviate in any significant way from the expected. However, one of the more interesting features of science is that the unexpected often turns out to be theoretically more significant than the predicted. So it is important that, from time to time, we provide students with experiences that are entirely unexpected by them. Through such experiences, students develop the skills of critical observation, admirably summed up by Pasteur's famous saying that, in scientific observation, chance favours only the prepared mind.

However, the real problem is that inductive generalizations just cannot be relied upon, because they derive directly from a series of single observations. As David Hume (1854: 390) reminds us, 'There can be no demonstrative arguments to prove that those instances of which we have had no experience resemble those of which we have had experience'. In other words, induction is not logically valid. A general-ization derived from singular statements, however numerous, may still turn out to be wrong.

Towards an alternative model of science

If there are so many difficulties and absurdities with this traditional model of science, we should discard it in favour of a more realistic account of how science proceeds. Such an account starts with existing theory and knowledge, and attempts to explore it, think about it, use it, criticize it, test it, doubt it, modify it and replace it. It gives a more faithful description of how new ideas generated during these activities are refined, developed and tested by criticism based on internal consistency and consistency with other accepted theories, and by observa-tion and experiment.[1]

One such account is Karl Popper's hypothetico-deductive model, in which science proceeds by successive cycles of imagination and criticism (Popper 1968). First, a hypothesis is produced by intuition, by inspired guesswork from an existing theoretical background. From the hypothesis, certain conclusions are deduced and compared among themselves for internal consistency. Next, the conclusions are tested by observation or experiment. If the predictions are borne out, the hypoth-esis is corroborated; if not, the hypothesis must be modified or discarded. Thus, scientific reasoning is a constant interplay among hypotheses, the logical expecta-tions (predictions) they give rise to, and experimental or observational evidence; a constant dialogue between 'what might be' and 'what is'. In Popper's language, science proceeds by means of a series of conjectures and refutations until it arrives at a theory which satisfactorily explains the evidence (or, more precisely, is not refuted by it). This is not a random 'hit or miss' procedure; there is constant feedback for the modification and restructuring of hypotheses. Each conjecture is made in the light of previous experience.

There are several important differences between Popper's view of science and the traditional inductivist view: observation is placed much later; imagination and speculation based on existing theoretical understanding is placed first; falsification, rather than verification, is the central feature of hypothesis testing. In other words, every test of a theory is an attempt to falsify it, rather than an attempt to prove it correct. The significance of falsification in Popper's model is a consequence of the asymmetry between confirmation and refutation: while universal statements cannot logically be confirmed by single observations, no matter how numerous, they can be refuted by a single observation. The observation of one black swan falsifies the hypothesis that all swans are white. In other words, falsification is decisive.

By exposing hypotheses to a fierce struggle for survival, we ensure that only the fittest hypotheses survive. 'Fittest' means those that best fit the facts, the observational evidence. By rejecting hypotheses that fail to stand up to observational and experimental test, scientists make progress towards a truer description of the world, because they have ruled out some possible explanations. Of course, we could never know if we had arrived at the truth; we are all prisoners of our senses, confined by our environment, and limited by our imaginations. Scientific truth is simply our current 'best shot' at explanation. The theories that we hold are no more than provisional, those that we have not yet managed to falsify.

An alternative to Popperian ideas is presented in *The Structure of Scientific Revolutions*, where Thomas Kuhn (1970) argues that science is not the orderly, systematic and continuous activity that Popper describes. Rather, it proceeds by successive phases of revolution and consolidation. The disorganized and diverse activities that precede the emergence of a particular science become structured and directed when the community of practitioners reaches agreement on certain theoretical and methodological issues, that is, when the disciplinary matrix (the paradigm, as Kuhn calls it) becomes established and accepted. Workers then practice 'normal science' in an attempt to explore and develop the particular paradigm they have adopted, and the basic validity of which they have accepted. Inevitably, unsolved problems and apparent falsifications are encountered. Such anomalies are to be expected and tolerated. However, if they resist solution for a long time, if they strike at the very core of the paradigm, or if they have some pressing social or economic significance, then a 'crisis' develops. The crisis is resolved when a new paradigm emerges which can satisfactorily solve the problems and provide guidelines for a new normal science. Thus, according to Kuhn, the path of science is discontinuous; it proceeds through a series of major conceptual revolutions interspersed with periods of stability and consolidation.

There are some interesting features in Kuhn's model of science. First, there is a tolerance of anomaly and falsifying evidence. Provided that these are not 'serious', they are accepted as normal. The paradigm is given 'breathing space' in which to accommodate anomaly through modification and development. If scientific theories were not remarkably resilient in the face of apparently falsifying data, we would have to live with new theories all the time. Theories are resilient because they can accommodate counter observations in many ways. Indeed, according to Lakatos (1978), scientists engage in all kinds of pragmatic, intellectual manoeuvres to defend a favoured theory. Second, Kuhn argues that rival paradigms are incommensurate. Because they involve different concepts and ideas, they direct attention to different things, and in different ways. Even when the new paradigm uses words from the old, it does so in a new way. Compare, for example, the use of concepts such as 'mass', 'time' and 'energy' in the Newtonian and Einsteinian paradigms, or 'acid' and 'base' in the Lowry–Bronsted and the Lewis theories.

> The proponents of competing paradigms practice their trades in different worlds … In one, solutions are compounds, in the other mixtures. One is embedded in a flat, the other in a curved, matrix of space. Practising in different worlds, the two groups of scientists see different things when they look from the same point in the same direction.
>
> (Kuhn 1970: 149)

It follows that direct comparison of rival paradigms is difficult, perhaps even impossible. There are no paradigm-independent concepts that can be used; there are no paradigm-independent observations that can be made or experiments that can be performed. So much for the decisiveness of Popper's falsificationist model! If it isn't possible to perform critical experiments capable of furnishing theory-free data, it follows that there are no purely empirical criteria for establishing the superiority of one paradigm over another. In other words, science is not entirely objective and rational, at least not in the sense that rationality is conventionally portrayed in science education. A message that we do not build into the science curriculum, or into the public image of science, is that scientific theories are empirically underdetermined. Empirical adequacy is insufficient, in itself, to establish validity. Consistency with the observable facts does not confer truth status on a theory. Such consistency simply means that a theory may be true. But so may lots of other theories that also correspond with the observations (Duhem 1962). Moreover, empirical inadequacy is frequently ignored by individual scientists fighting passionately for a well-loved theory and is often considered subordinate to the 'context of discovery' by the community-appointed validators (Knorr-Cetina 1983). Additional factors that may play a part in bringing about the shift of paradigm allegiance that constitutes a scientific revolution include:

- Elegance and simplicity (the aesthetics of science)
- Similarity and consistency with other theories
- 'Intellectual fashion', in the sense of compatibility with trends in other disciplines
- Social and economic considerations
- Cultural considerations

- The status of the researchers
- The views of 'significant others' – influential and powerful scientists, journal editors, publishers, and so on
- The priorities of research funding agencies.

If one takes the view that science is a communal activity, and that the ideas of particular scientists only become accepted as scientific knowledge when they achieve consensus within the community of scientists, it follows that many of the sociological, psychological, political and economic issues that influence individuals could, and sometimes will, influence the decisions that the community makes. By failing to address these influences, the simple-minded accounts of theory acceptance and rejection presented in some school science textbooks are insulting to students and often flatly contradict what they read, elsewhere, about real scientists like Galileo, Albert Einstein, Barbara McClintock, Francis Crick and Jim Watson. What these accounts omit is people, and their views, attitudes, passions and prejudices. By contrast, Fuller (1988) writes about the rather wider issues that influence the ways in which scientists present their own work and evaluate each other's. Prominent among them are strong presuppositions or feelings about the way things work, sometimes before evidence is collected, sometimes despite the evidence that has been collected (Holton 1978; 1986).

It would be more appropriate for the school curriculum to emphasize the ways in which knowledge is negotiated within the community of scientists by a complex interplay of theoretical argument, experiment and personal opinion, than to try to project the view that science is independent of the society in which it is located. Criteria of judgement include factors outside pure logic and empirical adequacy, including the social, economic, political, moral and ethical factors that impact on the decision-makers. In other words, science is not value-free and 'people-proof'. As Robert Young says:

> Science is not something in the sky, not a set of eternal truths waiting for discovery. Science is a practice. There is no other science than the science that gets done. The science that exists is the record of the questions that it has occurred to scientists to ask, the proposals that get funded, the paths that get pursued.... Nature 'answers' only the questions that get asked and pursued long enough to lead to results that enter the public domain. Whether or not they get asked, how far they get pursued, are matters for a given society, its educational system, its patronage system, and its funding bodies.
>
> (Young 1987: 18)

What is important is that we achieve a sensible balance between the view that science is absolute truth ascertained by value-free, disinterested individuals using entirely objective and reliable methods of inquiry (a view that, unfortunately, is still quite widespread in school science curriculums), and the dangerously relativist view that 'scientific truth' is that which is in the interests of those in power or, as Slezak (1994: 269) lampoons it, 'truth is what you can get away with'. While we should reject the notion that science is entirely determined by a combination of scientists' self-interests and political expediency, we should recognize that it is profoundly influenced by social, economic and moral–ethical considerations and so is, to a large extent, a product of its time and place. While it would be absurd to claim that scientific knowledge is less reliable or valid simply because it is developed in furtherance of particular interests, or that the products of scientific inquiry and theory-building cannot be understood apart from their socio-historical contexts, appreciation of the socio-cultural milieu within which particular scientists work (or worked) provides the context for understanding their priorities, working styles and criteria of judgement. This applies just as much to a full understanding of the elegant rationalist work of Isaac Newton as it does to understanding the theory of phrenology, a set of beliefs and values held by many prominent scientists and non-scientists in Victorian England (Hodson and Prophet 1986).

The role and status of scientific knowledge

Rather than being a collection of well-established facts, strict definitions and non-negotiable rules and algorithms, scientific knowledge is a network of inter-related concepts and propositions that stand or fall on their ability to describe, explain and predict a range of observable phenomena, without being dependent on any single observation. Moreover, these complex structures are tentative and temporary. History shows us that they grow and develop over time in order to meet the various purposes of science. Consideration of these purposes is beyond the scope of this chapter, save to say that what needs to be established clearly in the minds of students is that:

- Conceptual structures are designed for diverse purposes
- Role and status are inextricably linked.

At the very least, students should be made aware of the crucial distinction between explanatory theories and instrumentalist models. Theories can be described as our 'current best shot' at explaining 'how things are' in the physical world. They should not be regarded as 'true' or as 'proven'. Rather, they should be taken as a more tentative scientific truth: knowledge that has been subjected to, and has survived, critical scrutiny by other scientists using the distinctive procedures and criteria legitimated by the scientific community. Inevitably, theories will change as a consequence of the complex interactions among theoretical speculation, experiment and observation. Models are imaginary conceptual devices for predicting, calculating, manipulating events and generally achieving a measure of control of the environment. Models have no pretensions towards 'truth'; they merely have to work (i.e. do their job satisfactorily). Whether they correspond to reality or not is irrelevant.

An intriguing feature of science is that models that are initially introduced as predictive devices are sometimes elaborated and developed into theories. On occasions, scientists discover that the entities they had earlier created for instrumental purposes actually exist. Put another way, and somewhat more cautiously, they accumulate observational support for the existence of these entities.[2] More frequently, explanatory theories that are superseded by better theories revert to the status of model and continue to fulfil a useful predictive function. It is not illogical or unscientific to retain a falsified or superseded theory in an instrumental capacity, provided that its status is recognized and acknowledged. Within a restricted domain of application, and this applies particularly to school science, it may be simpler to use than current theory. Nor is it illogical or unscientific to use alternative (even seemingly incompatible or contradictory) instrumental models for different aspects of the same phenomenon if all that is sought is a prediction or calculation of a numerical quantity. In a school context, it is common for conflicting wave and particle models to be used side-by-side in accounting for different properties of light.

Understanding and successfully using scientific knowledge entails knowing something about the justification for, and status of, different conceptual structures, and knowing when their use is appropriate and inappropriate. Just as it is important for students to learn that in day-to-day life the appropriateness of language and behaviour is dependent on the social context, so it is important for them to recognize that the appropriateness of scientific models and theories is dependent on the kind of issue or problem being addressed. It is important, also, to recognize that the variety of specific purposes that motivate theory building and model building within the sciences ensures that the precise meaning attached to a concept will depend on the specific role that it has within a particular knowledge structure. As suggested earlier, the differences in meaning of mass and energy in the Newtonian and Einsteinian views of the world, and the shift in meaning of acid and base between the Lowry–Bronsted and Lewis theories, illustrate this point very clearly.

Achieving a balanced view of science and scientists

The purpose of this chapter is to show how a more personalized view of science and scientific inquiry might be promoted in school. Replacing inductivism by Popperian methods puts imagination and creativity back into what is still a rigorous method, but a method driven by people and their particular interests, knowledge and values. Including the Lakatosian notion of rival 'research programmes', each with its particular protagonists, puts passion back into science; acknowledging Kuhn's views about the revolutionary nature of scientific progress opens the door for a consideration of sociocultural forces. Finally, Feyerabend's (1962) so-called 'anarchic view of science' recognizes the significance of intuition and tacit knowledge in scientific expertise or connoisseurship. Scientific inquiry is not the simple application of an all-purpose algorithm comprising a series of content-free, generalizable and transferable steps, as advocates of the so-called Process Approach to science education allege (see Wellington 1989). Real science is an untidy, unpredictable activity that requires each scientist to devise their own course of action. In that sense, there is no method. In approaching a particular situation, scientists choose an approach they consider to be appropriate to the particular task-in-hand by making a selection of processes and procedures from the range of those available and approved by the community of practitioners. Further, scientists refine their approach to a problem, develop greater understanding of it and devise more appropriate and productive ways of proceeding all at the same time. As soon as an idea is developed, it is subjected to evaluation (by observation, experiment, comparison with other theories, etc.). Sometimes this evaluation leads to new ideas, to further and different experiments, or even to a complete re-casting of the original idea or reformulation of the problem. Thus, almost every move that a scientist makes during an inquiry changes the situation in some way, so that the next decisions and moves are made in an altered context. Consequently, scientific inquiry is holistic, fluid, reflexive, context-dependent and idiosyncratic, not a matter of following a set of rules that requires particular behaviours at particular times. It is best summed up by Percy Bridgman's (1950: 351) remark that 'the scientific method, as far as it is a method, is nothing more than doing one's damnedest with one's mind, no holds barred'.

In making their choices and in implementing their chosen strategy, scientists make use of a kind of expertise that has been variously labelled tacit knowledge, scientific intuition and scientific flair. It is the kind of knowledge, often not well articulated, or even consciously applied, that can be acquired only through the experience of doing science. It constitutes the central core of the art and craft of the scientist. It is not distinct from the possession of laboratory skills, on the one hand, and the possession of conceptual understanding, on the other. Rather, it is the capacity to use both in a purposeful way, in order to achieve particular goals. It combines conceptual understanding and bench skills with elements of creativity, experimental flair (the scientific equivalent of the gardener's 'green fingers') and a complex of affective attributes that provide the necessary impetus of determination and commitment. With experience, it develops into what Polanyi (1958) and Oakeshott (1962) call 'connoisseurship'. Thus, scientists proceed partly by rationalization (based on their theoretical understanding) and partly by intuition rooted in their tacit knowledge of how to do science (connoisseurship): 'A practising scientist is continually making judgements for which he can provide no justification beyond saying that that is how things strike him' (Newton-Smith 1981: 81).

It is not my wish to portray all scientists as self-serving, cynical opportunists, and it would be a disaster if the science curriculum did so. There is no doubt that scientists' personal, political and religious views impact on the kind of science they choose to do; there is no doubt, either, that intuition, luck (both good and bad), self-interest, personal ambition, academic and publishing pressures will, from time to time, influence the way they do it. The key question, as Loving (1997: 436) reminds us, is 'whether these are the predominant factors driving good science or factors that make science simply a human (and thus imperfect) endeavour'. Above all, I want to remind students that science is carried out by people, and that these people, like everyone else, have views, values, beliefs and interests. I want the curriculum to show students that these people (scientists) can be warm, sensitive, humorous and passionate. More importantly, I want them to realize that people who are warm, sensitive, humorous and passionate can still become scientists,

though they are required to conduct their work in accordance with codes of practice established, scrutinized and maintained by the community of scientists.

Once we put people back into science, we open up the possibility that science
can be and has been different. Different groups of people have different priorities,
they identify different problems, which they approach in different ways, using
different theories, instruments and methods. They may even have different criteria
of validity and acceptability. If science has different goals, methods and criteria of
judgement, it is inevitable that it will generate different knowledge and different
theories. This new curriculum message is that science is not propelled exclusively
by its own internal logic. Rather, it is shaped by the personal beliefs and political
attitudes of its practitioners and reflects, in part, 'the history, power structures, and
political climate of the supportive community' (Dixon 1973: 71). This can be highlighted by historical studies, by studies of non-Western science, and by studies of
the misuse of science for social and political purposes (Hodson 1993). By emphasizing that current ideas are no more than the latest in a series of views shaped and
influenced by personal and social conditions and attitudes, historical case studies
can reinforce understanding of the mechanisms of scientific practice and imbue
students with a healthy scepticism regarding scientific claims – an important
element in developing critical scientific and technological literacy. When reinforced by consideration of some current thinking concerning feminist science and
ethnoscience, for example, these activities will help to impress on students that we
can re-orient, re-prioritize and re-direct our science and technology towards more
socially-just and environmentally-sound practices.

Notes

1   What follows is a very brief account of several alternative views of scientific method. It is not
     intended to be a rigorous treatment; its purpose is to indicate some points that collectively
     constitute a more personalized view of science and, hence, a more appropriate image of science for
     the school curriculum.
2   This more cautious phrasing recognizes the theory-dependence of experiments and correlation
     studies, and of the interpretation of evidence provided by them.

References

Barlex, D. and Carre, C. (1985) *Visual Communication in Science*, Cambridge: Cambridge
    University Press.
Bridgman, P.W. (1950) *Reflections of a Physicist*, New York: Philosophical Library.
Cawthron, E. R. and Rowell, J. A. (1978) 'Epistemology and science education', *Studies in
    Science Education* 5: 31–59.
Dixon, B. (1973) *What is Science For?*, London: Collins.
Duhem, P. (1962) *The Aim and Structure of Physical Theory* (trans. P. P. Wiener), New York:
    Atheneum Press.
Feyerabend, P. K. (1962) 'Explanation, reduction and empiricism', *Minnesota Studies in the
    Philosophy of Science* 3: 28–97.
Fuller, S. (1988) *Social Epistemology*, Bloomington, IN: Indiana University Press.

Hodson, D. (1986) 'Rethinking the role and status of observation in science education', *Journal of Curriculum Studies* 18: 381–96.

Hodson, D. (1993) 'In search of a rationale for multicultural science education', *Science Education* 77: 685–711.

Hodson, D. and Prophet, B. (1986) 'A bumpy start to science education', *New Scientist* 1521: 25–8.

Holton, G. (1978) *The Scientific Imagination: Case Studies*, Cambridge: Cambridge University Press.

Holton, G. (1986) *The Advancement of Science and its Burdens*, Cambridge: Cambridge University Press.

Hume, D. (1854) 'Of the understanding', in *Philosophical Works, Vol. 1*, Edinburgh: Adam and Charles Black (reprinted by Scientia Verlag, 1964).

Knorr-Cetina, K. D. (1983) 'The ethnographic study of scientific work', in K. D. Knorr-Cetina and M. Mulkay (eds) *Science Observed*, London: Sage.

Kuhn, T. S. (1970) *The Structure of Scientific Revolutions*, Chicago: University of Chicago Press.

Lakatos, I. (1978) *The Methodology of Scientific Research Programmes*, Cambridge: Cambridge University Press.

Loving, C. (1997) 'From the summit of truth to its slippery slopes: Science education's journey through positivist–postmodern territory', *American Educational Research Journal* 34: 421–52.

Medawar, P. B. (1967) *The Art of the Soluble*, London: Methuen.

Medawar, P. B. (1969) *Induction and Intuition in Scientific Thought*, London: Methuen.

Newton-Smith, W. H. (1981) *The Rationality of Science*, London: Routledge and Kegan Paul.

Oakeshott, M. (1962) *Rationalism in Politics and Other Essays*, London: Methuen.

Polanyi, M. (1958) *Personal Knowledge: Towards a Post-Critical Philosophy*, London: Routledge and Kegan Paul.

Popper, K. R. (1968) *The Logic of Scientific Discovery*, London: Hutchinson.

Slezak, P. (1994) 'Sociology of scientific knowledge and scientific education: Part 1', *Science and Education* 3: 265–94.

Theobald, D. W. (1968) *An Introduction to the Philosophy of Science*, London: Methuen.

Wellington, J. J. (1989) 'Skills and processes in science education: an introduction', in J. J. Wellington (ed.) *Skills and Processes in Science Education*, London: Routledge.

Young, R. M. (1987) 'Racist society, racist science', in D. Gill and L. Levidow (eds) *Anti-racist Science Teaching*, London: Free Association Books.

3   What is science?

Michael Reiss

I have found Ms … has had to deal with another problem: the history of science is almost entirely the history of *Western* science, and Ms … has almost no knowledge of
European history since classical times. This is obviously a considerable drawback in
coming to a general view or coming to grips with many broader problems in the
development of science …

> (Copied from a 1981 end-of-term supervision report of
> a student from Pakistan doing the second-year undergraduate
> course in History of Science at Cambridge University)

Who are scientists?

A while ago, I happened to see a new set of postage stamps produced in the UK, titled
'Scientific achievements' (issued 5 March 1991). It's worth spending a few moments
imagining what you might expect (or hope!) to see on these stamps. Well, whatever
you thought, the Royal Mail produced four stamps under the heading 'Scientific
achievements' with the captions 'Faraday – Electricity', 'Babbage – Computer',
'Radar – Watson-Watt' and 'Jet Engine – Whittle' (Figure 3.1). I find it difficult to
imagine a narrower conception of what science is and who does it. The image seems
to be that real science is hard physics, with military applications, done by males who
are white and worked on their own between about 1820 and 1940. No wonder so
many students drop science at school as soon as they have the chance! Children
come to school science lessons with clear impressions of what science is, how it operates and who does it (Driver *et al.* 1985; Osborne and Freyberg 1985). There is a limit
to what science teachers can realistically be expected to achieve in terms of challenging social perceptions and changing received wisdom.

It seems sad that the Royal Mail could produce a set of stamps that portrayed
such a biased view of science. Stamps to feature scientists could convey the notion
that women do science, that science didn't start in the nineteenth century and
finish around the time of the Second World War, that it isn't a Western construct,
that it is done by people working in groups and that it permeates every area of life.

Countless examples could be given of the way we are all, including pupils and
students in school, bombarded with messages about who scientists are, but two

Figure 3.1 Presentation pack of UK postage stamps issued on 5 March 1991 under the title 'Scientific achievements'

more will suffice. The first is taken from a book titled *History of Science* published in 1985 by the American Institute of Physics (Weart and Phillips 1985). Some indication of the partiality of this publication is gleaned from the third sub-heading of the Introduction which modestly asserts 'History of modern science largely the history of physics'. Under this heading we read:

> Why was the history of modern science, so far as it has been written down, largely the history of physics? Perhaps it was for the same reasons that, ever since I. I. Rabi got together with Dwight Eisenhower, nearly all of the President's science advisers have been physicists. One reason might be that physics is a master-key to all the twentieth-century sciences; another, that nuclear weaponry has made scientists and the public especially watchful of physics; yet another, that physicists have often had broader viewpoints than other technically orientated people, with an interest in everything from music to social relations.
>
> (Weart and Phillips 1985:2 of Introduction)

Unless you are from the USA and a physicist and have had a remarkably narrow education, it is unlikely that you will believe this. The worrying thing is, that evidently a number of important and influential people really do believe that the history of modern science is largely the history of physics and that 'physicists have often had broader viewpoints than other technically-oriented people'!

The second example of how we are all bombarded with messages about who scientists are comes from the broadcasting by the BBC World Service of a major series called *They Made our World*. To quote from the book that accompanies the series:

[The series was] broadcast around the world in twenty-six episodes Autumn 1990–Spring 1991. It features a gallery of great scientists, engineers, inventors and thinkers who contributed massively to the development of world [*sic*] we live in today.

(Hamilton 1991: inside front cover)

One might have thought that a World Service series would at least have striven to be international in flavour, but the list of chapter titles is so distinctive that it is worth giving in full:

Sir Francis Bacon (1561–1626)
Sir Isaac Newton (1643–1747) [*sic*]
Joseph Priestley (1733–1804)
Antoine-Laurent Lavoisier (1743–1794)
Michael Faraday (1791–1867)
James Clerk Maxwell (1831–1879)
Sir Charles Lyell (1797–1875)
Charles Darwin (1809–1882)
Father Gregor Mendel (1822–1895)
Edward Jenner (1749–1823)
Louis Pasteur (1822–1895)
Sir Alexander Flemming (1881–1955)
James Watt (1736–1819)
George and Robert Stephenson (1781–1848) (1803–1859)
Sir Alexander Graham Bell (1847–1922)
Thomas Alva Edison (1847–1931)
Wilbur and Orville Wright (1867–1912) (1871–1948)
Henry Ford (1863–1947)
Professor Wilhelm Röntgen (1845–1923)
Guglielmo Marconi (1874–1937)
John Logie Baird (1888–1946)
Leo Hendrik Baekeland (1863–1944)
Alan Turing (1912–1954)
Albert Einstein (1879–1955)
Ernest Rutherford (1871–1937)
Robert Oppenheimer and the Manhattan Project (1904–1967).

Of the twenty-eight people listed, none is a woman and none comes from outside Western Europe and the USA. Now the point I wish to make is that who a great scientist is partly depends on one's point of view. There are no absolute or universal criteria by which scientific excellence can infallibly be judged. It is all too easy for excellent scientists to be omitted from such lists. The Royal Mail, the contributors to *History of Physics* and the BBC World Service are guilty of sins of omission, rather than of commission. And, of course, what such people and institutions do is to

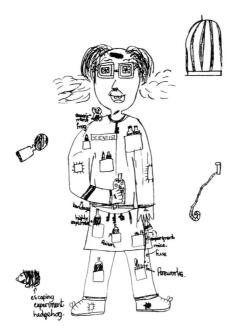

Figure 3.2 A portrayal of a scientist by Caroline Allen (aged 9)

reflect society's view of who scientists are. Powerful organizations such as the BBC and the Post Office reflect, perpetuate and even generate myths.

The effect that all this has can be seen by asking children to draw or describe a scientist. The results are consistent (Wyvill 1991). Most scientists are portrayed as being white, male, middle-aged to old and wearing white coats (Figure 3.2). To determine whether or not this is a distortion or an accurate reflection of the community of scientists, we need to go beyond the question 'Who are scientists?' and examine the nature of science.

The nature of science

The popular view of what science is and how it proceeds probably goes something like this:

> Science consists of a body of knowledge about the world. The facts that comprise this knowledge are derived from accurate observations and careful experiments that can be checked by repeating them. As time goes on, scientific knowledge steadily progresses.

Such a view persists, not only among the general public, but also among science teachers and scientists despite the fact that it is held by most historians of science,

Figure 3.3 What is the relationship between science and that which it describes?

philosophers of science, sociologists of science and science educationalists to be, at best, simplified and misleading and, at worst, completely erroneous (Latour 1987; Woolgar 1988; Wellington 1989; Harding 1991).

It is not too much of a caricature to state that science is seen by many as *the* way to truth. Indeed, a number of important scientists have encouraged such a view by their writings and interviews (e.g. Peter Atkins and Richard Dawkins). It is generally assumed that the world 'out there' exists independently of the particular scientific methodology used to study it (Figure 3.3). The advance of science then consists of scientists discovering eternal truths that exist independent of them and of the cultural context in which these discoveries are made. All areas of life are presumed amenable to scientific inquiry. Truth is supposed to emerge unambiguously from experiment like Pallas Athene, the goddess of wisdom, springing mature and unsullied from the head of Zeus. This view of science is mistaken for a number of reasons, which I now want to go on to discuss.

Scientists have to choose on what to work

What scientists 'choose' to work on is controlled partly by their background as individuals and partly by the values of the society in which they live and work. Most scientific research is not pure but applied. In particular, approximately one half of all scientific research funding is provided for military purposes. To give just one specific example of the way society determines on what scientists should work: the

1980s saw a significant reduction in Great Britain of research into systematics, taxonomy and nomenclature (the classification, identification and naming of organisms). This was a direct result of changes in government funding which, for instance, required the Natural History Museum in London, the major UK centre for such research, to generate much of its own income. As a result, the number of scientists working there in these disciplines more than halved as such scientists generate very little income.

Now, my point is not specifically to complain at the demise of systematics, taxonomy and nomenclature in the UK, but to point out that society and individual scientists have to choose on what to work. To a very large extent that choice is not determined on purely scientific criteria (if such criteria exist), but by political machinations and by the priorities (some would describe them as quirks) of funding bodies.

Scientists do not discover the world out there as it is

Scientists approach their topics of study with preconceptions. There is no such thing as an impartial observation. In the classroom this is seen to be the case every time a group of pupils is asked, for the first time, to draw some cells or sulphur crystals under the microscope. It isn't possible until you know what to draw. Unless you know that a leaf of pondweed consists of numerous small, brick-like structures, all you *can* see is a mass of green with lines and occasional air bubbles. In the same way, the first time the German artist Dürer saw a rhinoceros, he drew what, by his normal standards, could be described as a fat armour-plated horse (Figure 3.4). To expect pupils to draw regular epidermal cells the first time they see them is to expect more of them than Dürer could manage.

Instances where we can look back and see how scientists have unconsciously interpreted what they have seen in the light of their cultural heritage are legion. In his book *Metaphors of Mind*, Robert Sternberg points out that much of the present confusion surrounding the concept of intelligence stems from the variety of standpoints from which the human mind can be viewed (Sternberg 1990). The geographic metaphor is based on the notion that a theory of intelligence should provide a map of the mind. This view dates back at least to Gall, an early nineteenth-century German anatomist and perhaps the most famous of phrenologists. Gall investigated the topography of the head, looking and feeling for tiny variations in the shape of the skull. According to Gall, a person's intelligence was to be discerned in the pattern of their cranial bumps. A second metaphor, the computational metaphor, envisions the mind as a computing device and analogizes the processes of the mind to the operations of a computer. Other metaphors discussed by Sternberg include the biological metaphor, the epistemological metaphor, the anthropological metaphor, the sociological metaphor and the systems metaphor. The point is that what scientists see and the models they construct to mirror reality depend very much on where their point of view is.

A clear example of how the work that scientists do is inevitably affected by who they are is provided by Jane Goodall's seminal (if that is not too sexist a term!) research on

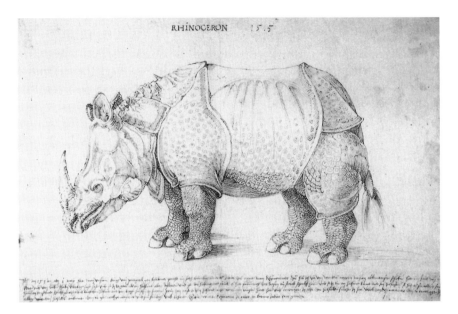

Figure 3.4 Albrecht Dürer's rhinoceros. Pen and ink, 1515

chimpanzee behaviour. When Jane Goodall first arrived to study the chimpanzees on the banks of Lake Tanganyika, the game warden who took her round made a mental note that she wouldn't last more than six weeks. She has stayed for forty years, producing the definitive accounts of chimpanzee social organization and behaviour in her fascinating and moving books *In the Shadow of Man* (van Lawick-Goodall 1971) and *The Chimpanzees of Gombe: Patterns of Behavior* (Goodall 1986).

An important point about Jane Goodall is that she had no formal training in ethology (the science of animal behaviour), having trained as a secretary after leaving school. As she herself wrote, 'I was, of course, completely unqualified to undertake a scientific study of animal behaviour' (van Lawick-Goodall 1971: 20). However, she spent some time with the celebrated palaeontologist Louis Leakey and his wife, Mary, on one of their annual expeditions to Olduvai Gorge on the Serengeti plains. Louis Leakey became convinced that Goodall was the person he had been looking for for twenty years – someone who was so fascinated by animals and their behaviour that they would be happy to spend at least two years studying chimpanzees in the wild. Leakey was particularly interested in the chimpanzees on the shores of Lake Tanganyika as the remains of prehistoric people had often been found on lake shores, and he thought it possible that an understanding of chimpanzee behaviour today might shed light on the behaviour of our Stone Age ancestors.

Goodall couldn't believe that Leakey was giving her the chance to do what she most wanted to do – watch chimpanzees in their natural habitat. She felt that her lack of training would disqualify her. But, as she later wrote:

Louis, however, knew exactly what he was doing. Not only did he feel that a university training was unnecessary, but even that in some ways it might have been disadvantageous. He wanted someone with a mind uncluttered and unbiased by theory who would make the study for no other reason than a real desire for knowledge; and, in addition, someone with a sympathetic understanding of animal behaviour.

(van Lawick-Goodall 1971: 20)

Now the point, of course, is not that Jane Goodall could approach chimpanzees with a mind 'uncluttered and unbiased by theory' but that the clutter and theory in her mind was crucially distinct from that in someone who emerged from a university course in ethology. In the 1960s one of the great heresies of academic ethology was to be anthropomorphic – to treat non-humans as if they had human attributes and feelings. That is precisely what Jane Goodall did, and it allowed fundamentally new insights into chimpanzee behaviour. A flavour of Jane Goodall's approach can be obtained by reading the following quote:

One day, when Flo was fishing for termites, it became obvious that Figan and Fifi, who had been eating termites at the same heap, were getting restless and wanted to go. But old Flo, who had already fished for two hours, and who was herself only getting about two termites every five minutes, showed no signs of stopping. Being an old female, it was possible that she might continue for another hour at least. Several times Figan had set off resolutely along the track leading to the stream, but on each occasion, after repeatedly looking back at Flo, he had given up and returned to wait for his mother.

Flint, too young to mind where he was, pottered about on the heap, occasionally dabbling at a termite. Suddenly Figan got up again and this time approached Flint. Adopting the posture of a mother who signals her infant to climb on to her back, Figan bent one leg and reached back his hand to Flint, uttering a soft pleading whimper. Flint tottered up to him at once, and Figan, still whimpering, put his hand under Flint and gently pushed him on his back. Once Flint was safely aboard, Figan, with another quick glance at Flo, set off rapidly along the track. A moment later Flo discarded her tool and followed.

(van Lawick-Goodall 1971: 114–15)

Other writers at the time did not give names to their animals; nor did they use language like 'getting restless', 'wanted to go', 'set off resolutely' and 'pottered about'; nor did they impute to their subjects the ability consciously to manipulate one another.

Apart from her lack of formal training, there is another factor about Jane Goodall that may well be significant. She is a woman. The longest-running studies on animal behaviour have all been carried out by women including: Jane Goodall on chimpanzees (1960 to present); Dian Fossey on gorillas (1966 to 1985 when she was murdered, probably because of her dedication to the gorillas); and Fiona Guinness on red deer (1972 to present). All three worked/work quite exceptionally long hours with what can only be described as total dedication. In 1978 and 1979, I spent a couple of months working alongside Fiona Guinness. On average she worked fourteen hours a day, seven days a week.

My point is not that research scientists ought to work this long, nor that only women can show the empathy with animals that these three did or do. Rather, it is that the personal and social pressures that shaped Jane Goodall, Dian Fossey and Fiona Guinness were crucial to the type of science that they carried out or do carry out. And this is true for all scientists. It's just that it is easier to see in these three cases. Donna Haraway in her book *Primate Visions: Gender, Race and Nature in the World of Modern Science* argues that scientific practice is story-telling. The work that primatologists do is moulded by the environment in which they operate and by the sort of people they are, so that the stories that primatologists tell reflect the social agendas that surround them (Haraway 1989).

It is possible to suppose from the above that only bad science is affected by the presuppositions of the individuals that carry it out, influenced by the hidden assumptions of the society in which they live and move and have their being. Indeed, most practising scientists are happy with the notion that this is the case. However, many sociologists of science want to go much further than this. They argue that every science inevitably reflects the interests, the values, the unconscious suppositions and the beliefs of the society that gives rise to it (Longino 1990). For an example of how even what is almost universally acknowledged as being among the best of science may have critically been influenced by what might be described as extra-scientific forces, consider some of Newton's thinking in his *Principia* (Freudenthal 1986; discussed by Chalmers 1990).

One of Newton's key advances was to argue that the properties of wholes are to be explained in terms of the essential properties of their parts. For instance, Newton asserted that the extension, hardness, impenetrability, mobility and force of inertia of the whole result from the extension, hardness, impenetrability, mobility and force of inertia of the parts. From this, he concluded that the smallest of particles are also all extended, hard, impenetrable, moveable and endowed with their proper forces of inertia.

Newton's assertion that the whole is simply the sum of its component parts provided the crucial foundation stone for his pivotal work on gravity, but from where did he get the idea? The assertion cannot, of course, be proved. Indeed, every biologist knows that the properties of an organism (say, a giraffe) cannot be deduced from the properties of the molecules of which it is comprised. Biology is all about understanding that the properties that one level of organization has are not necessarily apparent from studying lower levels of organization.

Freudenthal traces Newton's assumptions back to the individualistic understanding of society that emerged in the seventeenth century as European feudal society came to be replaced by early forms of capitalist society. Freudenthal points out that, while the various new conceptions of society formulated in the seventeenth century by Thomas Hobbes, John Locke and others differ from each other in significant respects, they have one thing in common. They all attempt to explain society by reference to the properties of the individuals that make up the society.

Further, individuals are assumed to have these properties independently of their existence in society.

At this point, it may be worth pointing out that accepting the essential premise of sociologists of science that science and society are inevitably, inexorably intertwined, does not necessarily require one to abandon all belief in the objectivity of science. As Alan Chalmers puts it: 'The natural world does not behave in one way for capitalists and in another way for socialists, in one way for males and another for females, in one way for Western cultures and another for Eastern cultures' (Chalmers 1990: 112). This seems reasonable. However, a scientist's *perceptions* of the natural world, as well as her interpretations, come through their senses, themselves as a person and their culture. What is of significance for science education is that there can be no single, universal, acultural science. Rather, every sort of science is an ethnoscience, as I shall now go on to argue.

Science as a collection of ethnosciences

The term 'ethnoscience' first became widely used in the anthropological literature of the 1960s (Bulmer 1971). It has been used in two ways:

> It refers firstly to the 'science', in the sense of modes of classification of the material and social universe, possessed by societies unaffected or little affected by modern international scientific thinking and discoveries. Secondly, it refers to a particular anthropological approach which has as its objective the systematic scientific investigation of ways in which particular societies classify the universe …

Such ethnoscientific research has contributed much that is of value to those hoping to fashion a science education for a pluralist society, but we need to broaden this definition slightly. To restrict the term 'ethnoscience' to societies 'unaffected … by modern international scientific thinking and discoveries' is both to misunderstand the nature of science, and to risk adopting a patronizing and racist attitude to such ethnosciences. It misunderstands the nature of science because, as I have argued above, *all* science is set in a cultural milieu, so that we cannot validly distinguish a number of ethnosciences from a single international non-ethnoscientific science. It risks being patronizing and racist because accepting such a definition of ethnoscience inevitably makes it likely that a writer, however impressed she or he is with a particular ethnoscience, ends up comparing it with 'modern international scientific thinking and discoveries', which then act as a benchmark against which the particular ethnoscience is judged.

Further we should not assume that within a particular society, all scientific thinking operates within the same paradigm. By virtue of differences between individuals in such important characteristics as gender, religious beliefs, ethnicity, age and disability, individuals may differ significantly in their scientific understanding and conception of the world. There are two extreme ways in which a teacher may react to such differences. The more common is to adopt, implicitly, what we can call a 'deficit' model of science. Here all inter-individual (and inter-cultural) differences in scientific understanding and practice are held to exist because individuals and cultures differ in the extent to which they understand and practise the one, true science. The role of a science teacher is clearly then to remove obstacles to the understanding of this single true science, and then teach it (cf. Layton 1991).

The second extreme way in which a teacher could react to inter-individual and inter-cultural differences in scientific understanding and practice is to adopt what we can call an 'all sciences are equal' model. Here, there is no objectivity in science. All scientific methodologies and findings, however much they differ, are of equal validity.

I suspect it is because this second model leads to conclusions which, to practically every science teacher, are so manifestly absurd, that the first model – with its assumptions of the one, true science – is so often adopted.

What I will attempt to argue is that there is a middle ground between these two models, a middle ground which genuinely allows for inter-individual and inter-cultural differences without abandoning all claims to real scientific progress.

Published or be damned

Once a scientist or group of scientists has discovered something or produced a new model to interpret a phenomenon, it is necessary for their work to be disseminated in some form, usually through publication. Getting work published, read, recognized and cited depends greatly on the personalities of the individuals involved and on what society values.

As a single example of the importance of society's world view in accepting a scientific theory, consider the circumstances that surrounded the publication of William Harvey's ideas on the circulation of the blood. Although the circulation of the blood had been established in China by the second century BCE at the latest, in Europe the idea was proposed by Michael Servetus (1546), Realdo Colombo (1559), Andrea Cesalpino (1571) and Giordano Bruno (1590). These men had read of the circulation of the blood in the writings of an Arab of Damascus, Ibn Nafis (died 1288) who himself seems to have obtained at least some of his ideas from China (Temple 1991). Harvey published his 'discovery' in 1628. It is possible that the early seventeenth century accounts of a huge diversity of pumping engines for mine drainage and water supply caused the scientific community and general public to be in an appropriate frame of mind to accept the notion of the heart as a mechanical pump (cf. Russell 1988). In other words, most people remember Harvey as the person responsible for the discovery of the circulation of the blood because earlier proponents of the idea published them at times when their understanding and acceptance were more difficult for people.

Mention can also be made of the importance of the language that scientists use. Some scientists are simply much better at writing their work up so that it is more likely to be published, read and cited. What people then remember is the language used as well as the science. Indeed, the two cannot be separated. We cannot sift out the language of corruption to reveal a pure, unsullied science.

An illustration of the intimacy of the relationship between language and science was provided by the attempts of newspapers and magazines in the UK on 24 April 1992 to describe the reported discovery by a Nasa satellite of radiation from the Big Bang. The word most often used was 'ripple'. The first two paragraphs of the *Independent* report (which dominated the front page of the paper) were as follows:

> Fourteen thousand million years ago the universe hiccuped. Yesterday, American scientists announced that they may have heard the echo.
> A Nasa spacecraft has detected ripples at the edge of the Cosmos which are the fossilised imprint of the birth of the stars and galaxies around us today.

Even the *Sun* weighed in. Under a headline 'We find secret of the creation' (page 6) the ripples were said to 'look like wispy clouds'. The publicity attending the news was heightened by Stephen Hawking who was reported on the front page of the *Daily Mail* as describing the finding as 'the discovery of the century, if not of all time'.

It's easy to make fun of reports which talk of wispy clouds and the universe hiccuping, but my point is that all science has to be reported in a language, even if it is the language of mathematics. And all languages, including the language(s) of mathematics, are human constructs.

Changing conceptions of science

The notion as to what constitutes science differs over time and between cultures (Hiatt and Jones 1988; Brooke 1991). Attempts by certain historians and philosophers of science to identify a distinctive 'scientific method' which demarcates science absolutely from other disciplines have not proved successful. Though certain principles, such as testability and repeatability, may be central to modern science, it is now widely held that the question 'What is science?' can only be answered: 'That which is recognised as such by a scientific community.' Although this answer, being somewhat tautologous, may appear distinctly unhelpful, its truth may be seen by examining what other times and cultures include in science.

Figure 3.5 shows the early classification of Islamic science. To many readers the inclusion of such things as syntax, grammar, pronunciation, poetry, metaphysics, jurisprudence and rhetoric may appear surprising. But one should remember that, throughout the Middle Ages, Western philosophy operated within a framework of the seven liberal arts. These consisted of the verbal arts (the trivium) – grammar, rhetoric and logic or dialectic – and the mathematical quadrivium – arithmetic, music, geometry and astronomy (Wagner 1983). The twentieth-century Western understanding of science is just that – a twentieth-century Western understanding. In particular, school science is all too often seen as being absolutely distinct from other domains of knowledge such as the creative arts and economics, despite the fact that practising scientists, historians and philosophers of science agree that creativity and financial constraints are of prime importance in science.

Science is also often seen in conflict with religion, despite the fact that other

Science of language

syntax
grammar
pronunciation and speech
poetry

Logic

necessary conditions for premises
    which would lead in a syllogism
    to certain knowledge
definitions of useful syllogisms and
    the means of discovering
    dialectical proofs
examination of errors in proofs
definition of oratory
study of poetry

Propaedeutic sciences

arithmetic
geometry
optics
science of the heavens
music
science of weights
science of tool-making

Physics and metaphysics

Physics

knowledge of the principles which
    underlie natural bodies
knowledge of the nature and
    character of the elements
science of the generation and
    corruption of bodies
science of the reactions which the
    elements undergo in order to
    form compounds
science of compound bodies
    formed of the four elements
science of minerals
science of plants
science of animals

Metaphysics

knowledge of the essence of beings
knowledge of the principles of the
    particular and observational
    sciences
knowledge of noncorporeal beings,
    leading finally to the
    knowledge of the Truth, that
    is, of God, one of whose names
    is the Truth

Science of society

jurisprudence
rhetoric

Figure 3.5 The early classification of the sciences according to the Iḥṣā' al-'ulūm of al-
    Fārābī

models of the relationship between science and religion exist and many
outstanding scientists have a religious faith (Barbour 1990; Brooke 1991).

Much school science operates on the assumption that 'real science' consists in
doing laboratory experiments to test hypotheses. I should like to relate an anecdote
to illustrate this. When I started teaching social biology to 16–19-year-olds in a
school in England, the Examinations Board that set the syllabus included a project
in its scheme of assessment. One of my students was a very fit athlete who lived in
Bahrain out of term time. He carried out on himself measurements of such

physiological variables as body temperature and body mass just before and just after completing a number of runs of predetermined distance, both in the UK and in Bahrain. Another student was interested to see whether a person's astrological sign (determined by their birth date) correlated with their choice of school subjects (e.g. sciences versus humanities) or with their personality. Accordingly, she carried out a large survey of fellow students. The Examinations Board marked its projects on a 1 (top) to 9 (bottom) scale. Both students were given a 9, which meant that their project contributed nothing to their overall mark: in other words it was scored zero, their projects being deemed to have had no scientific worth.

I'm not claiming that either of these projects was the finest I have ever seen. But I am convinced that the marks they were given (and these marks were not changed on appeal) reflected too narrow an assumption in the Examiners' minds about what constituted a scientific project.

In England and Wales, successive versions of the Science National Curriculum Attainment Target 1 have had a model of science which, while there is much that is good about it, would disqualify, for instance, much of the work done by astronomers, taxonomists, palaeontologists and theoreticians from being included within its compass. Mayr has argued that after the time of the Middle Ages (in Western Europe) the physical sciences were the paradigm of science:

> As everyone was willing to concede, the universality and predictability that seemed to characterize studies of the inanimate world were missing from biology. Because life was restricted to the earth, as far as anyone knew, any statements and generalizations one could make concerning living organisms would seem to be restricted in space and time. To make matters worse, such statements nearly always seemed to have exceptions. Explanations usually were not based on universal laws but rather were pluralistic. In short the theories of biology violated every canon of 'true science', as the philosophers had derived them from the methods and principles of classical physics.
>
> (Mayr 1988: 9)

Sadly, it is still the case that much school science has too narrow an understanding of the *methods* of science. This, I suspect, is one reason why pupils too often find their school science unsatisfying. They know that it's too restricted a way of looking at the world. And they're right.

References

Barbour, I. G. (1990) *Religion in an Age of Science: The Gifford Lectures 1989–1991, Vol. 1*, London: SCM.

Brooke, J. H. (1991) *Science and Religion: Some Historical Perspectives*, Cambridge: Cambridge University Press.

Bulmer, R. N. H. (1971) 'Science, ethnoscience and education', *Papua and New Guinea Journal of Education* 7(1): 22–33.

Chalmers, A. (1990) *Science and its Fabrication*, Milton Keynes: Open University Press.

Driver, R., Guesne, E. and Tiberghien, A. (eds) (1985) *Children's Ideas in Science,* Milton Keynes: Open University Press.

Freudenthal, G. (1986) *Atom and Individual in the Age of Newton,* Dordrecht: Reidel.

Goodall, J. (1986) *The Chimpanzees of Gombe: Patterns of Behavior,* Cambridge, MA: Belknap Press of Harvard University Press.

Hamilton, J. (ed.) (1991) *They Made Our World: Five Centuries of Great Scientists and Inventors,* London: Broadside Books.

Haraway, D. (1989) *Primate Visions: Gender, Race and Nature in the World of Modern Science,* London: Routledge, Chapman and Hall.

Harding, S. (1991) *Whose Science? Whose Knowledge? Thinking from Women's Lives,* Milton Keynes: Open University Press.

Hiatt, L. R. and Jones, R. (1988) 'Aboriginal conceptions of the workings of nature', in R. W. Home (ed.) *Australian Science in the Making,* Cambridge: Cambridge University Press, pp: 1–22.

Latour, B. (1987) *Science in Action: How to Follow Scientists and Engineers through Society,* Milton Keynes: Open University Press.

Lawick-Goodall, van, J. (1971) *In the Shadow of Man,* Glasgow: Collins.

Layton, D. (1991) 'Science education and praxis: the relationship of school science to practical action', *Studies in Science Education* 19: 43–79.

Longino, H. E. (1990) *Science as Social Knowledge: Values and Objectivity in Scientific Inquiry,* Princeton, NJ: Princeton University Press.

Mayr, E. (1988) *Towards a New Philosophy of Biology: Observations of an Evolutionist.* Cambridge, MA: Belknap Press of Harvard University Press.

Osborne, R. and Freyberg, P. (1985) *Learning in Science: The Implications of Children's Science,* Birkenhead, Auckland: Heinemann Education.

Russell, N. (1988) 'Teaching biology in the wider context: the history of the disciplines as a method 2: worked examples', *Journal of Biological Education* 22: 129–35.

Sternberg, R. J. (1990) *Metaphors of Mind: Conceptions of the Nature of Intelligence,* Cambridge: Cambridge University Press.

Temple, R. (1991) *The Genius of China: 3000 Years of Science, Discovery, and Invention,* London: Prion/Multimedia.

Wagner, D. L. (ed.) (1983) *The Seven Liberal Arts in the Middle Ages,* Bloomington, IN: Indiana University Press.

Weart, S. R. and Phillips, M. (eds) (1985) *History of Physics: Readings from Physics Today – Number Two,* New York: American Institute of Physics.

Wellington, J. (ed.) (1989) *Skills and Processes in Science Education: A Critical Analysis,* London: Routledge.

Woolgar, S. (1988) *Science: The Very Idea,* Chichester: Ellis Horwood.

Wyvill, B. (1991) 'Classroom ideas for antiracism through science in primary education', in A. Peacock (ed.) *Science in Primary Schools: The Multicultural Dimension,* Basingstoke: Macmillan Education, pp. 11–27.

4 Practical work in science
Time for a re-appraisal

Jerry Wellington

School science is now firmly embedded in the laboratory. The Third International Mathematics and Science Study (TIMSS 1997) report compared the curriculums of 13-year-old pupils in a range of countries – practical, laboratory activities in science were more frequent in England than in any other country. This may be a cause for celebration – but is the practical, hands-on approach to science working? The aim of this chapter is to begin to look behind the TIMSS data and to ask what is going on in practical laboratory activities, and why.

The laboratorizing of school science

The process of locating school science education in the laboratory has taken place over a period of at least a century. In tracing the history of practical science education, Nott (1997: 49) argues that, by 1897, the laboratory had already 'been identified as an essential item for school science education'. In the century that has followed, the school laboratory has become a symbol of the status of Science in the curriculum, 'rather than a space appropriate for teaching and learning science' (Nott 1997: 54).

In 1988, an article written by three sociologists (Delamont *et al.* 1988) described a view of secondary school science from an outsider's perspective. The title of their article ('In the beginning was the Bunsen') was used to signal what they call the 'ritualistic or fetishistic' way in which the Bunsen burner has become the icon of school science. They describe how pupils' first few lessons in secondary science are an initiation into a new domain. The subject becomes consecrated and demarcated, away from other curriculum areas because of features like its danger and its precision:

> The laboratory is introduced to pupils as an esoteric locale, with its own special objects, ceremonial observances, demands and dangers. Entry into the world of school science is managed as a *rite de passage*: the initiates embark on a perilous and closely supervised adventure. In the course of their initiation they are introduced to artefacts which are endowed with special status.
>
> (Delamont *et al.* 1988: 316)

This is the way science lessons are seen by outsiders, albeit sociologists. Surely, there must be some justification for these rites, icons and artefacts? There must be more to laboratory life than Nott's cynical end remark:

> Why do we do so much practical work in science in English schools? Perhaps because there are so many laboratories.
>
> (Nott 1997: 60)

Recent phases and fads in practical work

It is inevitable that science education and its practical work will, and should, change over time. It is as much a function of its social, historical and technological context as science and scientific method itself. Articles such as Nott (1997) and Gee and Clackson (1992) give an account of its history over a long period, in the latter case going back to the days of John Locke in the late seventeenth century. More recently, Hodson (1996) has talked of 'three decades of confusion and distortion', starting from the 1960s. In my view, from a UK perspective, there have been three important movements in that period which could (rather cruelly and with hindsight) be called phases or fads. I will term them: the discovery approach, the process approach, and 'practical work by order'.

The discovery approach

The discovery phase involved pupils in 'being scientists for the day' and invoked slogans such as 'I do and I understand'. Hodson (1996: 116–19) gives a full account of this phase and its origins in the US, in the writing of Schwab and Bruner. Courses, curriculums and publications were born and were most evident in the Nuffield programmes developed in the late 1960s. Those who taught with the Nuffield materials will have fond memories of the creativity embedded in the approaches, the ideas and the practical work of the Nuffield movement. Many of the 'experiments' and the newly-designed items of apparatus live on and have become institutionalized – more icons of school science. The approach has been criticized largely for its distorted view of scientific enquiry, i.e. it presented scientists rather like 'Sherlock Holmes in a white coat' (Wellington 1981). Observation was presented as theory-free; the jump from experimental data to laws and theory was presented as an inductive process. Hodson (1996: 118) summed up the discovery movement up as 'philosophically unsound and pedagogically unworkable'.

The process approach

The second recent phase, in my view, deserves less attention than the discovery era, which although based on a shaky image of science, did at least produce a number of valuable teaching ideas and materials. The so-called process approach was based not only on a totally distorted view of science, but also led to a range of published teaching materials in the 1980s that promoted a totally one-sided and potentially harmful approach to science education. The distorted view of science was based on the myth that the skills and processes of science (observing, inferring, predicting, and so on) could be divorced from the knowledge base, i.e. the laws and theories, of science. Processes were to be disembodied from their context and content, learnt and taught separately, in the hope that they could become transferable to other contexts. The so-called 'less able' learners, it was felt, could cope with these transferable processes even if they could not grasp the difficult concepts of science 'content' – thus science would be accessible to all. With hindsight, it seems remarkable that in 1989 a whole book (Wellington 1989) was considered necessary as one effort to counter this flawed approach to science and science education.

'Practical work by order'

The third phase, from an England and Wales perspective, although similar orders have been laid down elsewhere, came with National Curriculum legislation, which decreed not only the content to be covered in science education, but also the approach which should be taken to practical and investigative work. Indeed 'approach' is too weak a term for, since 1988, different templates have been made law which dictate how investigative work should be done and which model of science and scientific method it should follow. The first template relied heavily on a control-of-variables model of science that bore no resemblance to the history of science or to its current practice. The model was ridiculed by some (discussed in Wellington 1994) since its application to the work of scientists such as Mendel, Hawking, Newton or Einstein (who probably never controlled a variable in his life) condemned them to reaching barely level one on the statutory ten-point scale. More seriously, its imposition in schools led to the hostility, resentment and 'bitterness' (Donnelly 1995: 99) of teachers who were forced to implement and assess this rigid model of scientific enquiry. The model was later revised and re-christened 'Experimental and Investigative Science'. There is less emphasis on variables and their control and, quite rightly, the importance of evidence and its evaluation are stressed – but it still promotes *one* model or template for science and scientific enquiry. The idea of having one format or one algorithm for science is, as other authors and I argue, flawed.

Reasons for doing practical work now – and their limitations

I find that teachers are always surprised, even shocked, when asked to consider what is the purpose of practical work in science education. Donnelly (1995: 97) reports the same reaction in asking teachers in a research project to suggest the purposes of pupil laboratory work:

> I haven't even thought about it … I mean, that's what science is.

> It's what science is all about really, is getting on with some experiments. Science is a practical subject … you know, end of story I think.

I recently asked a sample of forty-eight science graduates embarking on a teaching career to write down on a small, blank piece of paper why we do practical work in school science. Inevitably, I received a wide range of answers to such an open question, for example: 'to back up the theory', 'to give pupils something to remember the theory by', 'to make theory more visual and accessible to kids', 'makes things easier to remember', 'to give experience – seeing is believing', 'to bring science to life', 'develop manipulative skills', 'to develop skills useful to life and to home', 'to develop practical skills', 'to develop an enquiring mind', and 'to learn transferable skills like a fair test, or planning and observation'. On a more practical level, some wrote: 'to make a change from theory work', 'something else to do apart from lessons', 'keep kids quiet', 'make lessons more interesting', 'they break up lessons to keep the kids entertained', 'fun – sometimes!', 'nice change', 'to make boring, dry topics more fun', and 'give interest and variety'.

This wide range of responses is interesting to consider in the light of research over the last thirty years into teachers' reasons and rationales for doing practical work. The research and critical analysis of Kerr (1964), Buckley and Kempa (1971), Thompson (1975), Beatty and Woolnough (1982) and others have indicated a range of important reasons for doing practical work in science. These were summarized and critically discussed nowhere more clearly than in Hodson (1990). The reasons and rationales put forward can be grouped into three main areas: one relating to knowledge and understanding (the cognitive domain); one relating to skills and processes, often deemed to be transferable; and a third relating to attitudes, enjoyment and motivation (the affective domain). I found it interesting that all the free-range responses given by the learner teachers above fall into these three groups.

Below, is a brief summary of the arguments in each area and counter arguments to them.

1   Cognitive arguments

It is argued that practical work can improve pupils' understanding of science and promote their conceptual development by allowing them to 'visualize' the laws and theories of science. It can illustrate, verify or affirm 'theory work'.

The counter argument to this, of course, is that practical work can confuse as easily as it can clarify or aid understanding (especially if it 'goes wrong'). Hence the counter-slogan which came from an unknown source in the 1980s: 'I do and I become confused'. It can be argued that theory comes first and is needed in order to visualize – not the other way round:

> Experience does not give concepts meaning, if anything concepts give experience meaning.
>
> (Theobald 1968)

This may be a good argument for doing practical work after teaching and discussing theory. But practical work is still not a good tool for teaching theory –

theories are about ideas not things. Theories involve abstract ideas that cannot be *physically* illustrated:

> In the context of the school laboratory it is clear that students cannot develop an understanding through their own observations, as the theoretical entities of science are not there to be seen.
>
> (Leach and Scott 1995: 48)

2   Affective arguments

Practical work, it has been argued, is motivating and exciting – it generates interest and enthusiasm. It helps learners to remember things, it helps to 'make it stick'.

Few who have taught science would deny this. But this is not the case for all pupils – some are 'turned off' by practical work, especially when it goes wrong or they cannot see the point of doing it. All teachers can relate to the lovely quote from the pupil in Qualter *et al.* (1990: 5): 'Oh no, Sir! Not another one of your problems', as she responds to her teacher's attempt to turn a piece of practical work into a 'problem-solving' investigation. Evidence from Murphy (in Woolnough 1991) indicates that more girls than boys react negatively to practical work in science.

3   Skills arguments

It is argued that practical work develops not only manipulative or manual dexterity skills, but also promotes higher-level, transferable skills such as observation, measurement, prediction and inference. These transferable skills are said to be valuable, not only to future scientists but also because they possess general utility and vocational value.

There may be some truth in the claim for manipulative skills and possibly measurement, but there is little evidence that skills learnt in science are indeed general and transferable, or that they are of vocational value. As one of the leading writers in the field of situated cognition puts it:

> The results of learning transfer experiments range from positive to negative ... as a whole perhaps equivocal and unstable describes them best. But when we investigate learning transfer directly across situations, the results are constantly negative, whether analysing performance levels, procedures or errors.
>
> (Lave 1988: 68)

In a slightly different area of skill (personal skills and teamwork) it has been claimed that the small-group work which inevitably goes on in practical science can develop such skills as communication, interaction and cooperation. Again, this may be partially true, but when group work is closely observed and analysed, it often reveals domination by forceful members, competition, lack of engagement for some and a division of tasks which may leave one pupil simply recording results or drawing out a neat table without even seeing, let alone touching, any apparatus (discussed in Wellington 1994: chp., 8).

Finally in this domain, it has been argued that practical science develops the general skill of 'scientific enquiry' or scientific method. This training or inculcation into the method of science is said to be transferable and, again, of vocational value to all students, even if they choose other career paths (as the vast majority do). Counter arguments to this claim have been put forward in many publications (e.g. several chapters in Wellington 1989; and Chapman 1993, who talks of the 'over-selling' of science education). But perhaps the most telling quote comes from Ausubel (1964), whose work ironically has been used to support certain phases in practical work in the recent past:

> Grand strategies of discovery do not seem to be transferable across disciplines … it hardly seems plausible that a strategy of inquiry, which must necessarily be broad enough to be applicable to a wide range of disciplines and problems, can ever have sufficient particular relevance to be helpful in the solution of the specific problem at hand.
>
> (Ausubel 1964: 298)

'Real' science, teachers' science, pupils' science and school science

One of the accusations levelled against practical work in school science is that it has failed to reflect 'real' science. This, in my view, begs two questions: first, how could it and anyway, why should it? Second, what is 'real' science?

Take the second question first. The world of science covers a huge range of diverse activities. If we consider all the activities or disciplines that we would prob-ably list as 'sciences', it is likely to include astrophysics, biochemistry, biotech-nology, botany, cosmology, ecology, and zoology. From this list, it is almost impossible to define or distil out the essential, defining features of being 'a science' or those of 'scientific method'. Each will have certain features in common but these are more like 'family resemblances' (Wittgenstein 1953) than a single, unifying feature or an essential core. The methods they use are different; the culture and the history vary from one science to another. In some ways, considering sciences as a family is like considering the range of games that exist. Different games have different rules, different numbers of players and different times of duration. Some games use a board, some have teams, while others need individuals, some involve physical contact, and some do not. We all know a game when we see one, but we would all be hard pushed to state the defining features of games as a family.

So it is hardly surprising that the various 'phases and fads' in practical work in science education over the decades have failed to mimic or to capture 'scientific method'. It is not just a difficult task for school science – it is an impossible one. This is the reason why a single, prescriptive framework for experimental and inves-tigative work in practical science will never succeed, and why any attempt to impose a single format or prescription for practical work receives resentment, cynicism and scepticism from the science teaching profession.

However, this does not imply that science education can convey nothing about the nature of science. Indeed, this is still one of its most important roles, especially if it is to improve the public understanding of science (Millar 1996, gives a full discussion of a science curriculum aimed at fostering public understanding). There are certain messages about science as an activity that can be conveyed (either implicitly or explicitly – 'caught *and* taught'). These can be summarized as follows:

1   In science, experiments are not conducted which are independent of theory, i.e. experiments are not done in a theoretical vacuum.
2   As a result, predictions, observations and inferences are theory-laden.
3   Scientists normally work as members of communities, often in institutions – science is a social activity that involves people. These people have personal attitudes, views, opinions and prejudices.
4   Scientists work in a social, cultural, historical and political context. This context determines what methods they are able to use; what questions get asked; how far they are funded and pursued. The research pursued and methods used in Victorian England or Nazi Germany have not been, and will not be, acceptable in other eras.
5   Scientific theories do not follow logically from experimental data (the fallacy of induction). Experiments may be derived or suggested by theories – but theories are not fully determined by or derived from experiments (things like human beings and 'leaps of the imagination' are needed in the middle).
6   Unlike Premier League football managers, established theories are not dismissed just because of a few bad results. Similarly, the choice between competing theories is not made purely on empirical/experimental grounds. Theories are not confirmed or proven, but can be supported, by experimental results. Theories can be shown to be false (falsified) by experimental data.
7   Science has methods but does not have *one method*. No scientific method follows a set, algorithmic procedure or a set of rules. Science also involves tacit, implicit, personal knowledge.

It is a tall order to expect science teachers, most of whom will have spent little or no time during their science degrees considering the nature of science, to convey all these messages about science in busy laboratories – or to find the time and the strategies to teach these ideas explicitly. This is made especially difficult for teachers by the fact that pupils' perceptions of science, and indeed those of the public generally (Wellington 1991 on media science), are totally at odds with the seven statements above. Young people's views and beliefs about science pose a challenge for the science teacher in the laboratory – the place where a number of cultures meet. So what strategies and approaches can be used to address this problem? First, learners need to be shown or taught how to observe things. They will not see a field around a magnet or reflection/refraction in a ripple tank or a cell under a microscope unless they know what they are looking for. Children need to learn the observational language of science – they need to 'see things as …'. This is why science processes cannot be separated from science content – all the processes of science e.g. inferring, classifying, predicting, hypothesizing, seeing and observing, are embedded in science knowledge and theory (Wellington 1989). Science processes are situated in science, they are not context-free and transferable.

For similar reasons, science teachers cannot teach theory through practical work. Pupils cannot just be exposed to phenomena or events or observations in the hope that they will somehow induce or discover 'the theory'. Discovery learning may work for teaching *knowledge that*, e.g. a metal bar expands when you heat it, but cannot be expected to teach knowledge *why*, e.g. theories such as the particle model of matter which can help to explain expansion. Practical work can illustrate phenomena but it cannot explain why they happen. Pupils need to be taught that not everything in science can be related to laboratory experience and to doing things. This is why conversation, discussion and imagination are so important, i.e. working with the ideas, concepts and principles of science.

A third point that pupils need to be told when doing practical work is that a few 'dodgy', i.e. anomalous, results do not lead to the abandonment of a theory – it takes a lot more than that. However, a lot of judgement, i.e. prior theoretical knowledge, is required to decide which results are 'dodgy' or anomalous. Teachers do this all the time when they collect results in at the end of an 'experiment' and decide which ones to write on the blackboard and which ones 'don't fit' and can be ignored (especially when looking for lines of best fit). This leads to the next point – very few 'experiments' in school science are really experiments. It is just that we have all (teachers and pupils) got into the habit of calling them that.

'Experiment' – the all-purpose word

One of the issues which teachers *and* pupils need to become clearer about is the range of different types of practical work and the purposes they serve. There is a tendency for both teachers and pupils to call every type of practical activity they do in a school laboratory an 'experiment'. In fact, many of the practical activities done in school science are plainly not experiments. They may be illustrations of a phenomenon (either done in small groups or on the front bench); they may simply be providing experiences or giving pupils a feel for a phenomenon; they may simply be exercises or routines for pupils to follow, aimed perhaps at developing a particular skill or becoming used to a piece of equipment or an instrument (categories such as these were discussed helpfully by Woolnough and Allsop in 1985).

Equally, there are all sorts of 'experiments'. Some may (quite rightly since this goes on in 'real science' all the time) simply involve replicating a piece of practical work which has already been done, either recently or in many cases a few hundred years ago. Replication is an important part of scientific activity. Others may be genuine investigations, although these are probably far less common. Some, incidentally, do not involve any apparatus (e.g. thought experiments).

Whatever practical work is done in school laboratories, teachers should be wary of using the blanket term 'experiment'. This is more than a semantic point – pretending that all activity is experiment has generated much of the cynicism amongst pupils towards laboratory work which is summed up so well in this quote from a children's story:

> We were supposed to be reading the instructions for an experiment we were going to perform in class that day. Now there's another stupid thing. Year after year, this same teacher makes his students perform the same experiments. Well, if the experiments have been done so many times before, how can they still be experiments? The teacher knows what is going to happen. I thought experimenting meant trying new things to see what would happen. We weren't experimenting at all. We were playacting.
>
> (Martin 1990: 2)

The different types of practical work are all horses for courses. If we observe typical science teaching laboratories we see at least six types of activity going on that we would probably all class as practical work: teacher demonstrations; class practicals, with all learners on similar tasks, working in small groups; a circus of 'experiments', with small groups engaged in different activities, rotating in a 'carousel'; investigations, organized in one of the above two ways; and problem-solving activities. Another way of classifying practical work was suggested by Woolnough and Allsop (1985: 47–59). They gave a useful breakdown using three categories: exercises, experiences and investigations.

Each type of practical work serves a different purpose: different type, different aim (Gott and Duggan 1995: 21). We need to convey this to pupils, e.g. if they are going to replicate what someone already knows tell them – don't kid them that they are discovering something.

Institutionalized practicals – icons, rituals and malpractice

One of the legacies of the past in practical work has been the growth or evolution of 'standard' practicals that are passed on from one generation of teachers to the next, and by teacher-training institutions. They become embedded in published schemes and programmes, and are even transferred, without checking, from one textbook to another. There are many good reasons for this, of course, and part of it involves the inheritance of the considerable 'craft knowledge' required to carry out an effective piece of practical work.

However, there is also a slightly more sinister side to this generation game. As Kirschner puts it:

> Years of effort have produced 'foolproof' experiments when the right answer is certain to emerge for everyone in the class if the laboratory instructions are followed.
>
> (Kirschner 1992: 278)

More recent research by Nott and Smith (1995) has highlighted the interesting behaviour of science teachers in the 'rigging' and 'conjuring' of so-called experiments in order that things do not go wrong. The ability to rig, of course, could be put down to craft knowledge, but the tendency to conjure, e.g. to inject oxygen from a tank in order to 'prove' that photosynthesis of pondweed has occurred, is a rather more dubious practice. Further work by Nott and Wellington (1996) has shown that the practice of conjuring may well be widespread and is often passed on by mentors in schools (or just as often by laboratory technicians) during teacher training.

The imposition of 'Investigations by order' has led to the development of similarly institutionalized practicals, but in this case masquerading as investigations, all designed and tailored to fit the national template and its assessment framework. An alien observer travelling around the schools of England and Wales would soon begin to wonder why so many pupils were dissolving jellies, bouncing ping-pong balls and watching coffee cool in the laboratories of the nation.

Time for a re-appraisal

No one doubts that the experiences of practical work and getting a feel for materials, apparatus, events and phenomena are a vital part of science education. There is, however, a need to examine where we have come from with practical work, to assess its value, to search for more 'authentic' practical work and to suggest ways of improving it for the future (Wellington 1998).

A full re-appraisal of the role of practical work should strive to develop a *balanced science curriculum*. Of course, this would include practical work, and indeed many of the current approaches and practices in practical science are educationally valuable and well worth preserving. However, a balanced science curriculum would *not* be dominated by a *single* set framework or format for practical work – and it certainly should not pretend that the practical work in a teaching laboratory mirrors the nature of 'real' science. This balance would include several elements. At least one element of the practical curriculum would involve looking at someone else's data, preferably someone pupils don't know. It could be a figure from the past, it could be from another learner, e.g. via the Internet, or it could be a piece of contemporary science. It could involve some kind of historical case study.

A balanced, practical curriculum would include the critical use of simulations. The simulation could be computer based, e.g. on disc or CD-ROM, from the Internet, or handled using paper-based materials. Students at a later phase could learn how to look closely and critically at how the simulation is constructed, which model or models it is based on, and what its limitations are.

Practical activity in the future would sometimes involve the use of ICT and the use of data-logging even if not carried out as a whole-class practical. It should be used to show the benefits (and possible drawbacks) of using computers in practical science. It should emphasize the interpretation of the data rather than its collection and processing.

At least one element of work (probably as project work) should look at a contemporary, controversial issue that is science-based. For example, this could be the BSE debate, the use of mobile phones, the issue of cloning and genetic engineering, global warming, pollution, or the use and supply of energy. Practical activities would include: looking at data, who collected it and how; the interpretation of data and the concept of evidence; media coverage of the issue, the 'evidence' and the experimental work; and the perspectives and prejudices of the people involved (the scientists included).

As part of a re-appraisal, we should consider how pupils could carry out at least one *genuine* scientific investigation, i.e. a research project, over an extended period of time, which does not follow a set format or template. If this could be based in the community or local environment, involve fieldwork, or even link with local employment, that would be an added bonus. It could certainly involve extended observations over a period of time, e.g. fieldwork, environmental monitoring, or astronomical work such as observing the sky. Whatever its focus, it should require pupils to use secondary sources.

Finally, and most generally, a re-appraisal of practical work could lead to teachers and pupils becoming clear about different types of practical work and why they are doing them. The purpose of any practical activity needs to be clear and explicit to both teachers and their pupils – how can students be expected to see the point of a practical exercise if they are not given some indication from the teacher who asks them to do it? Pupils will also need to be shown and told that not everything in science is connected with doing. Time needs to be allocated to discussing ideas, to interpreting data, and to making the link between things observed and ideas. Science is a practical subject, but it is also a theoretical subject.

There is a need for curriculum change and development, for technological as well as educational reasons. However, changes and improvements will come about only if due account is taken of teachers' viewpoints and practical concerns. As past experience has shown, there is a vital need for careful professional development. Science teachers in the 1990s became bruised and bitter about the impositions made on them in the area of 'experimental' science. The days of investigations by order, and of dropping ICT onto school doorsteps, must be seen as past mistakes, not to be repeated.

References

Ausubel, D. P. (1964) 'Some psychological and educational limitations of learning by discovery', *The Arithmetic Teacher* 11(5): 290–302.

Beatty, J. and Woolnough, B. (1982) 'Practical work in 11–13 science: context, type and aims of current practice', *British Educational Research Journal* 8(1): 23–30.

Buckley, J. G. and Kempa, R. F. (1971) 'Practical work in sixth form chemistry', *School Science Review* 53: 24–36.

Chapman, B. (1993) 'The overselling of science education in the eighties', in E. Whitelegg, J. Thomas and S. Tresman (eds) *Challenges and Opportunities for Science Education*, London: Paul Chapman.

Delamont, S., Beynon, J. and Atkinson, P. (1988) 'In the beginning was the Bunsen: the foundations of secondary school science', *Qualitative Studies in Education* 1(4): 315–28.

Donnelly, J. (1995) 'Curriculum development in science: the lessons of Sc1', *School Science Review* 76(277): 95–103.

Gee, B. and Clackson, S. (1992) 'The origin of practical work in the English school science curriculum', *School Science Review* 73(265): 79–83.

Gott, R. and Duggan, S. (1995) *Investigative Work in the Science Curriculum*, Buckingham: Open University Press.

Hodson, D. (1990) 'A critical look at practical work in school science', *School Science Review* 70(256): 33–40.

Hodson, D. (1996) 'Laboratory work as scientific method: three decades of confusion and distortion', *Journal of Curriculum Studies* 28(2): 115–35.

Kerr, J. F. (1964) *Practical Work in School Science*, Leicester: Leicester University Press.

Kirschner, P. (1992) 'Epistemology, practical work and academic skills in science education', *Science Education* 1: 273–99.

Lave, J. (1988) *Cognition in Practice*, New York: Cambridge University Press.

Leach, J. and Scott, P. (1995) 'The demands of learning science concepts – issues of theory and practice', *School Science Review* 76(277): 47–51.

Martin, A. M. (1990) *Claudia and the Great Search*, New York: Apple Paperbacks, Scholastic.

Millar, R. (1996) 'A science curriculum for public understanding', *School Science Review* 77(280): 7–18.

Murphy, P. (1991) 'Gender differences in pupils' reaction to practical work', in B. E. Woolnough (ed.) *Practical Science*, Milton Keynes: Open University Press.

Nott, M. (1997) 'Keeping scientists in their place', *School Science Review* 78(285): 49–61.

Nott, M. and Smith, R. (1995) '"Talking your way out of it", "rigging" and "conjuring": what science teachers do when practicals go wrong', *International Journal of Science Education* 17(3): 399–410.

Nott, M. and Wellington, J. (1996) 'When the black box springs open: practical work in school science and the nature of science', *International Journal of Science Education* 18(7): 807–18.

Qualter, A., Strang, J. and Swatton, P. (1990) *Explanation – A Way of Learning Science*, Oxford: Blackwell.

Theobald, D. W. (1968) *An Introduction to the Philosophy of Science*, London: Methuen.

Thompson, J. J. (1975) *Practical Work in Sixth Form Science*, Oxford: Oxford University Press.

TIMSS (1997) *Third International Mathematics and Science Study*, Slough: NFER.

Wellington, J. J. (1981) '"What's supposed to happen, Sir?": some problems with discovery learning', *School Science Review* 63(222): 167–73.

Wellington, J. J. (ed.) (1989) *Skills and Processes in Science Education*, London: Routledge.

Wellington, J. J. (1991) 'Newspaper science, school science: friends or enemies?', *International Journal of Science Education* 13(4): 363–72.

Wellington, J. J. (ed.) (1994) *Secondary Science: Contemporary Issues and Practical Approaches*, London: Routledge.

Wellington, J. J. (ed.) (1998) *Practical Work in School Science. Which way now?*, London: Routledge.

Wittgenstein, L. (1953) *Philosophical Investigations*, Oxford: Oxford University Press.

Woolnough, B. E. (ed.) (1991) *Practical Science*, Milton Keynes: Open University Press.

Woolnough, B. E. and Allsop, T. (1985) *Practical Work in Science*, Cambridge: Cambridge University Press.

Section 3

Curriculum innovation

Introduction

Changing the curriculum is difficult. It cannot simply be brought about by decree. It requires teachers to give up practices which they have developed over many years and which, for them, have proved to be effective in the classroom. It may require them to acquire new subject knowledge, or to think of existing knowledge in new ways, or to use new teaching strategies. Change that is brought about too fast, with insufficient preparation and without building on existing practice, simply results in 'de-skilling' teachers. Changes in society, in scientific knowledge, and in the pupils themselves, mean that continual curriculum innovation is essential, but there is also an understandable resistance to change. The current curriculum is the outcome of this tension between the need for change and the need for continuity.

The 1980s saw a growing concern that the provision of science education was too focused on the minority of pupils who would go on to specialize in science. A broader approach was required to meet the needs of all pupils. This movement towards 'science for all' has had many consequences, and despite the criticisms against the curriculum raised in the last section, the picture is not all gloomy. There have been many successes. Science is now taught to a wider range of pupils; there has been a huge expansion of science in the primary school, more science is studied by more pupils in the secondary school, and there is a broader range of post-16 provision. There have also been major changes in the nature of the curriculum. There has been a significant shift in the balance towards investigational work as an assessed component of the curriculum. And there has been at least some recognition of the importance of learning about the nature of science itself and the context in which it is done. The National Curriculum includes requirements about the ways in which scientists work, how scientific ideas develop, the social and historical contexts, and considerations of ethical issues. Much attention has also been paid to issues of gender and ethnicity. Accompanying these curriculum changes has been a broadening in the teaching strategies used in science classrooms. The first four chapters in this section give some examples of curriculum innovations, and the final chapter proposes a possible direction for the science curriculum in the future.

Alan Peacock discusses the development of primary science, from the point where it hardly existed in the primary school to the present position, in which science is one of the core subjects in the curriculum. Key issues in primary science are the balance between scientific knowledge and investigational skills, the value of formal assessment and its possible negative effects on teaching, and the extent to which the science that is studied is of interest or relevance to primary pupils. Understanding what happens in primary schools, and the science which pupils have been taught, is essential for secondary teachers. This may seem an obvious point, but evidence from, for example, inspection reports suggests that few secondary schools are effective in building on the work that pupils have done in the primary school. Mike Coles explores the nature of vocational science, and how both the nature of the science studied and the ways that students are expected to work are different from those in other science courses. He argues that the traditional science curriculum is dominated by its existing knowledge base to an extent that introducing new areas of knowledge becomes difficult. Vocational approaches, such as thinking about the knowledge needed for action, and paying attention to what scientists do in work, have much to offer the general science curriculum. Joan Solomon examines some of the influences on the growth of 'science, technology and society' (STS) education in schools. She identifies a number of different movements, each of which has its own effects on the nature of the courses introduced – a broader view of science education seeing science as part of the general culture, an emphasis on social responsibility and knowledge for political action, an interdisciplinary approach dealing with issues in a holistic way from different perspectives, or an instrumental view of science education as aiming to meet the needs of industry. Though the elements of STS included in the original proposals for the National Curriculum in science were successively dropped, she suggests that there are positive signs in its inclusion in the latest version. Alongside the growth in interest in STS education in the 1980s was the increased attention paid to multi-cultural and anti-racist education. Reg Dennick argues that much of the writing about the history of science devalues or ignores the contributions made by other cultures. He stresses the universality of science as a human activity; pupils should learn how different sciences developed in different cultures, as a response to specific needs and dependent on the socio-economic context. Moreover, science education has a responsibility to challenge racist ideology. He argues that anti-racist, multi-cultural science education should aim to 'reduce prejudice and conflict between individuals, ethnic minorities, cultures and nations'.

In the final chapter in this section, Robin Millar proposes some key aspects of a curriculum that aims to develop a better public understanding of science. He examines critically some of the arguments which have been put forward about why all pupils should study science, and argues that, while some of these reasons may be valid, the present curriculum is failing to meet the challenges. A curriculum that can justifiably call itself a 'science for all' needs to reduce much of the content and focus more on practical, technological knowledge and on the powerful explanatory 'stories' of science. It needs to develop a better understanding of the methods by which scientific knowledge is constructed, and of the social dimensions of the creation and application of that knowledge. This is a major task for the science education community.

5 The emergence of primary science

Alan Peacock

The origins of primary science

Until the 1950s, the term 'science' was hardly ever used in primary schools; in my small-town primary school in Yorkshire, we had 'Nature Study', went for nature walks to look at trees and flowers and to collect frog-spawn; back in the classroom we would draw the developing tadpole, keep weather records and make a display of fruits at harvest time. In grammar school, we did chemistry and physics – no biology, it was a boys school! – by watching the teacher demonstrate experiments, starting in week 1 with 'the parts of the Bunsen burner'. The secondary modern schools did a watered-down version of this called General Science or Rural Science.

In the early 1960s, however, like everything else, science curriculums in Britain began to change. In the USA, anxiety about the irrelevance of school science to the real world, and about their falling behind the Russians in the space race, led to massive resources being committed to developing new science programmes for high school children. In Britain, we followed suit with the Nuffield Science materials, which pioneered a new approach to science teaching. Pupils actually undertook investigations themselves, rather than simply doing practicals to verify the results the teacher had written on the board. Prime Minister Wilson threw his weight behind these changes, stressing the importance of effective science education if Britain's economy was to be revitalized and new industries forged in the 'white heat of the technological revolution'.

It took longer for these ideas to trickle down as far as primary schooling, however. Nuffield Junior Science developed from its senior siblings, but the first major impact on the primary school curriculum in Britain was made by the Schools' Council, a body made up of teachers and educationists from across the whole spectrum of education, charged with reviewing and developing new approaches to the curriculum and examinations. In the early 1970s, the Schools' Council published 'Science 5–13', an approach to science for primary and middle schools which adopted the, then fashionable, Objectives Approach which had been the basis of most American developments in science curriculums. The key volume, *With Objectives in Mind* (Harlen 1975), set out the philosophy of the programme and established, for the first time, a discussion about what science in primary schools ought to be trying to achieve. The objectives of Science 5–13 were on the processes of science rather than teaching facts, as Wynne Harlen, the major author of the project stated:

> to observe, raise questions, propose enquiries to answer questions, experiment or investigate, find patterns in observation, reason systematically and logically, communicate findings and apply learning.
>
> (Harlen 1975)

The approach was consistent with the child-centred approach at the heart of 'good primary practice', embodied in the influential Plowden Report of the late 1960s, but despite this, it was never used by more than a quarter of primary schools. It marked the first attempt in Britain to foster the teaching of science as a process to primary age children; some commentators such as Paul Black have suggested that, for this reason, teachers lacked the confidence to take up the new philosophy. However, the project's materials have enjoyed a remarkably long shelf-life, and many of today's commonplace notions in primary science (such as Minibeasts) had their origins in Science 5–13.

Rumblings of discontent

Up until the late 1970s, there had been no requirement that primary teachers must teach science; the primary curriculum was largely school- and teacher-determined, and as a consequence, science was still a Cinderella subject. In 1976, Prime Minister Callaghan instigated what has come to be called the 'Great Debate' about education and the curriculum and science was again thrust to the fore of curriculum concern. However, the Inspectorate report on Primary Schools in England in 1978 only served to emphasize the problems of science practice in primary schools, asserting that few schools had effective science programmes; there was lack of equipment; the teaching of science skills was often superficial or non-existent; teachers had little confidence and lacked a working knowledge of elementary science; and that in hardly any classrooms did children investigate scientifically the questions and problems which arose from their everyday experience and interests. All this at a time when the economy had been struggling for five years after the oil crisis and when science education was seen by politicians as a crucial element in the long-term strategy for recovery.

These events inevitably provoked an increase in the amount of science on the primary curriculum. However, over the next ten years, all evidence pointed to the fact that little change took place in the actual science achievement of children, particularly in the direction of skills learning which Science 5–13 and the Inspectorate had sought to foster. For example, the Assessment of Performance Unit (APU) showed in the early 1980s that most children at age 11 were not competent in science skills such as recognizing patterns in observations, hypothesizing and controlling variables. The Department for Education and Science (DES, now DfEE) claimed in 1984 that science in primary schools was falling far short of the effectiveness claimed for it; and HMI in 1989 found that weaknesses identified in 1978 still persisted, placing some of the blame at the door of teachers' lack of science knowledge.

Accordingly, in 1985, the DES took the unprecedented step of publishing a Policy Statement on 'Science for All' (DES 1985) which can now be seen as the precursor of the Science National Curriculum, and which stated clearly not only that all primary teachers had to include some science in their teaching, but also stipulated in broad terms the science knowledge and skills which children ought to be taught in primary schools. The stage was thus set for Kenneth Baker to instruct the Science Working Group to establish the first ever prescription of the science that teachers must legally teach in English and Welsh primary schools.

The development of primary science in other countries

Meanwhile, what had been happening in the rest of the world? In Europe, there had been no parallel upheaval in the science curriculum for primary schools. The German Grundschule continued to teach 'Sachkunde', which was, in effect, local environmental studies and which emphasized general knowledge, but none of the investigation skills pioneered by Science 5–13. Likewise in France, science did not figure as a subject in the primary curriculum. The International Science Survey of Science attainment in nineteen countries in 1970 had served to emphasize the deficiencies that had become only too apparent in Britain, and many countries realized the need for change. Yet the science curriculum in England and Wales was very different from that in most other countries, where the emphasis tended to be on environmental rather than science education in the primary phase (Peacock 1993).

The main developments came in those areas of the world most influenced by American and British systems, such as the Commonwealth countries and the Pacific Rim. In anglophone Africa, for example, the Africa Primary Science Programme in the 1970s developed materials which were modified and used in many African countries, materials which emphasized science problem-solving through 'Science 5–13' approaches, and which were of a very high standard. Commercial publishers in individual countries, such as Kenya, took this a step further by commissioning high quality textbooks for primary schools based on the newly developed syllabuses: good examples are the *Beginning Science* series from Kenya (Berluti 1981 onwards) and *Primary Science for the Caribbean: a Process Approach* (Douglass and Fraser-Abder 1984). In some ways, then, countries like Kenya, already having science as a compulsory subject in the primary school and having excellent teachers' and pupils' materials, were moving ahead of us. The materials were strongly influenced by 'North Atlantic' curriculum developers and had strong family resemblances to materials in the USA and Britain; it only remained for them to be effectively implemented in the classroom.

UNESCO meanwhile had also been active in the field of primary science, producing its valuable *Resource Book* (UNESCO 1973). This activity was followed by a major UN report in the late 1970s that began to consider the role of science education in national development (UNESCO 1980).

Various authorities, however, began to question the (Western) assumption, prevalent up to this stage, that science was somehow 'culture-free' and that a Western science curriculum was thus appropriate in all contexts. Links began to be made between economic development, locally-appropriate vocational skills and the skills of science; and for many developing countries where primary education was terminal for the great majority of children, this meant looking again at the science content of the primary curriculum. Thus the debate about the relative importance of knowledge, process skills and attitudes in science came to the fore, not only in Britain in the lead-up to the National Curriculum, but also in many developing countries. In many such countries where science was already well established, skills and attitudes useful in health, agriculture, mining, conservation, tourism and other aspects of the economy of developing countries were now being seen as just as important to primary leavers as factual knowledge or examination passes, hitherto the ticket to an office job.

The National Curriculum in science and its impact on primary teachers

Back in Britain, the Education Reform Act in England and Wales gave 'Core' status to science and the Science Working Group moved quickly to work on the prescription of content, so that from 1987 onwards, science became the 'guinea pig' subject in Kenneth Baker's strategy for statutory curriculum development. Assessment strategies were being simultaneously developed by the Task Group on Assessment and Testing (TGAT) and subsequently by the Schools' Examinations and Assessment Council (SEAC), so that versions of proposals came and went with alarming frequency. Commercial publishers raced to adapt their schemes or to develop new ones; more than one expensive new science package had to be abandoned or re-jigged at the eleventh hour because of changes in the number and wording of Attainment Targets.

Primary teachers waited apprehensively for the outcomes. Most of them had experienced little science teaching themselves in primary school; most were women who had rarely studied physical sciences. The big question was, would the profession be able to 'deliver' the new science curriculum? In anticipation of a 'no' answer, the DES was already making available relatively large amounts of money for in-service training through the new Education Support Grants (ESG) and GRIST (Grant-Related In-Service Training) systems of funding in-service work. Local authorities all over the country appointed Science Advisory Teachers to run courses and provide school-based support for teachers. At the same time, the Council for the Accreditation of Teacher Education, which was appointed to approve all initial training courses for teachers, stipulated that trainees must receive the same minimum 100 hours' training in science as in English and maths (increased to 150 hours in 1993), which precipitated changes in the way primary teachers were trained to teach science. Research such as the SPACE Project (Science Processes And Concept Exploration) (SPACE Project 1990 onwards) was providing valuable evidence, in forms accessible to teachers, about children's science learning and ways of assessing it in the classroom.

A major effort appeared to have been made, then, to make primary teachers ready to teach the new science National Curriculum (although cynics might argue that the actual money available was no greater than it had been before). Has it been successful? The evidence of most evaluations so far is not encouraging. In their evaluation of the ESG initiatives, for example, the ASE evaluators found that teachers tended to revert to 'old' habits as soon as the in-service support was withdrawn (IPSE 1988). The first evaluation of the pilot trials of Standard Attainment Tasks found that teachers themselves did not fully understand what was required, especially in open-ended investigation. Also, studies of teachers' science knowledge continue to show widespread misunderstandings of science phenomena, and lack of confidence in teaching the subject (e.g. Wragg *et al.* 1991; Summers and Mant 1992). Research in the 1990s continued to show that the teaching of science in primary schools was often characterized by frequent errors of fact; tight teacher control leading to aimless activity; missed opportunities to elaborate on pupils' responses; explanations and discussions which compound pupils' own misconceptions; and increased 'teaching to the test'.

Yet there is also evidence to show that, where teachers do have background knowledge and confidence, their practice is frequently in line with accepted notions of good science practice. In other words, they plan a clear framework for teaching both content and skills; have appropriate materials available; explain expectations clearly; match tasks to different abilities; listen to and challenge pupils' responses; respect their prior knowledge; and use authentic models and representations for instruction. Support for primary teachers has come in the form of the recently introduced Scheme of Work for Science by the Qualifications and Curriculum Authority (QCA 1998), which provides teachers, in term-by-term detail, with a comprehensive six-year plan for science through Key Stages 1 and 2. How does the achievement of our primary children compare, therefore, with children in other countries?

Comparisons with science achievement in other countries

The most recent comparable evidence comes from the Third International Mathematics and Science Study (TIMSS 1998), data for which was gathered in the mid-1990s. At that time, despite formally testing primary pupils more than in any other country, our combined rating in mathematics and science for 10–11-year-olds was eighteenth, above the United States but below many countries in the Pacific Rim and Eastern Europe. Coming just before the election of New Labour, the results generated the new government's interest in teaching methods used in Japan and Korea, who topped the table: an Ofsted team visited these countries and produced reports which have had an influence across the whole approach to the core curriculum in primary schools (Reynolds 1996).

The illustrations above indicate that attainment in science is not related simply to one or two factors in the education of children. Improving attainment in science in primary schools – and linking it to science in secondary schools – has proved to be a difficult thing to achieve, despite the prescription and support which the National Curriculum for science was intended to provide. What then are the current concerns about science teaching in the primary classroom and what political and professional issues have a bearing on these? What are the main conflicts – it is probably not too strong a word – that persist within primary science?

The knowledge–process debate

An enduring concern during the past twenty-five years or more has been about what should be the relative emphasis on science knowledge, on the one hand, and science processes on the other. The Science Working Group resolved this (and successive Secretaries of State have concurred in their creation of statutory requirements) by requiring the primary curriculum to focus equally on 'Knowledge and Understanding' and 'Enquiry'. However, there has been an increasing opposition from both researchers and teachers over the years to the idea of trying to teach, or even specify, investigation skills independently of a particular context: some authors, such as Millar and Driver (1987) and Claxton (1991), would argue that this is at the root of teachers' difficulties. Researchers in other countries would also agree. For example, it has been shown in Nigeria that children's observational drawings in science are powerfully influenced by the cultural significance of the objects being drawn (Jegede and Okebukola 1991).

The Statements of Attainment against which children were initially assessed were specified separately for knowledge and skills; yet a major lesson from research over the years has been the powerful way in which assessment methods affect what and how teachers teach. Increasingly, standard tests have moved away from practical (skills) to written (knowledge) testing. Thus the question of the relative importance of knowledge and skills, and their integration in practice, remains at the centre of primary science practice. Politically, there has also always persisted a sub-text, which somewhat naively associates knowledge acquisition with 'real' learning and investigation with the 'child-centred' (or so-called 'discovery') approaches much derided by the right. In recent years, discussion in the media has been increasingly characterized, not by evidence from research (of which there has been a great deal) but by the shrill protestations of journalists of fairly extreme political persuasions. It is increasingly difficult, therefore, for the parent or interested observer to distinguish professional opinion from partisan prejudice, especially as Ministers and Chief Inspectors themselves often appear to be deliberately eroding the professionalism of educators in general.

Assessing science in primary schools

The problem above is compounded because it is almost impossible to separate this question from the controversial issue of assessment. At present, children still have to be assessed in science in primary schools in England and Wales (not in Scotland, interestingly, where only English and mathematics are assessed) and their levels of attainment reported at age 7 and age 11. Assessment is by a combination of Teacher Assessment (TA) and Standard Attainment Tasks (SATs). The process has been associated with controversy from the beginning, and numerous interventions have only served to increase the complexity of the testing and reporting procedures. One contentious issue is the assessment of enquiry skills.

It had been convincingly argued from the beginning by TGAT and all other informed opinion, that enquiry skills can only be satisfactorily assessed through practical means. But such standardized practical tests are both expensive and time-consuming, never mind being difficult to administer fairly (witness the 7 year-old asked to predict if the melon would float, who answered 'yes, because Kate's melon floated this morning'!). In the initial trialling of practical tests with 7-year-olds, there was wide concern amongst teachers about the time taken and the consequent disruption of learning; accordingly, reliance on pencil-and-paper tasks now dominates the standard tests, therefore dominating the teaching prior to the tests.

Of course, this does not, in theory, prevent continuous practical assessment of skills by teachers throughout the year (although the main impact of the Literacy and Numeracy Hours on science teaching has been to reduce the time available, so that teachers rarely do more than one or two 'practicals' per term). But the whole development of National Curriculum requirements has been paralleled by a growing distrust of teachers by legislators, culminating in the recent initiation of tests in mathematics, English and ICT for all primary teachers-to-be. Meanwhile, teachers find that the outcomes of all this extra assessment work do not, by and large, tell them anything they didn't know already about their pupils' science attainment.

Thus, the assessment process is clearly not yet satisfactory; the question is, do we need it in science in the primary phase? For some, it is clearly motivated only by political desires to identify and weed out 'bad' teachers and schools, a fear accentuated by the Chief Inspector's repeated comments about 15,000 teachers needing to be sacked. Others in England have argued that one positive outcome has been an increase in teachers' professionalism relating to planning, assessment and reporting skills. In Australia, the decision has already been taken to abolish all forms of standard assessment in the primary phase; whilst in some countries, all assessment at the end of primary schooling, including science assessment, is by computer-marked multiple-choice tests. In which direction are we, or ought we to be, moving? Would it help if we dropped science from the core and stopped assessing it at Key Stage 2?

Specialist teaching of science in primary schools

If primary teachers have continued to have difficulties with teaching science effectively, is there then a case for the specialist teaching of science in primary schools? At present, only a small minority of children receive specialist teaching of science, although it has been commonplace in some subjects, such as music, for many years. The 'Three Wise Men' report (Alexander *et al.* 1992) advocated moves towards specialization at the top end of the primary school, and clear evidence has been referred to which shows that teachers with adequate subject knowledge and confidence teach science more effectively. The postgraduate certificate route into primary teaching is now seen by the government as the preferred way of training primary teachers with a science background; and yet that science background may not always be appropriate to primary school work. DfEE legislation now requires that all training courses incorporate elements relevant to the role of specialists as Curriculum Leaders in their subject area; in many schools, such specialists play a role in the professional development of their non-science colleagues. Often, however, they find that increased pressure on their time, brought about by demands of National Curriculum legislation, prevents them from adequately fulfilling this role, denying them, for example, time to work collaboratively with colleagues in their classrooms. Is the science specialist in a primary school (if there is one) best used as a specialist science teacher or as an in-service supporter of generalist teacher colleagues?

Under Local Management, schools have to settle for do-it-yourself INSET, with less and less access to specialist input from outside. In many countries, professional development in science is in the hands of non-governmental organizations (NGOs), funded by international aid agencies or industrial conglomerates and it is, therefore, also at the mercy of political fashions and the goals of multinational companies. The role of the science specialist within the school thus becomes more and more crucial, for though there is prescription of the 'what' of science by national or centralized curriculums, the 'how' is still largely in the hands of individual schools and teachers, despite the impact of Ofsted. So, we still have to decide how science should best be 'packaged' in the interests of the learners and the teachers. The issue has been addressed in such documents as the *Beyond 2000* report (Millar and Osborne 1998), but has not received widespread attention in schools themselves. Despite the introduction of the QCA Science Scheme mentioned above, many primary teachers still prefer science to be taught through cross-curricular topics. Should we go for 'explanatory stories'? For holism or specialism? For 'citizen science' (Jenkins, 1999)?

The relevance of primary science

For many years, the primary curriculum was seen as a preparation for work in the secondary phase and culminated for many in the hurdle of 11-plus verbal reasoning and other such tests. In many countries throughout the world, however, science is still examined at the end of the primary phase, which is, in effect, the end of schooling for the majority. In the 1960s, comprehensive education and the Plowden Report institutionalized notions of integration and child-centred approaches, which only a few local authorities such as Leicestershire and the West Riding of Yorkshire had previously adopted. But, despite this move to start from where the child was and develop work out of each child's capacities and interests, the HMI Report of 1978 expressed anxiety about how rarely this happened in science, even though such initiatives as 'Breakthrough to Literacy', to take just one example, had been successful in individualizing language work.

At that time, teachers by and large took little trouble to find out what children's science interests and knowledge were, and did less to use them as starting points. We now have much clearer ideas about children's science knowledge when they begin school and their increased interaction with mass media has also provided insights into children's science beliefs, interests and concerns. Yet, we still have in primary schools a 'school science' that is, in many ways, only tenuously linked to the 'real world' concerns and problems which science can and should help pupils deal with. And, of course, in the developing world, with its far more serious political, resource and teaching constraints, relevance is far more difficult to achieve (Knamiller 1984). The turning away from science which is evident at the secondary and tertiary phases, particularly amongst girls, is of great concern; recruiting sufficient high-quality scientists into teaching not only continues but is increasing as a problem, in the UK as elsewhere. In South Africa, for example, it has been estimated that only 1 in 10,000 children who begin primary school matriculate in a science subject. Would these critical situations be ameliorated if primary school science were seen to be concerned with the urgent questions of environment, health, nutrition, exercise, conservation, climate, energy consumption, bioethics and other questions which preoccupy professional scientists as well as many children?

For example, would it concern children to know that the average British citizen uses about fifty times more energy and twenty times more water than the average citizen of the world's poorest countries, such as Nepal? If so, what else should children know and do in science that might help them deal with this constructively? Energy and Water are both in the National Curriculum: the question for teachers is whether to focus merely on what is required for children to do well in tests and achieve the required levels, or whether to 'go for' science learning which has a 'realness' about it. The two are not, by definition, exclusive; but in practice, the former still tends to push out the latter, particularly as teachers struggle and juggle with the literacy and numeracy requirements, demands for more use of IT, and the attainment targets of all the other National Curriculum subjects as well as science. Children are not likely to develop a genuine enthusiasm and scientific curiosity if, as often happens, they are asked to copy down a diagram of 'The Water Cycle' every year.

Postscript

I have tried to do two things: first, to show briefly how we got to where we are in primary science (and by implication, to show also that we still have a long way to go); and second, to pose some important questions about the role of the primary science teacher, in the wider cultural and political context. You may try, as you progress into your career as a secondary science teacher, to develop your own thinking on some of these issues, using questions such as those raised above as pegs on which to hang your developing ideas. In addressing the key question of how we best help children construct science ideas, it is, in the end, the teacher's and the child's world-views that determine how science is perceived:

The notion of world-view incorporates the constraints of both language and culture on concept learning in an interdependent relationship. Consequently, teachers are dealing with the development, enrichment or change of world-views rather than simply science concepts.

(Lynch and Jones 1995: 118)

As a science teacher, then, to what extent do you teach what you believe? The evidence referred to briefly above suggests that primary science teachers no longer have the option to 'teach' (which usually means to 'get across') ideas which may not connect with children's existing world-views, simply in order that these ideas be retained, briefly, for the sole purpose of being tested. The alternatives, however, are still to be fully explored.

References

Alexander, R., Rose, J. and Woodhead, C. (1992) *Curriculum Organisation and Classroom Practice in Primary Schools; A Discussion Paper*, London: Department of Education and Science.

Berluti, A. (1980 onwards) *Beginning Science* (5 volumes; standard 4–standard 8), Nairobi: Macmillan Kenya.

Claxton, G. (1991) *Educating the Enquiring Mind: The Challenge for School Science*, London: Harvester Wheatsheaf.

Department of Education and Science (1985) *Science 5–16: A Statement of Policy*, London: HMSO.

Douglass, R. and Fraser-Abder, P. (1984) *Primary Science for the Caribbean: A Process Approach* (7 volumes; standard 1–standard 7), London: Macmillan Caribbean.

Harlen, W. (1975) *With Objectives in Mind (Science 5–13 Series)*, London: Macdonald Educational.

Initiatives in Primary Science Education (IPSE) (1988) *An Evaluation Report*, Hatfield: Association for Science Education.

Jegede, O. and Okebukola, P. (1991) 'The relationship between traditional African cosmology and students' acquisition of a process skill', *International Journal of Science Education* 13(1): 37–47.

Jenkins, E. W. (1999) 'School science, citizenship and the public understanding of science', *International Journal of Science Education* 21(7): 703-10.

Knamiller, G. (1984) 'The struggle for relevance in Science education in developing countries', *Studies in Science Education* 11: 60–78.

Lynch, P. P. and Jones, B. L. (1995) 'Students' alternative frameworks: towards a linguistic and cultural interpretation', *International Journal of Science Education* 17(1): 107–18.

Millar, R. and Driver, R. (1987) 'Beyond processes', *Studies in Science Education* 14: 33–62.

Millar, R. and Osborne, J. (1998) *Beyond 2000: Science Education for the Future*, London: King's College.

Peacock, A. (1993) 'A global core curriculum for primary Science?', *Primary Science Review* 28: 8–10.

Qualifications and Curriculum Authority (QCA) (1998) *Science Scheme of Work for Key Stages 1 and 2*, London: QCA.

Reynolds, D. (1996) *Worlds Apart? A Review of International Surveys of Educational Achievement Involving England*, London: Ofsted/HMSO.

SPACE Project (1990 onwards) *Research Reports* (14 titles, various authors), Liverpool: Liverpool University Press.

Summers, M. and Mant, J. (1992) 'Some primary school teachers' understanding of the earth's place in the universe', *Evaluation and Research in Education* 6(2–3): 95–111.

Third International Mathematics and Science Survey (TIMSS) (1998) *Assessing Mathematics and Science Literacy (TIMSS Monograph No. 4)*, Vancouver: Pacific Education Press.

UNESCO (1973) *Source Book for Science Teaching*, Paris: UNESCO.

UNESCO (1980) *Final Report of the Meeting of Experts on the Incorporation of Science and Technology into the Primary School Curriculum*, Paris: UNESCO.

Wragg, E. C., Bennett, S. N. and Carré, C. G. (1991) 'Primary teachers and the National Curriculum', *Research Papers in Education* 4(3): 17–45.

6   Science education

Vocational and general approaches

Mike Coles

Science has a special position in education and training because it is considered to be general (for everyone) and vocational (a preparation for those who think they will seek scientific/technical work). This chapter examines the nature of vocational science and argues that general education could pay more attention to the content and approaches used in vocational courses for the benefit of all students.

Applied science

The word *vocational* is so imprecise when it comes to science education that using it in a conversation or when constructing an argument is asking for trouble. School science is strongly *vocational* since success in it is a prerequisite for many technical jobs. Science A levels are *vocational* because higher education course entry largely depends on them and, these days, a science degree is the main route into science jobs.

It is certainly accurate to describe some science courses as *pure* or *applied:*

- *pure* in the sense that the drive is for a systematic construction of a knowledge and skills base;
- *applied* because applications of science are the focus of study or because the courses require students to apply knowledge and skills.

However most courses are hybrids. It (almost) goes without saying that students must have something to apply before they can solve problems, and there will be application even in a pure study of science, for example, ideas about the conservation of energy will be applied to learning about bond-making and bond-breaking in chemical reactions.

The word *vocational* can mean more than *applied* to many people and I will go on to try to demonstrate this distinction.

Vocational science

What are the distinctive characteristics of general vocational science courses?

1 General vocational science courses concentrate on the *broad purposes of scientists' work* – such as extracting substances from raw materials, synthesizing substances, manufacturing products, characterizing materials, analysing substances, observing phenomena, managing people and facilities, communicating with colleagues, and monitoring and controlling plant and situations. This is a very different focus from that in pure courses and from that in most applied courses. The knowledge and skills needed by students in order that they can do the things that scientists do is gathered *en route*. This is thought to bring relevance and motivation to learning. The approach also encourages students to be better information seekers and information handlers.

2 *Contexts for study are work-related* and based on problems encountered in businesses and public services. Once more, relevance is the aim. However, using real contexts also brings home the varied nature of science in real life and the ways people have to work with others to solve problems. There is a theoretical argument that proposes that students need to practise science in a range of settings if they are to begin to think as working scientists do. Applied courses often use a work-related context as a vehicle for teaching facts and principles associated with pure science.

3 *Active learning methods* are encouraged. This is not because they are the most effective means of learning. As much as some would believe this to be true, there is no proof of their dominance over other methods. Active learning methods are of prime importance in vocational courses because they allow students to develop general skills such as planning, information-seeking and teamwork. Other methods will not work because the student needs room for manoeuvre; they have to be able to make their own decisions about such things as approaches to assignments, sources of information and how to contribute best in a group exercise. Here, it is difficult to argue that vocational courses have this characteristic and pure courses do not. However, it is reasonable to say that active learning methods are often a requirement of vocational programmes whereas learning methods are often not specified in pure (or applied) courses.

4 *Assessment of students' progress is continuous* and based on coursework, it often includes a project or assignment. This is not because continuous assessment is generally the best way of measuring attainment, rather that it is more fit for the purpose of measuring the capability of students for scientific work in diverse settings and in terms of skills such as planning, information-seeking and working with others. Projects lend themselves to teacher assessment. A student's scientific knowledge and skills can be assessed through paper-based examination, but this can be problematic. This is because every student's knowledge base has been developed in a range of settings and varies in depth according to the problems they have solved. Continuous assessment is often a dominant part of assessment practices used in vocational programmes.

5 There is *more scope for the student to impose a structure* on the work. This is because the student needs to show their project management skills. They have to demonstrate they appreciate the meaning of criteria for success and the

importance of deadlines. In pure and applied courses, the structure is often based on the structure of the knowledge and skills base – which in turn is often closely related to the facts and principles. In vocational programmes, the knowledge and skills base will focus on practical knowledge and the processes of learning and working.

Why these characteristics?

These characteristics are key features of vocational courses, as they are perceived to relate closely to scientific ways of working. Employers have a strong influence on the structure and content of vocational courses – stronger than their influence over general science courses. What is it they want from science education that leads to the characteristics 1 to 5 above?

The changing nature of work

The first thing employers would want to impress on science educators is that the work situation is constantly changing. Many companies have described new working practices and the needs that brought them about. The Chemical Industries Association (CIA) described today's workplace in the following way:

> Less and less people doing jobs; jobs disappearing. Work will be completed by people employing sets of skills and competencies. Employees will work in teams across functions, they might manage a project one day and be a subordinate the next, they will need to be multi-skilled and work to objectives and outcomes.

The Ford Motor Company has responded to the current business environment, and in particular the power and potential of high technology, by operating a flatter management structure with empowerment of staff at local level. It has reduced its workforce dramatically in the last fifteen years. High technology means it puts greater emphasis on the quality of staff inputs, needing proportionately more high-level thinkers. To do this, it has improved the staff selection processes, employed more women (particularly able women previously not in employment) and begun to develop the concept of a worker willing to adapt and learn through a commitment to lifelong learning.

Scientific research in universities is also changing. The use of IT networks has accelerated team working. Collaboration with businesses is being encouraged and is now a key factor for public funding. The Technology Foresight scheme aims to give a more economic focus to areas of research.

These examples signal a deep change in the way business operates today. Other changes, such as the dramatic increase in the number of people working to short-term contracts, and the expansion of consultancy and teleworking, with the consequent development of a smaller number of 'core' staff (centrally employed, full time, permanent administrative and strategic managers), further illustrate how many companies are adapting to the business environment.

General skills or attitudes

The next focus for employers would be to ensure that everyone recognizes that general skills, including the personal qualities of individuals, are very important. There have been many attempts at listing these general skills. The following table summarizes research evidence in this area – the skills in the table are specific to people in scientific employment. These people include plant managers, research managers, medical practitioners, animal technicians and scientists 'on the bench' in universities, companies and public service laboratories. The general skills are listed in order of the frequency in which they were identified.

Generic skill or attribute	*Observations*
Communication	This is a broad field. Recent research has found fifty-two different types of communication identified by employers and higher education tutors. There are often comments from employers on poor levels of communication skills.
Team work	Everything that signals good teamworking potential is highly valued (see Management below). Seen as a weakness in science graduates.
Mathematics including number skills	Critical for most scientific work. Concerns about weak algebra and the effect of calculators on feel for numbers, estimating, etc. Particular worries over maths abilities of physics and engineering undergraduates.
Self motivation, commitment	See personal skills below. Training to degree level seen as indicator of commitment to subject area. Needed for person to learn, develop and progress. Ambition is valued.
Business awareness	Usually about adjusting to business environment (opportunities and constraints).
Information technology skills	Increasing dependence on IT in research and management.
Adaptability and flexibility	Needed in teamwork and in work environment.
Management	Commonly project management, people (team) management and sometimes time management.

Creativity	Linked to progress and gaining commercial advantages.
Problem solving	Some would regard this as a scientific skill. Seen as a composite by many. May include the management of problems.
Initiative	Often limited to managing one's own work programme. Other times about taking opportunities for development.
Leadership	Links with teamwork.
Planning	Varies considerably between different types and levels of work.
Legal awareness	Arising more frequently because of health and safety responsibilities but also because some areas are becoming subject to increasing regulation.
Personal effectiveness	Often used as an overarching phrase to cover communication, teamworking, time management.
Decision making	Some would regard this as a scientific skill. Good decision-making based on evaluation of data is seen as crucial. A key skill in managers.
Foreign language skills	Often rated as an advantage rather than crucial.

These general capabilities are particularly important to working scientists. The new working environment means that organizations require people with these broad capabilities to make them effective.

Scientific capability in the work place

What do employers look for in terms of scientific capabilities? The Consortium of Science and Technology Institutes (CSTI) commissioned an analysis of the function of scientists in a wide range of occupations (CSTI 1995). The CSTI analysis was wide-ranging in its sampling of types of science work. The report lists forty-six occupations where science is the main part of the job (such as a medical technician), or is critical to the job being carried out effectively (such as a nurse). Some 2.7 million people fall into these categories in the UK workforce. This is about 10 per cent of the UK workforce. Their report of the work contained the following broad description of the task of scientists.

> To explore, establish, apply, manage and administer safe and ethical practices and procedures of science, technology and mathematics to generate new knowledge, and to exploit this knowledge to serve the economy, the environment and society.

Table 6.1 The Consortium of Science and Technology Institutes' analysis

Applying scientific abilities	Communication	Managerial
Generate own ideas, hypotheses & theoretical models and/or utilize those postulated by others	Determine current and projected requirement from within and outside the organization, for science mathematical and technological skills/ services	Develop policies and strategies which will lead to the achievement of objectives (set by self and others) and the efficient, effective and safe execution of the operation/organization
Design investigations, experiments, trials, tests, simulations and operations	Research all potential sources of information to establish current knowledge, understanding, practices and procedures	Determine appropriate policy/practices for the safe and effective utilization of resources
Conduct investigations, experiments, trials, tests and operations	Communicate the results and outcomes of present and previous scientific, technological and mathematical investigations and/or activities	Administer policy/strategies to ensure achievement of objectives
Evaluate data and results from the processes and outcomes of investigations, experiments, trials, tests and operations	Teach, train and assess students/clients/trainees in the knowledge, understanding and practices (both new and established) of science, technology and mathematics	Monitor and evaluate the efficient and effective running of an investigation, programme, initiative, section, department, branch or organization

This job purpose was broken down into subcategories. Three layers of sub-categories were described. In the first (least detailed) layer, the essential function of applying scientific, technological and mathematical knowledge, methods, tests, and trials is accompanied by a communication function and a managerial function. These are then broken down into the next layer of detail as shown in Table 6.1.

Clearly, vocational science courses need to give strong emphasis to these capabilities. Other research conducted by the author and based on the same cross section of scientists led to the following broader description of these basic components of scientists' activity (Table 6.2).

These two tables can be regarded as a checklist for identifying the key aspects, the building blocks, of vocational science programmes. There is also a case that other types of science programme include some (or all) of these aspects. The difference between different types of programmes might be measured in terms of the difference in emphasis given to these aspects.

Table 6.2 The broad characteristics of scientific capability

Characteristics of scientific capability	Comment
Knowledge of facts, principles, laws and theories	Knowledge is needed at all levels of work. The knowledge required is often specialized and personalized.
Generic (non-scientific) skills	Such is the ability to communicate well with individuals and groups, the ability to seek out relevant information, the ability to work well with others.
The ability to manipulate skilfully equipment and materials	Measurements and creating observations. Appropriate accuracy, good consistency and knowledge of the underlying principles on which the measurement or observation is based are important.
Understanding how to experiment	The ability to solve a problem by analysing the nature of the problem, creating a hypothesis to test it and constructing an experimental procedure which is well controlled and is likely to yield data of optimum value.
The ability to analyse data	Data arising from different sources and in different forms (words, numbers, graphical, images) to create statements which can be shown to have a basis in the data. Logical thought and open-minded consideration of evidence is part of this feature.
Appreciating the nature and structure of science work	This includes appreciation of different approaches to creating new, reliable knowledge. On a local scale, it includes such things as understanding how the parts of a science work group interact and the ways such groups contribute to more general purposes within companies and public services. On a wider scale, it involves knowledge of how science makes progress.

Science education and the work of scientists

Evaluating science education against what scientists do in work shows that there is potential for science curriculums to become broader, more varied, more relevant and allow students to become more aware of the practice of science and, if it is their intention, more employable in scientific work.

The scientific knowledge-base

One of the problems of modernizing the knowledge base is that science educators see a core of ideas as central to most scientific activity, for example the concepts of the conservation of energy, and the notion of a dynamic equilibrium or homeo-stasis. These are important parts of science courses. The problem is that there are many of them and they quickly fill the space available in the core. Furthermore, they are basic ideas and are usually well established. This can lead to a feeling that the core is dated. During the definition of a core for A level physics syllabuses in 1992, a commentator speaking for the Institute of Physics felt moved to remark that it was a pity a core for advanced physics education in the late twentieth century contained no twentieth-century physics. When a core is large, the non-core material to be included has to be limited. This additional material is usually drawn from a bank of explanatory concepts, which are traditionally part of a partic-ular area of science. The introduction of new areas of science knowledge becomes very difficult. These problems may be eased by using a knowledge base determined through the analysis of action knowledge. There is also the possibility that educa-tionalists can be persuaded that a knowledge base derived from science practice is at least valid in the sense it will prepare students better for scientific work. This may be more convincing than arguments that may appear to teachers to be about what content seems most fashionable at a particular time.

Another issue that arises as a result of having at large core of knowledge is that the assessment of knowledge can dominate the overall assessment regime in a given qualification. Knowledge can be assessed by straightforward methods of written answers to questions. The assessment method can require recall of facts, application of ideas and analysis of data. The examinations can be shown to be fair and yield reliable data. However, fairness and reliability may be more difficult to establish in the examination of the scientific skills associated with experimenta-tion. The same will apply to the examination of general skills – for example those associated with managing a project. The examination of aspects of scientific capa-bility (and general skills), which complement cognition of explanatory concepts, can become complex and expensive to operate. Outcomes of these relatively complex procedures often command less public confidence than those derived from written examinations. This is not the place to discuss the advantages and disadvantages of various assessment instruments, but the issue is important because there will be pressure to give more weight to written papers focused on explanatory knowledge. This will lead to less time and effort being applied to the examination of other aspects of scientific capability. The size of the core of explan-atory concepts which is included in a qualification, and the weight given to the concepts in examination, needs to be held in check so that the important skills of science, which are not generally assessed through examination, are not under-valued. Of course, these skills do not function in isolation from the knowledge base. In scientific activities there is extensive interplay between cognition associ-ated with explanatory concepts, the cognition associated with experimentation and data, and a range of manipulative skills.

The development of practical skills

Research with practising scientists has shown that school, college and university courses were considered to offer low levels of relevant practical experience. Scientists generally want more attention to be focused on the ability to manipulate equipment and materials and the ability to measure and create observations, including the need for accuracy and consistency. Evidence suggests students need to be able to:

- practice and improve skills;
- explain the background to the measurements and observations and also to the levels of instrument error and human error;
- appreciate the importance of this type of skill in laboratory work.

It might be argued that practical skills are best learned on-the-job. When a person joins a science-based team they will be inducted into the specialist procedures used by the laboratory. Often, they will shadow an experienced worker until they become proficient in these skills. There is no substitute for this on-the-job training, but it may be to the advantage of students considering scientific work if they had had experience of aiming for consistency and optimizing accuracy in school or college practical work. They can then recognize the demands likely to be made of them in work. The beginning of their working career is likely to be predominantly practical in nature. This might add further weight to an increased focus on practical work in the later stages of full-time education.

Educating analytical thinkers

Evidence from research with working scientists shows this to be a very important aspect of scientific capability. Analytical thinking is important because it is a key aspect of problem solving and many scientists are employed as problem solvers. Most, if not all, advanced courses in education require students to be analytical. What is special about the way analytical thinking is developed in the context of science and how is it best developed though the education and training system?

There are possibly three dimensions of scientific subject matter which make analysis particularly challenging. The first dimension is that the subject matter could be practical or physical in nature. This introduces the need for decisions about such things as manipulation, sequences of actions, spatial orientation and costs. This may be the only concrete aspect of the analysis. The second dimension is that mathematical thinking may be required. The third dimension is that the explanatory concepts (facts, principles and theories) involved may be demanding in themselves. They are certainly largely abstract in nature. Some of these explanatory concepts are susceptible to change when applied in certain conditions. Analysis in scientific contexts can involve all three dimensions and can be very demanding.

The development of general skills

In the UK, there has been a strong and consistent pressure from business organizations for a better foundation in general skills to be established in schools and colleges. The priority given to the practice and refinement of these skills in scientific work raises more questions for general science education, where they are often, at best, implicit.

The distinction between science and technology

In life and in work, science and technology interact strongly; to be effective in work, people need to have scientific skills and be able to use them to solve problems, improve products and optimize processes. They need to have a firm grasp of explanatory concepts and of concepts of evidence, and be able to apply them both. The literature on technical work rarely distinguishes between science and technology. Working scientists often prefer to use the terms such as 'technical skills' as they described their work. Many are involved in the technical enterprise of production and improving processes.

If people work by integrating science and technology activities – even research scientists carry out technological functions – why are the distinctions so persistent in training? Is a science education the best way to train someone who will eventually work as a technologist? These questions are not new, yet we still have a strong commitment to maintain a distinction between the two fields. In education today, from the primary phase through to support for higher degrees, science and technology are largely planned and taught separately. They seem to be based on the philosophy 'first you study science and then you can learn some ways of using the science'.

The evidence from this research work is that the divisions between science and technology are maintained by education whilst work practice calls for a more integrated view of science, technology and engineering in school education.

The importance of context

In recent years there has been increasing research interest in the transferability of knowledge and skills from one domain to another. Research evidence suggests that, at best, a student will learn to apply a skill more quickly in a new context if they have practised the skill previously elsewhere. Evidence of complete transfer is weak. The area of school mathematics has been the focus of much research into transfer. Teachers have found that the process of learning an idea or technique in a mathematics lesson and, at some later time, applying the learning to a problem in a lesson in another subject is more problematic than it might seem. The same problem is likely to beset transfer of scientific skills to, say, technology settings. Science education needs to be reviewed from the perspective of how well teaching approaches encourage knowledge and skill transfer between contexts.

The proponents of the theory of situated cognition would explain poor transfer by proposing that knowledge (explanatory concepts, concepts of evidence and general skills) is linked to the situations in which it is learned *and* to the situations where it is applied. When students learn facts, principles and skills in situations that are distant from those where they will be applied, they have difficulty in transferring their abilities. Scientific work settings are not accessible to most students and it might therefore be expected that, whilst some students will have learned useful science in school and college, they will have a problem applying it in practice. There are many examples of school and college science programmes where the situational base is extended to enhance transfer (e.g. teacher placements in industry in vocational science courses). The need for real contextual experience does put some doubt on the long-term value in teaching scientific investigation in schools as an academic construction rather than as a problem-solving activity. Another way of developing contexts with a greater chance of allowing transfer to work situations is to use discourse or problem-based methods. The method has advantages in that it has a closer fit to the way people may learn in work and this may increase potential for transfer from one situation to another.

Problem-solving is a key feature in the literature describing employers' needs. Contexts for problem-solving are therefore important and science education needs to be reviewed from this perspective. Problem-solving in science education can be very different from that practised in business. Problem-solving situations in schools are often characterized by short timescales, use of limited pre-specified resources, and work being done by individuals and their peers with little technical support. On the other hand in business, longer timescales will often be involved, resources will be available for work done by teams of people with different skills and experience and technical support and expert advice is likely to be ready at hand. Problem-solving in schools and colleges suffers many constraints and it would be unrealistic to believe the process of problem-solving in business could be faithfully replicated in schools and colleges. Nevertheless, there are business practices that could be adapted to educational settings and this might enhance transfer.

One implication of Lave's work (Lave 1988; Lave and Wenger 1991) for education is that, if chances of transfer from school to work are to be optimized, it may be effective to explore a range of learning approaches that have different objectives. For example, including group activities where each member has a personal agenda and a shared one.

Work experience is a useful way of introducing a different context and is a feature of most curriculums, at all levels of education.

Conclusion

By describing science in terms of the work of scientists, a new way of analysing the form of scientific qualifications becomes available. This perspective highlights the importance of general skills, using technological contexts for problem-solving and recognizes three different features of doing science (practical manipulative, designing experiments and analysing data). It is clear that there is room for debate about whether school science courses offer a sufficient grounding in these aspects. It is also clear that, whilst vocationally-oriented science courses generally meet the needs of employers, there is scope for pure and applied courses to pay greater attention to some of these aspects, since they are potentially motivating to young people and have features which can be useful to students who may have ambitions outside scientific or technical careers.

References

CSTI (1995) *Occupational Mapping and Initial Functional Analysis of Occupations in Science, Ttechnology and Mathematics,* London: Council of Science and Technology Institutes.
Lave, J. (1988) *Cognition in Practice,* New York: Cambridge University Press.
Lave, J. and Wenger, E. (1991) *Situated Learning: Legitimate Peripheral Participation,* New York: Cambridge University Press.

7 The dilemma of science, technology and society education

Joan Solomon

Development and dilemma

The growth of Science, Technology and Society (STS) in the school curriculum was no tidy and well-planned affair. It arose from a variety of causes, most of which were unimpeachable in purpose. And yet the subject is often contentious, both in its nature and its method. It also highlights contradictions within science education itself. To some extent, all educational theory is bound to entertain controversy: indeed it may well be healthy for it to do so. For STS the controversy – political as well as educational – is particularly sharp. Even for the student who participates in STS lessons there are tensions which attend other aspects of science to a much slighter degree.

This chapter will trace some of the main influences for the introduction of STS courses in our schools. In his book *Teaching and Learning about Science and Society* (1980), Ziman identified seven different possible approaches to the teaching of an STS course at tertiary level. All of these he managed to justify as valid and acceptable in some important sense. Looking back over recent history of STS at school level, we find not just rationales proposed by innovating teachers but also the external pressures of politics and educational theory influencing curriculum. These forces contributed, from the start, to some inner conflicts and dilemmas of purpose.

The name STS for the whole genre of courses may be attributable to the influential collection of papers published under the name *Science, Technology and Society* by Spiegel-Rosing and Price in 1977. By this date, there was a small but vigorous international scholarly movement in *Science Studies* which examined the economic and political aspects of current science-based issues, as well as the history, sociology and philosophy of science itself. In Europe as EASST, and in North America as 4S, such associations continue their work but, with few exceptions, there is precious little contact between them and the various educational groups which have sought to promote similar studies within school. This schism has been much to the detriment of the latter. The majority of school curriculum materials have been designed either by enthusiastic and self-taught teachers, or by professional industrialists and scientists without this science studies dimension to their thinking. On too many occasions this has produced courses with an intellectually flat, but content and evaluation rich, approach.

The cultural approach

The claim of science to be an integral and important part of the general culture is often traced back to C.P. Snow's influential lecture on *The Two Cultures*. This gave visibility to a claim which had been growing slowly since the beginning of the century and accelerating sharply since the Second World War. It was to have two different effects on education. In Britain, the claim was gradually taken over by the science education community and used to argue that all children should have some science in their school curriculum, at least up to the age of 16.

But the kind of science education on offer was also to be changed. In the discussion paper of the Association for Science Education (ASE), *Alternatives for Science Education* (1979) and its later paper, *Education through Science* (1981) the emphasis was moved away from the kind of science education designed to prepare the most able for a university degree in science, towards a science for the citizen. The earlier paper proposed a whole year, at grade 8, entirely devoted to *science and society*. In the USA, the report to the National Science Foundation by Hufstedler and Langenberg in 1980 shows a similar emphasis on developing a curriculum which would be more relevant to the community. It was a period when American education had been suffering from the *Back to Basics* movement and this report heralded a backlash which warned that science was diminished by being taught in this way, and urged the inclusion of scientific information related to personal, societal and vocational problems. The phrase 'scientific literacy' began to be heard and it was clear that some measure of real concern about the public understanding of science was being expressed. The National Science Foundation responded with recommendations for instruction on such themes as energy and the environment which would range 'from drill and practice to the simulation of complex problem situations'.

This comparatively modest movement towards relevance in science education was just one historical reaction to the growing importance of science in the curriculum. Another was more academic and cultural; it advocated a 'liberal studies in science' approach to secondary- or tertiary-level science education. Of the 'science greats' course at Manchester University, Jevons (1967) wrote,

> The precise core is provided by physical science, and it is supplemented by the more open-ended treatment of science considered from the economic, social, historical and philosophical points of view.

The emphasis on the history and philosophy of science claims a kind of continuity of thought with such venerable studies which had previously been embedded in other disciplines. Of course, the history of science had never been totally excluded from the school science courses. Many textbooks were in the habit of including references to the 'Great Men' of science. Even the British school Nuffield courses, which flourished in the 1960s, drew attention to the historical development of a few scientific ideas, mostly in cosmology. The American PSSC and BSCS courses, dating from the same period, contain similar historical references. The objective, however, seemed to be more of a glorification of scientific progress than of an understanding of the problematic interactions between science and society.

The social history of technology is a more likely starting point for STS courses, and some classic school books did mention the industrial revolution in connection with energy and engines, or the production of explosives and fertilizers in connection with the chemistry of nitrates. Holmyard's widely used textbook of school chemistry (first published in 1925 and virtually unchanged up to 1960) is a particularly good example of an approach which might include both science and technology but had absolutely no ambition to foster interest in contemporary or controversial social issues.

Two of the earliest courses in school STS did, in their own ways, use philosophical or historical approaches. In 1972, Aikenhead and Fleming (1975) began work on a new tenth grade course for Canadian students – *Science: A Way of Knowing* – which would allow them to make sense of their rapidly changing society. But Aikenhead wrote that the students made no progress without some instruction on different kinds of knowing.

> In our experience grade 10 students can seldom deal with the complex and sophisticated issues related to the interaction of science and society without having first achieved … a way of recognising and handling the different types of knowledge involved.
>
> (Aikenhead 1979)

At approximately the same time, the Schools' Council Integrated Science Project (SCISP) was developing a course in Britain which was similarly self-conscious about making explicit the thinking processes which might be used. Their textbooks spoke about searching for 'patterns' as the root activity of all science. In contrast to the previous example, they included under this procedural banner the economic and social factors involved in the application of science, for example, *Science and Decision-making* (Hall 1973).

The STS course which makes the most conscious use of historical preamble for teaching about topical issues is the later British course for grade 11 students, *SISCON-in-Schools* (Solomon 1983). In each one of the eight different booklets, recent history is used to show either how similar problems have been dealt with in the past, or how the quandaries of the present situation arose. The reason for this strategy is:

> to stand back from the present and to see how technology and science (have) serve(d) a community …
>
> (Addinell and Solomon 1983)

This historical dimension is then used to establish a new perspective in matters which may be almost too controversial for useful immediate discussion.

Political education for action

The next influence for STS also came from outside the domain of school science. This was a movement which could be called 'Science for the People' and traced a heritage both from the left-wing scientists of the 1920s and 1930s (Haldane, Hogben, etc.) and also from those educationalists of the post-Second World War period who, like Skilbeck, wrote of education for 'social reconstruction'. The first SISCON *(Science In a Social CONtext)* movement for the teaching of STS within the tertiary sector shared many members with the British Society for Social Responsibility in Science. This, in turn, had been influenced by the international Pugwash movement and was permeated by many of the same ideals. For these activists, it followed that the new science education should focus upon those issues about which citizens need to be educated for appropriate political action. Indeed, the action itself was sometimes an explicit aim of the course.

In America, environmental education was in many ways the precursor of STS education. It identified three kinds of skills to be developed in their students – cognitive skills which would enable them to understand issues, evaluative skills in which their affective reactions would be modified, and changes in behavioural action.

> Responsible action denotes those behaviours engaged in for the purpose of achieving and/or maintaining a dynamic equilibrium between quality of life and quality of the environment. Developing an environmentally literate citizenry who are both willing and able to engage in environmental action, is considered to be the ultimate goal of environmental education.
>
> (Hines and Hungerford 1984)

Since most of this environmental education was subsumed under social studies, rather than science, its influence on later STS courses in Europe has been regrettably small although more apparent in the growing movement for STS in the States.

In countries such as Holland and Canada, this more political theme became apparent in the movement for STS within schools at much the same time as public pressure groups became a common phenomenon, and laws to allow freer public access to scientific knowledge, were formulated and debated. Acid rain pollution of the Great Lakes, the introduction of nuclear power in Holland, Austria, and Sweden, mining for uranium in Australia and Canada – all of these were local issues of problematique which merit an STS category of their own in the next section of this chapter. They are placed in the present context because the issues were politically contentious and the courses based upon them were strongly influenced by a public education objective to enable citizens to partake in decision-making action.

> It is necessary, in STS courses, to recognise (social) forces, otherwise you could be reduced to a puppet … to exert any real influence, which is necessary to realize your social responsibility, is to transform (insight from these courses) into action.
>
> (quoted in Rip 1978)

Interdisciplinary education and the problematique approach

All STS courses should be interdisciplinary and embrace elements from any of the traditional science areas, as necessary. The justification for this assertion becomes clear enough if we examine narrow efforts to show the application of knowledge from one science discipline which touch on an STS theme. The laudable idea of showing the relevance of school physics may, for example, lead to a discussion of the electrostatic precipitation of solid particles in a factory chimney flue. However, if the physics orientation prevents the discussion from spreading into a consideration of acid rain, the desulphurization processes and the subsequent disposal of sulphur, the effort is revealed as a very weak version of real STS.

In most countries, science education in the secondary school has developed along disciplinary lines. Layton (1982) has outlined the long and chequered history of integrated science in British education, but it is clear that modern British schooling has called for, and is very slowly acquiring, a new kind of science teaching which does not measure its effectiveness by the demands of the most able. This permits its content to spread out beyond the usual subject limits. In other countries, school science has always been multi-disciplinary up to grades 8 or 9. This leads readily to an issue-based approach to STS teaching. But STS knows no frontiers and readily spills over into social studies, geography, religious studies and history, as well as the natural sciences. Many teachers have welcomed this as in keeping with a more holistic approach to education itself

Interdisciplinarity can be a powerful enabler of STS and it is also linked with it in more deeply theoretical ways. Ziman (1980: 117) has pointed out how borrowing from different subject areas can dislodge 'the myth of scientism that there is a "science" (actual or potential) for dealing with every problem'. In the school arena, the ethical, cultural, and political aspects of any issue which cries out for STS treatment go further than debunking myths; they resurrect the vision of the great educators of every age.

But basing school STS education on the consideration of a series of issues has drawbacks as well as advantages. The issues are chosen because of their topicality, local, national or international, but the very heat engendered by such contentious issues, which may raise the students' motivation to learn, also all too often drives out any general lessons which may be drawn about the nature of science, technology or social decision-making. The danger is all the stronger if the issues are taken in small packages, such as the British *Science and Technology in Society* (Holman 1987). Here there is no definable course at all, just series of detachable leaflets each of which represents one lesson which is to be fitted into the 'interstices' of the normal school science curriculum in an order to be decided by the teacher.

The most attractive feature of the problematique approach to STS education is its extension to local topics which touch the students' community closely. Most of these materials have been produced by school teachers for their own pupils and are usually only printed by school reprographic centres. On a slightly larger scale we may find, for example, units from Israel on the development of fertilizers from the

Dead Sea and the construction of a Mediterranean–Dead Sea canal. Sometimes, a particular theme from health education may seem to be treated in the style of an STS issue, for example, fluoridation of water, or drugs and smoking (Zoller 1985). But here we have topics which are not only important and close to the students' own experience, but which also carry a strongly didactic message from the teacher. It may be claimed that informed decision-making is the objective of such a course; yet the existence of a predetermined goal in terms of the students' final frame of mind, reveals such units as different in spirit from those STS courses which aim to show that social decision-making has no obvious *right answer*.

Vocational or technocratic

The fourth and final strand comes out of an instrumental view of science and technology as the engine of industry which is itself the essential wealth-producer of society. In this kind of STS course, the structure of industry is often studied for its own sake, e.g. *Science in Society* (Lewis 1980) and not as that of a factional interest in the community's concerns. For the consideration of energy generation, environmental control, and the monitoring of new technology – all topics which figure largely in STS courses – the role of industry is too intimately identified with one line of argument for it to come credibly into the educational marketplace as a purveyor of STS courses. Many industries – Shell, BP and ICI to name but a few – have spent considerable sums on educational materials, but teachers of STS courses need to exercise care in their use if the students are to learn about all points of view of the topic.

In a wider context, it has always been possible to view all education as a national investment. While the old belief in the 'trained mind' prevailed, no particular course of study needed to be specified so long as it was sufficiently taxing to stretch and train the mind. Science and technology were always too challenging and content-laden to fit comfortably into this scheme, and education adopted what Jevons (1967) has called the 'all or nothing' attitude towards science in the curriculum. Now that an education in science and technology is more highly valued for its contribution to industry, the attitude to their place in the general curriculum has changed in corresponding ways. It has been argued that some knowledge of the social and economic facets of science is essential for the mandarins of finance and the captains of industry. So, some schools may believe that they face a challenge to begin the education of an elite who are destined to lead in the new science-based industries. This is STS for the technocrats – yet another dimension of vocational education.

Out in the cold and back again?

The 1980s were a particularly good time in the UK for informal curriculum innovation by teachers. There was still no National Curriculum and the SSCR (School Science Curriculum Review) had set out in 1983 to produce guidelines for a new curriculum by simply using the initiatives of the country's force of science teachers. It did not last. Successive Conservative Secretaries of State for Education took over the reigns of power and, as they did so, it was clear that STS did not meet with approval either. Keith Joseph announced that the forthcoming National Curriculum would not have any mention of 'social and economic issues' in its science. Margaret Thatcher had already given her opinion that 'there is no such thing as society, only people'. Both of these were body blows to the existing STS courses. Moves to include it as 'Attainment Target 23' in the original proposals were simply ignored.

The first final version of the National Curriculum had no fewer than seventeen of these Attainment Targets, each of which had ten statements of objectives. The last of these, Attainment Target 17, *The Nature of Science* (NoS), survived an interesting two years before being pruned down to the present format. It included extracts from the history of science which showed both how the processes of science produced new theories which superseded the old ones, and also how these were affected by social influences. It was a way of teaching STS indirectly through history and there was evidence from research carried out in the classroom that it worked well (Solomon *et al.* 1993; 1994). Pupils at Key Stages 3 and 4 enjoyed the stories, and their understanding of the scientific processes moved quite painlessly from an idea that the results of experiments were always a surprise, to seeing that they were designed to test out a hypothesis. Even the more difficult idea that scientists at other times had come up with different ideas was beginning to be understood in terms of different influences from society.

The 2000 Science Curriculum reinstated elements of both these historical and social aspects of science under the rubric *Ideas and Evidence in Science*. In Key Stage 4 it is to be seen at both single and double award – Sc1 1(a), (b), (c) and (d). To a lesser extent it is also present in Key Stage 3 – Sc1 1(a), and even through an historical example in the Programme of Study for Key Stage 2 – Sc1 1(a).

Looking back on the early days of STS, what stands out most clearly was the grass roots reaction to hugely important topical issues. Teachers had reacted to Rachel Carson's call for action to preserve wildlife (1962), and there were fierce campaigns to 'Ban the Bomb' or to close down nuclear reactors. However, the last move has come from cool governmental curriculum planning, as it mostly does in other countries. In the USA, a comprehensive programme of reform 'Project 2061' was launched in 1989, the same year as our first National Curriculum. Understanding the *Nature of Science,* which included its social and industrial relations, took first place in the project's later programme *Benchmarks for Scientific Literacy* in 1993. Perhaps it is possible to argue that the future of STS is now more secure within the National Curriculum than it was before as a go-it-alone progressive feature, or the odd exercises to be added on to a lesson, if there was time. Its purpose is to build a better science education which will 'belong to our own times and to our own form of civilisation', as John Ziman (1980) wrote about the first wave of STS education.

This is a good educational spot to watch!

References

Addinell, S. and Solomon, J. (1983) *Science in a Social Context, Teachers Guide*, Hatfield: Association for Science Education.

Aikenhead, G. (1979) 'Science: a way of knowing', *The Science Teacher* 46: 6.

Aikenhead, G. and Fleming, R. (1975) *Science a Way of Knowing*, Saskatoon: University of Saskatchewan, Department of Curriculum Studies.

Association for Science Education (1979) *Alternatives for Science Education*, Discussion Paper, Hatfield: Association for Science Education.

Association for Science Education (1981) *Educating through Science*, Policy Document, Hatfield: Association for Science Education.

Carson, R. (1962) *Silent Spring*, Greenwich, CT: Fawcett Publications.

Hall, W. (1973) *Science and Decision-making*, London: Longman and Harmondsworth: Penguin.

Hines, J. M. and Hungerford, H. R. (1984) 'Environmental educational research related to environmental action skills' in ERIC, *Monographs in Environmental Education and Environmental Studies* (1971–1982), Columbus: Ohio State University, pp. 113–30.

Holman, J. (1987) 'Resources or courses? Contrasting approaches to the introduction of industry and technology to the secondary curriculum', *School Science Review* 68(244): 432–8.

Hufstedler, S. M. and Langenberg, D. N. (1980) *Science Education for the 1980s and Beyond*, Washington, DC: National Science Foundation and the Department of Education.

Jevons, F. (1967) 'A science greats', *Physics Education* 2: 196.

Layton, D. (1982) 'Science education and values education – an essential tension', in Proceedings of an International Seminar, London: Chelsea College.

Lewis, J. (1980) *Science in Society. Readers and Teachers' Guide*, Hatfield: Association for Science Education and London: Heinemann.

Rip, A. (1978) 'The social context of science, technology and society courses in the universities', in E. Boeker and M. Gibbons (eds) *Science, Society and Education*, Amsterdam: Vrie Universiteit, pp. 135–52.

Solomon, J. (1983) Eight titles in the *SISCON in Schools* series and a Teachers' Guide, Hatfield: Association for Science Education and Oxford: Basil Blackwell.

Solomon, J., Duveen, J. and Scott, L. (1993) 'Pupils' understanding of science: description of experiments or "A passion to explain"?', *School Science Review* 75(271): 19–30.

Solomon, J., Duveen, J. and Scott, L. (1994) 'Pupils' images of scientific epistemology', *International Journal of Science Education* 16(3): 361–73.

Spiegel-Rosing, I. and Price, D. de S. (eds) (1977) *Science, Technology and Society: A Cross-disciplinary Perspective*, Beverly Hills, CA: Sage.

Ziman, J. (1980) *Teaching and Learning about Science and Society*, Cambridge: Cambridge University Press.

Zoller, U. (1985) 'Interdisciplinary decision-making in the science curriculum in the modern socio-economic context' in G. Harrison (ed.) *World Trends in Science and Technology Education*, Report on Second International Symposium, Nottingham: Trent Polytechnic.

8 Analysing multi-cultural and anti-racist science education

Reg Dennick

Introduction

We are confronted by the problems of racism and xenophobia on a daily basis, in our own society and around the world. Overt racist behaviour can be minimized by legislation, but education clearly plays an important role in helping future generations to respect other people, whatever their country or culture. However, the educational system itself can sometimes be the source of racist ideas and stereotypes. There are many subtle ways in which children's attitudes are influenced and these can often be found embedded within the content and processes of the curriculum. Strenuous efforts have been made in the past twenty years to eradicate such influences across the curriculum spectrum. Many teachers feel that the science curriculum is probably the last area that could be tainted by racist ideas, but they would be wrong.

It is the purpose of this chapter to examine the underlying assumptions and concepts on which a multi-cultural and anti-racist science curriculum could be based. In order to do this, it is necessary to briefly examine the debate between multi-cultural and anti-racist education in the context of science education. Next, the relationships between racism and the ideological distortions of scientific knowledge and methodology will be examined. The influence of ideas concerning the nature of scientific thinking, technology and the scientific method on the way science is taught will be looked at next. Finally, the assumptions underpinning anti-racist science education will be analysed in more detail.

Multi-cultural and anti-racist education

Multi-cultural education can be seen as an attempt to provide a curriculum that allows children to explore other cultures as well as their own so that an ethical framework of respect and toleration is built up. In the context of science education, this could involve looking at the scientific contributions made by other civilizations, cultures or native peoples. It is essentially a process of curriculum development and alteration designed to challenge and educate children out of their prejudices, leading towards a state of social cohesion within cultural diversity (Lynch 1986). The 'problem' that multi-cultural education addresses is the conflict between different *cultures*.

Anti-racist science education, on the other hand, starts from the assumption that the whole of the curriculum, the school institution, the teachers and the pupils, the Local Education Authority and society in general are influenced, either consciously or unconsciously, by a racist ideology which not only causes the overt activities of prejudice and discrimination but also subtly distorts the contents of the curriculum, views on the nature of the scientific enterprise and claims to the origins of scientific and technological knowledge itself. Anti-racist education is specifically built on the premise that it is necessary to challenge and oppose racism in society and at school; tinkering with the curriculum does not solve the 'problem'; the 'problem' is racism.

Although the polarity between multi-cultural and anti-racist education has created considerable conflict in the past, with the 'anti-racists' accusing the 'multi-culturalists' of being woolly-minded liberals trying to replace one racist curriculum with another, and the 'multi-culturalists' seeing the 'anti-racists' as hopelessly idealistic, radical revolutionaries, it is now clear that the two perspectives are inextricably linked.

However, in order to discover the roots of racism in British culture, and the distorting influence that it has had on education, and especially science education, it is necessary to analyse the history of the past few hundred years and, in particular, the period of British colonialism and imperialism.

Racism and the ideological justification for slavery

The origins and history of European slavery are well covered in the literature and there is not space to cover it here. However, the three books produced by the Institute of Race Relations (IRR) (1982a; 1982b; 1985) are an ideal resource for dealing with this issue in the classroom. Of more relevance to this chapter is the fact that the economics and practice of colonial exploitation and slavery clearly needed justification which was provided by the ideology of racism. Similarly, there were more subtle ideological distortions of 'foreign' cultures, which attempted to view them as 'primitive' and underdeveloped.

Slavery has a long history and was the economic base of many ancient cultures including that of Egypt, Greece and Rome. From the sixteenth to the nineteenth century, the 'Slave Trade' reached new heights of inhumanity and barbarity, possibly only surpassed by the purges of Stalin and the Jewish Holocaust in the twentieth century. The destruction of flourishing African cultures and the decimation of African populations weakened the infrastructure of many African societie,s laying them open to the final indignity of imperial conquest and exploitation in the nineteenth century. Such a massive process, which had an enormous impact on the economies of Western Europe and particularly Britain, had to be justified to the population as a whole and it is in this process that we can find the roots of modern racism.

The development of a racist ideology, which legitimated slavery and colonial exploitation, essentially revolved around a racial hierarchy with 'Whites' at the top and 'Negroes' at the bottom. Thus a hierarchy of cultures, coupled with the concept that white society had made the most 'progress', could be used to justify negative attitudes towards the history and achievements of foreign countries as well as ancient civilizations, and constituted a pervasive cultural hegemony.

Religious ideology made a major contribution towards such attitudes and the 'white man's burden' was seen as an obligation to civilize and baptise primitive peoples and replace their culture with the 'White Anglo-Saxon Protestant work-ethic'. Similarly, the knowledge that Sub-Saharan Africans had been enslaved since antiquity, coupled with the biblical story of God's curse on Ham, that he should be 'a servant of servants', provided ideal justification for treating blacks as slaves. It was with that peculiar evangelical fervour that characterizes the Christian religion, that many missionaries took the 'Word of God' and the culture that went with it around the world. A systematic denigration and distortion of foreign cultures was assisted by the foreshortened historical perspective provided by the widely accepted chronology of Bishop Ussher, who, in 1650, put the origin of the Earth as 4004 BC. Such a lack of historical understanding over-emphasized the contribution made by Graeco-Roman civilization and ignored the contributions from the Near East, China, India and Africa. Africa was never considered to have had civilization. Despite Egyptian history and the history of many African cultures such as the Dogon, Songhay and the civilizations of Benin and Great Zimbabwe, the contemporary historian, Trevor-Roper, stated that Africa did not have a history until it was subjected to imperial rule (IRR 1982a). More recently Bernal (1987) in the controversial book, *Black Athena*, has shown how scholars in the nineteenth century constructed a view of Greek civilization which emphasized its white European origins and neglected its Egyptian and African roots.

The expropriation of scientific discoveries

Throughout European history since the Renaissance, there has been a tendency to disparage and downgrade the discoveries and achievements of other cultures, and historians have been very prone to give credit where it is not due. Needham (1969) points out that possibly the three most important scientific and technological advances of the last millennium, namely paper and printing, gunpowder and the compass, were not only discovered by the Chinese, in some cases a thousand years earlier than is commonly assumed, but were all popularly thought to have been discovered by Europeans. Thus, gunpowder is well documented in the ninth century AD in China, although its discovery is often ascribed to Roger Bacon in 1269. The introduction of gunpowder into Europe in the thirteenth century had an enormous effect on the change from feudal fiefdoms to nation states and created the initial conditions for the formation of many of the modern European states. The spread of printing in Europe has always been seen as a necessary precursor to the Renaissance, the Reformation and the rise of Capitalism, and its discovery is usually ascribed to Gutenberg in the fifteenth century. However, paper was developed in China in the second century AD and printing, using blocks, was known in 740 AD. The floating magnet was used as an aid to divination and geomancy in China for over two thousand years and was regularly used as a navigational aid by

Chinese mariners in the eleventh century. However, many textbooks of physics state that William Gilbert discovered this use of the magnet in the sixteenth century. Again the impact that the compass had on navigation and subsequent voyages of exploration, exploitation and colonization was enormous.

Needham (1969) cites literally hundreds of scientific discoveries and technological advances the Chinese made during their long history, and which inevitably filtered westwards over the millennia. But Chinese 'science' is often downgraded by historians to the status of 'technology' since, in their judgement, it did not display evidence of the hypothetico–deductive system coupled to mathematical generalizations characteristic of 'modern' science (Crombie 1959).

To reduce Chinese science to merely 'technology' is to ignore the evidence of Sinological scholarship that has emerged in the last few decades, particularly that of Needham and his monumental work on *Science and Civilization in China* (Needham 1954). Technology, when used in this sense, has the connotation of 'trial and error' and 'chance' discoveries made without any underlying theoretical understanding. However, all the evidence now available points towards the conclusion that what the Chinese carried out was genuine 'science', with all the modern attributes of accurate and systematic observation, meticulous recording and communications, and rigorous experimental technique, including the use of controls. In addition, theoretical structures, albeit different from our own, underpinned their activities.

It must also be made clear that not only have historians of science and textbook writers devalued Chinese science, but also Islamic, Indian, Egyptian and African science has frequently been reduced to the 'technological' level and their discoveries expropriated. The knowledge that eventually filtered back into European civilization through Moorish Spain after the so-called Dark Ages, is sometimes seen merely as a collection of ancient texts that had been copied by Arab and Islamic scholars. In fact, what was passed on was a sophisticated Islamic Culture uniting art, religion and science in a profound worldview which is still very much alive today (Nasr 1968). Thus Sardar (1980), Ashrif (1986) and Nasr (1968) cite many discoveries made by Islamic scientists, such as the pulmonary circulation of the blood, heliocentric theories of the solar system and important ideas in optics, which are frequently ascribed to European traditions. Studies of African science have revealed the presence of steel making in Tanzania 1,500 to 2,000 years ago, evidence of an agricultural civilization in the Nile Valley 7,000 years before the Egyptians, and many other astronomical, mathematical and medical discoveries produced by African scientists (van Sertima 1983).

Greek science, on the other hand, is frequently cited as the prototype of the scientific method because of its development of theoretical frameworks. However, these were never tested empirically and the legacy of Greek speculation, despite its advances in logical and geometrical reasoning, led to the absurdities of Ptolemaic planetary astronomy, a universe made of immobile, crystalline spheres and an overwhelming reliance on the writings of Aristotle and Plato which inhibited truly scientific investigation.

The scientific method

There is yet another important layer of ideological distortion that influences the thinking of teachers with respect to multi-cultural and anti-racist science, and that is the precise nature of the scientific method. That science is a human activity may appear to be stating the obvious, but to the public and children, too often the image of science is that it is an impersonal process which avoids value judgements and which operates objectively and impartially.

However, in recent years there has been a debate in science education concerning the precise nature of the scientific method and its relationship to science teaching, as ideas have shifted towards an emphasis on 'process science'. Some science schemes have been criticized for putting forward an inappropriate or 'philosophically inaccurate' view of the scientific method (Hodson 1985; Hodson 1988; Millar and Driver 1987). Modern formulations of the scientific method are essentially based on the 'hypothetico-deductive' model, which emphasizes the role of subjective conjectures, or hypotheses from which deductions can be made that are empirically testable (Chalmers 1967). It crucially stresses the creative role of the subject in the scientific process. As Albert Einstein said, 'Imagination is more important than knowledge'. The work of Kuhn (1964) has furthermore shown that sociological factors are important in the progress of science, and that communities of scientists do not give up their cherished theories without a struggle, even when there is overwhelming evidence that they are wrong. Science is anything but the coldly objective and rigid process that many people popularly believe, and which science education fosters.

Such changes from the 'traditional' view of science as 'objective knowledge' to science as a human and social construction have influenced science education and led to a greater emphasis on the processes rather than the 'facts' of science, and to real investigative work being at the heart of science teaching. These changes have occurred in parallel with changes to the way that children are believed to learn scientific concepts, and which have led to different approaches to classroom learning (Driver 1983; Driver *et al.* 1985; Osborne and Freyberg 1985).

Such a view of the scientific method, coupled with a 'constructivist' approach to learning, makes science a much more human and approachable subject. In addition, this modern view of science throws open the whole debate concerning the difference between 'science' and 'technology'. Wolpert (1992), for example, asserts that science and technology are fundamentally different because technology lacks the theoretical framework characterized by science and denies that science can be found in any early civilization other than the Greeks. As mentioned earlier, the developments of the Chinese, Egyptians, other ancient civilizations and native peoples are dismissed as mere technology. However, at the cognitive level, there is little difference. Scientists may mentally conjecture and hypothesize whereas the conjectures of technology are concrete events in the real world that are tested against reality. The difference between science and technology is merely one of degree and emphasis rather than a fundamental conceptual difference. Science and technology are both 'problem-solving' activities demanding the same intellectual rigour and using the same cognitive mechanisms.

It is now abundantly clear from Needham's work that what the Chinese practised was 'science', albeit with different theoretical structures and without the mathematical methods that characterized so called 'modern' science. Similar arguments can be made for India, the Islamic world and Africa, and once this is accepted, the way is open for a fresh look at the scientific discoveries and ideas from these cultures, not as peripheral contributions to 'Western Science' but as scientific innovations in their own right. The different types of science developed in different cultures can then be seen in relation to the socio-economic conditions prevailing, and as responses to specific needs. As Needham points out:

> Science is one and indivisible. The differences are essentially sociological – what you do science for, whether for the benefit of the people as a whole, or for the private profit of great industrial enterprises, or for the development of fiendish forms of modern warfare; in a word, your motive. The differences will also be great according to whom you get to do it, whether you confine it to highly trained professionals, or whether you can use a mass of people with only minimal training ...
>
> (Needham 1976: 103)

The universality of science

The idea that scientific thinking is a normal human function has been put forward strongly by Robin Millar (1987; 1989) who suggests that the scientific processes of observing, hypothesizing and inferring are general cognitive skills used routinely by everyone. Similarly Piaget suggested that the 'Logical Operation' stage of cognitive development, found in all human beings, is essentially characterized by the ability to perform scientific thinking. Chomsky (1980) speculated that all human beings possess an innate 'science-forming capacity' that lies at the core of the ability of human beings to develop scientific knowledge. Furthermore, the recent work of evolutionary psychologists has attempted to reconstruct the evolution of the human mind and to provide theories to account for the origin of logical and technological thinking as well as artistic and 'scientific' thinking (Mithin 1996). Atran (1990) argues for the existence of an innate 'intuitive biology' or 'natural history' intelligence while Spelke (1991) asserts that children are born with an intuitive knowledge of the behaviour of physical objects. These two 'content-rich mental modules' are contrasted with other innate cognitive abilities in the areas of language (Pinker 1994), and 'intuitive psychology' (Whiten 1991). Such ideas lead to the conclusion that 'scientific thinking' is a normal human cognitive function possessed by all people *at all times;* indeed that it is an innate capacity. These developments are further evidence against the assertions of Wolpert (1992) that scientific thinking is 'unnatural' or opposed to 'common sense'

Science is not just an activity carried out by white men in white coats; it is an activity that all children from all cultural and ethnic backgrounds can participate in and 'own'. In addition, if teachers do not see science as a worldwide and human-istic phenomenon, they will continue to see the science and technology of other civilizations, both in the past and the present, in an ethnocentric and patronizing way, reinforcing racist stereotypes. But, by recognizing the way in which ideological distortions deriving from racism have influenced the content and methodology of science education, they can begin to undertake curriculum change.

The developing world and 'green science'

No one culture has a monopoly of scientific achievement and textbooks and work schemes should contain a variety of examples of people and processes from different parts of the world. This 'global perspective' links anti-racist and multi-cultural science education into issues concerned with the developing world and 'green science' and provides an ideal opportunity to make cross-curricular links. Resources that encourage children to explore how people solve problems in different cultures are now available. However, it is important that teachers avoid reinforcing stereotypical views about 'primitive' and 'advanced' science and tech-nology in the developing countries and the Western world. The aim must be to demonstrate that science and technology throughout the world are 'problem-solv-ing' activities; that all human beings and cultures possess this capacity, but that it manifests itself in different ways depending on the historical and socio-economic conditions and the resources available.

Scientific investigations can branch out into geographical, environmental and economic issues. If problem-solving is discussed within the context of 'limited resources', it seems legitimate to discuss the reasons for this which will inevitably involve looking at past colonial exploitation, cash cropping, deforestation, debt and many other issues.

Similarly, the types of technology found in developing countries are often on a more human scale and are frequently less environmentally-damaging than some of the 'big' technologies of the developed world. Here, very important issues concerning 'green science' and appropriate technology can be investigated and the scientific issues brought out.

The assumptions of anti-racist science – science as ideology

The book, *Anti-racist Science Teaching* by Gill and Levidov (1987) was a milestone in this debate and brought together some powerful arguments for the primacy of anti-racist science education. The agenda of anti-racist science includes areas such as the refutation of 'race' as a valid biological category, the 'race' and IQ debate, biological determinism, the 'nature–nurture' debate, the claims of socio-biology, nutrition, hunger and poverty, exploitation and debt, sickle cell anaemia in Black populations, and culture-fair forms of assessment. It is a very important develop-ment in science education since it challenges many fundamental views and, at the same time, expands our view of relationships between science, society and culture. While it is not possible to deal with all those issues here, it should be mentioned that its fundamental assumptions are underpinned by a view of scientific knowledge as very much the reflection of the prevailing values of the culture in which it takes place, and hence influenced by political, ideological and economic priorities.

Thus Robert Young (1987a) in *Anti-racist Science Teaching* declares, 'There is no other science than the science that gets done.' He suggests a culturally-relative view of science and points to the way that different cultures have used science to develop different knowledge and belief systems and world views. He suggests that the anti-racist curriculum should include a study of the Western capitalist approach to science that led to the separation of 'fact and value, matter and mind, mechanism and purpose'. When studying science, all concepts and facts should be looked at in the context of 'origins, assumptions, articulations, benefits, alternatives'. Young furthermore shows that the Sociology of Knowledge is capable of undermining the claims of science to value-free and objective knowledge and concludes that nothing, no matter how detailed, abstract or general, escapes the structuring of the social world; all is mediation.

But if all is 'mediation', what is it mediation *of*? Young moves his argument into the 'base–superstructure' debate of Marxism and discusses whether the development of science has its own internal dynamic, resting on the history of ideas, or if it is connected to the social and material means of production in the economic base of society. Young concludes that:

> At the deepest level, world-views or philosophies of society are arguably historically constituted. Within a given mode of production different epochs call up different disciplines and topics, along with criteria for acceptable answers to the questions we put to nature. Within a given period different priorities and conceptual frameworks arise.
>
> (Young 1987b: 85)

The extreme view of the cultural relativism of science put forward by Young, and the Marxist view that science is ideologically compromised in many areas, seems to lead to a paradoxical situation. This concept of science is not only seen as a tool of the ruling capitalist class involved in furthering racist ideology, exploitation of the Developing World, uncontrolled economic growth and pollution, but at the same time, in terms of anti-racist science education, it is the only legitimate method of countering and challenging this domination. Since, as Young argues, there is no such thing as a neutral, objective science and that all cultures and ideologies use science for their own purpose, it is difficult to see how 'science' can be used to challenge such ideologies. This is a fundamental problem for all who adopt the approach that knowledge is socially, politically or ideologically constructed.

Young, or indeed any of the other authors contributing to *Anti-racist Science Teaching*, does not address this problem. However, I think it is extremely important, from a theoretical point of view, to establish to what extent science can be used to challenge racism and the scientific distortions and ideologies which lead from it. It seems essential to try to find some ground on which anti-racist scientists can stand when criticizing biological determinism, racism and other ideological distortions of science. Needham's assertion that 'science is one and indivisible' or the ideas of Piaget and Chomsky and the evolutionary psychologists that scientific thinking is an innate, human attribute, contradict Young's culturally-relative view of science and provide a point of departure for a wider view of science in relation to culture.

It must be an ideologically untainted scientific method that can be used to refute racism and biological determinism, and it is by challenging the way in which racists use their 'hypotheses', 'observations,' 'theories' and 'evidence' from within the discourse of science that racist ideology can be 'scientifically' refuted. To accept Young's culturally-relative view of science is to legitimize the ideology of racism as yet another 'valid' knowledge and belief system. Clearly this is not what Young or other anti-racist scientists would want to do, but by cutting the ground from underneath any possibility of an objective area within science, they destroy any attempt to challenge racism scientifically.

Although there are areas of science that are clearly subordinate to ideology of one sort or another, the fact that critics of racism and biological determinism can successfully refute such 'theories' from within the discourse of science implies that the scientific method can be used to fight the ideological penetration of science and that science can therefore remain 'liberating'.

Conclusions

It is hoped that all of the major assumptions that are relevant to multi-cultural and anti-racist curriculum development have now been outlined. Most schools now accept that a multi-cultural curriculum must go hand-in-hand with an anti-racist policy and the polarity between these views is gradually diminishing. Nevertheless, it is the recognition of racism and ethnocentrism in science that makes anti-racist science education of fundamental importance. Not only should anti-racist science teaching adequately challenge racist ideology in the classroom from a powerful scientific base, but it should also make people aware of the global economic and ecological connections between different peoples on this planet. However, the conflicts generated in the educational profession within the discourse of multi-culturalism and anti-racism are nothing in comparison to the real conflicts of racism, ethnocentrism, xenophobia, militant religious fundamentalism and nationalism which afflict the world daily and generate a constant stream of death, suffering, tragedy and political upheaval.

The resolution of these conflicts might be considered to be mankind's most pressing problem and, although political and economic changes must be necessary precursors, certainly one aspect of the solution must be in the area of education. Thus it is not too pretentious to suppose that anti-racist, multi-cultural science education can be at the forefront of educational attempts to reduce prejudice and conflict between individuals, ethnic minorities, cultures and nations. Science can be liberating when coupled to a strong humanistic, open-minded and truth-seeking philosophy. It can cut the ground from beneath ideologies that would seek to keep human groups in a state of conflict, feeding on ignorance and irrational fear. It can lay bare the economic and material connections that link cultures and nations in relationships of dominance and servility. It can monitor and challenge attempts to destroy the global environment and the ecological networks on which all life depends.

References

Ashrif, S. (1986) 'Eurocentrism and myopia in science teaching', *Multi-cultural Teaching* 5: 28–30.

Atran, S. (1990) *Cognitive Foundations of Natural History: Towards an Anthropology of Science*, Cambridge: Cambridge University Press.

Bernal, M. (1987) *Black Athena – The Afroasiatic Roots of Classical Civilization*, London: Free Association Books.

Chalmers, A. F. (1967) *What is this thing called Science?*, Buckingham: Open University Press.

Chomsky, N. (1980) *Rules and Representation*, Oxford: Blackwell.

Crombie, A. C. (1959) 'The significance of medieval discussions of scientific method for the scientific revolution', in M. Clagett (ed.) *Critical Problems in the History of Science*, Madison, WI: University of Wisconsin Press.

Driver, R. (1983) *The Pupil as Scientist*, Buckingham: Open University Press.

Driver, R., Guesnes, E. and Tiberghien, A. (1985) *Children's Ideas of Science*, Buckingham: Open University Press.

Gill, D. and Levidov, L. (eds) (1987) *Anti-racist Science Teaching*, London: Free Association Books.

Hodson, D. (1985) 'Philosophy of science, science and science education', *Studies in Science Education* 12: 25–57.

Hodson, D. (1988) 'Towards a philosophically more valid science curriculum', *Science Education* 72:19–40.

IRR (1982a) *Patterns of Racism*, London: Institute of Race Relations.

IRR (1982b) *Roots of Racism*, London: Institute of Race Relations.

IRR (1985) *How Racism came to Britain*, London: Institute of Race Relations.

Kuhn, T. S. (1964) *The Structure of Scientific Revolutions*, Chicago: University of Chicago Press.

Lynch, J (1986) *Multi-cultural Education Principles and Practice*, London: Routledge and Kegan.

Millar, R. (1989) 'What is scientific method and can it be taught?' in J. J. Wellington (ed.) *Skills and Processes in Science Education*, London: Routledge.

Millar, R. and Driver, R. (1987) 'Beyond processes', *Studies in Science Education* 14: 33–62.

Mithin, S. (1996) *The Prehistory of Mind*, London: Thames and Hudson.

Nasr, S. H. (1968) *Science and Civilization in Islam*, Cambridge, MA: Harvard University Press.

Needham, J. (1954) *Science and Civilization in China*, Cambridge: Cambridge University Press.

Needham, J. (1969) *The Grand Titration*, London: George Allen and Unwin.

Needham, J. (1976) 'History and human values: a Chinese perspective for world science and technology', in H. Rose and R. Rose (eds) *The Radicalisation of Science*, London: Macmillan.

Osborne, R. and Freyberg, P. (1985) *Learning in Science: The Implications of Children's Science*, Auckland: Heinemann.

Pinker, S. (1994) *The Language Instinct*, London: Penguin Books.

Sardar, Z. (1980) 'Can science come back to Islam?', *New Scientist* 23 October: 212–16.

Spelke, E. S. (1991) 'Physical knowledge in infancy: reflections on Piaget's theory', in S. Carey and R. Gelman (eds) *Epigenesis of Mind: Studies in Biology and Culture*, Hillsdale, NJ: Erlbaum.

van Sertima, I. (1983) *Blacks in Science: Ancient and Modern*, New Brunswick: Transaction Books.

Whiten, A. (ed.) (1991) *Natural Theories of Mind: Evolution, Development and Simulation of Everyday Mindreading*, Oxford: Blackwell.

Wolpert, L .(1992) *The Unnatural Nature of Science*, London: Faber and Faber.

Young, R. M. (1987a) 'Racist society, Racist science', in D. Gill, and L. Levidov (eds), *Anti-racist Science Teaching*, London: Free Association Books.

Young, R. M. (1987b) 'Interpreting the production of science', in D. Gill and L. Levidov (eds), *Anti-racist Science Teaching*, London: Free Association Books.

9   Towards a science curriculum for public understanding

Robin Millar

Concerns about science education

Within the past fifteen years, science has joined English and mathematics as core subjects in the school curriculum in the UK. There appears to be broad consensus, both within the education system and beyond, that all children should study science throughout the period of compulsory schooling, from 5–16. There has been little opposition within schools or beyond to this increase in prominence of science or to its allocation of 20 per cent of curriculum time at Key Stage 4, double that for other subjects.

Amongst the rare dissenting voices, Chapman (1991) has written of 'The overselling of science education in the 1980s', contesting the validity of arguments for compulsory 'science for all'. From outside the science education community, Simon Jenkins (1994), in a strongly written piece in *The Times,* argues that 'the adult world does not require deep knowledge of maths and science', and that the importance attributed to these subjects by politicians and industrialists is the result of a 'confidence-trick' played by the academic science community. Although outspoken critiques of this sort are relatively few, they are, I think, the visible sign of a wider and more general unease and concern about science education provision.

A major cause of this unease is the accumulation of evidence – not just in Britain but throughout much of the developed world – that little scientific understanding is actually assimilated by most students. The APU studies (Gamble *et al.* 1985) showed that only around 35 per cent of 15-year-olds could apply scientific knowledge to simple problem situations. Research into students' learning in specific science domains points in the same direction: very few young people by the age of 16 have a solid grasp of even the most basic scientific facts, principles, concepts and ideas. Ideas like the particulate theory of matter, the scientific model of the solar system, gas exchanges in plants and animals – all are poorly understood and there are many common and persistent misconceptions (for a summary of this sort see Driver *et al.* 1994).

A television programme, broadcast on BBC2 in 1994, based on work at Harvard and Leeds Universities, illustrated this dramatically, showing American engineering graduates unable to explain where the matter came from in a block of wood – and reluctant to accept that it could possibly have come from carbon dioxide in the air. The same research showed that students' lack of understanding of basics is apparently not noticed by their teachers, who consistently over-estimate their own students' understanding of basic ideas following instruction – perhaps because students find it possible despite this to obtain reasonable scores on conventional tests and examinations. Surveys of science understanding amongst the adult population (Durant *et al.* 1989) show much the same picture: little understanding and many potentially serious misunderstandings of basic science ideas.

Some have argued that the lack of effectiveness of science teaching is a consequence of the content of the curriculum on offer. Claxton (1991) writes of his:

> growing realization that we do not have a problem with science education; we have a disaster with it. Reading the literature, talking to teachers and students, and sitting in lessons,… it becomes obvious that what was being offered missed the mark of what the majority of students needed and wanted to know, not just by a bit but by a mile.
>
> (Claxton 1991: vii)

Do many students achieve little in science because they simply cannot see the point of it? And might their verdict be, as Jenkins argues, substantially correct?

To these I would add a third area of concern, about the uniform and unrelenting pace of most science programmes. Each lesson builds on the last, introducing new ideas. The 'big ideas' get lost in the mass of detail. For many students it is simply 'one thing after another' before you have fully grasped one idea you are on to another. There is no variety of pace, little time for consolidation, no learning 'rhythm', just, for most students, an out-of-control roller-coaster of ideas.

In this chapter I want to explore two questions:

- Why should science be taught to all school students?
- And (in the light of answers to that question) what should the science curriculum look like?

Why teach science, and why to all?

In the first *ASE Science Teachers' Handbook*, Milner (1986) addresses the question 'why teach science and why to all?' He argues that science, or for that matter any subject, can only lay claim to a place in the curriculum if we can show three things about it:

1   That it contributes distinctive skills, concepts and perspectives, not offered by any other subject.
2   That these would not be acquired informally, but only through formal instruction.
3   That it is important and of value to acquire them.

The first can be readily granted. Science has a distinctive area of concern – the behaviour of the natural world – and uses distinctive concepts and ideas to express our understanding. And there are distinctive features of its approach to enquiry, though these are not easy to specify in detail.

Scientific knowledge also meets the second criterion. It is very clear that many of the major ideas of science are counter-intuitive, as Wolpert (1992), for example, has recently argued; they are not simply acquired through experience. Teachers' experience of the problems of 'discovery learning' and of the persistence of misconceptions and 'alternative conceptions' despite evidence which conflicts, are persuasive evidence that this is so. The second criterion, however, may be more significant as regards so-called processes of science. I have argued elsewhere (Millar 1989; Millar and Driver 1987) that 'process skills' such as observing, classifying, predicting and so on *are* acquired informally – indeed are used by children from a very early age – and that the issue for science education is not teaching or developing these, but encouraging students to *use* capabilities they already possess in exploring scientific questions.

The third condition, that science is important and of value, raises the questions 'important and of value to whom?' and 'for what?'. Milner lays out a number of ways in which science is important and of value both to the individual leaner and to society.

Intrinsic justification

Scientific knowledge is a cultural product of great intellectual power and beauty. Humans have a curiosity about the natural world which scientific knowledge can help to satisfy. Many people have found the pursuit of science personally satisfying and rewarding.

Instrumental justification

Scientific knowledge is necessary in order to:

- make informed practical decisions about everyday matters;
- participate in decision-making on issues which have a scientific/techno-logical component;
- work in jobs which involve science and technology (at various levels).

Thomas and Durant (1987) approach the same question from a rather different perspective, in an article entitled: 'Why should we promote the public understanding of science?' They set out the different arguments which can be found in the literature on public understanding. These can be grouped into five distinct categories.

1   The *economic* argument: that there is a connection between the level of public understanding of science and the nation's economic wealth. In addition, scientific and technical achievement is seen as a sign of a nation's inter-national standing. Maintaining this depends on a steady supply of technically and scientifically qualified personnel.

2 The *utility* argument: that an understanding of science and technology is practically useful, especially to anyone living in a scientifically and technologically sophisticated society. They are better equipped to make decisions about diet, health, safety, and so on, to evaluate manufacturers' claims and make sensible consumer choices.

3 The *democratic* argument: that an understanding of science is necessary if any individual is to participate in discussion, debate and decision-making about issues which have a scientific component. Decisions have to be made about transport, energy policy, testing of drugs and treatments, disposal of wastes, and so on. There should be public accountability about the directions of some scientific research, and public involvement in decisions about whether or not to apply such knowledge.

4 The *social* argument: that it is important to maintain links between science and the wider culture. Specialization and the increasingly technical nature of modem science is seen as a social problem, leading to incipient fragmentation – and the alienation of much of the public from science and technology. A related argument is advanced from the science side: that improved public understanding will lead to more sympathy with, and hence greater support for, science and technology itself.

5 The *cultural* argument: that science is a major – indeed, *the* major – achievement of our culture and that all young people should be enabled to understand and to appreciate it. We should celebrate science as a cultural product.

These five arguments correspond closely to the justifications offered by Milner. I have simply stated the arguments above. In the next section, I want to look at them more critically, and use them to develop criteria for decisions about the science curriculum.

Considering the arguments for teaching science

Before considering each of the five arguments identified above, it is important to acknowledge that the school science curriculum has to do two jobs. For only a minority of young people, school science from 5–16 is the first stage of their training as scientists. They will go on to more advanced courses and perhaps to careers which involve science. For them, the 5–16 programme must provide a satisfactory basis for further study. The majority, however, will not study science further. For them, science is part of their general education, part of their preparation for life in a modern technical, industrialized democracy.

The science curriculum functions as:

first stages of a training in science	access to basic scientific literacy
for a minority	for the majority

At present in the UK, as in most other countries, the same science curriculum has to serve both ends. But it is far from clear that any one curriculum can do both these jobs effectively. It is, however, fairly clear that the present curriculum has evolved, in a fairly seamless line of descent, from curriculums designed for training in science. National Curriculum science is the son (or daughter) of GCSE science, and the grandson/daughter of GCE O level science. It has changed at the margins, some topics have been trimmed a little, it is less formal and mathematical – but its ancestry is clear. We have, in effect, assumed, through the period of comprehensivization and the ending of the GCE/CSE divide, that the route to a science curriculum for all was essentially to modify the 'training in science' curriculum to make it more accessible.

The result has been to make the 5–16 science curriculum less suitable as a preparation for more advanced study, whilst largely failing to make it motivating or accessible to the majority. The evidence for the former is the reducing proportion of students choosing to study science, particularly physics, in post-compulsory education, and the growing (and largely justifiable) perception that post-16 science is a difficult option, involving a considerable step-up in difficulty from pre-16 courses. For the latter, the evidence is the low level of understanding of basic science discussed earlier. The present curriculum falls between two stools; it is unsuited to either of its purposes.

Rather than considering further piecemeal modification, I think we need to ask: What would the science curriculum look like if it were designed with the needs of the majority in mind? What would a science curriculum designed to promote scientific literacy for the majority look like? These are the questions that I want to focus on in considering the five arguments for teaching science. Later, as a separate question, we might wish to ask: Would such a curriculum also be a reasonable preparation for further study in science for the minority who so chose?

The economic argument

The economic argument points to the connection between science and technology and industrial wealth-creation, and to the need for a continuing supply of science specialists to maintain and develop the technological infrastructure. This is a strong argument for making a 'training in science' curriculum available to *some* students, but, as relatively few highly-trained scientists are needed, it does not, as Chapman (1991) argues in detail, provide good grounds for teaching science to *all* students to age 16. The case for promoting public understanding of science will have to be made, and indeed is usually made, in terms of the other four arguments: the utility argument, the democratic argument, the social argument and the cultural argument.

The utility argument

The utility argument is that scientific knowledge is necessary for coping with aspects of everyday life. But most pieces of technical equipment can be used with little understanding of how they function and technological advance tends to make such understanding gradually less (rather than more) necessary. Few practical decisions are taken primarily on the basis of scientific understanding. When scientific knowledge is used in everyday settings, it is usually encapsulated in the form of a simple rule of thumb, like 'metals conduct', or 'if an electrical device stops working, it's probably a broken connection'. Layton (1993) shows how scientific knowledge invariably has to be reworked and reconstructed to enable it to be used to guide practical action.

There is also no evidence, so far as I know, that physicists have fewer road accidents because they understand Newton's Laws of Motion, or that they insulate their houses better than other comparable social groups because they understand the laws of thermodynamics. A study of Leeds pensioners (Layton *et al.* 1993) showed, not surprisingly, that their decisions about heating their homes were based on a host of factors, many of which were social, and not solely on their understanding of heat loss and insulation, which was frequently over-ridden by other practical and aesthetic considerations. These examples do not, of course, argue that no piece of scientific knowledge is ever practically useful. But they do suggest that the utility argument for understanding science is overrated.

Perhaps a utility argument can be constructed on a weaker interpretation of 'usefulness'. It might be argued that some understanding of how artefacts work, and even of natural phenomena, makes one feel more knowledgeable, and hence more 'comfortable' in everyday life. Indeed explanations of this sort feature prominently in popular science publications and appear to be quite widely seen as part of scientific literacy. It is, however, difficult to argue that an interest in such matters is more valuable, either to the individual or to society, than many of the other interests that people might have. Such an interpretation of 'utility' could scarcely justify compulsory science for all.

The value, I think, of the utility argument is that it challenges us to take the criterion of 'usefulness' of knowledge seriously. It points towards a science curriculum with a much stronger emphasis on a technological way-of-knowing about phenomena, on more immediately applicable knowledge rather than abstract general principles.

The democratic argument

The democratic argument is that an understanding of science is necessary to participate in discussion, debate and decision-making about science-related issues in society. Here again there are problems if we push this claim too far. First, we need to ask: What level of understanding is necessary if we are not to trivialize the issues? Even practising scientists often recognize that they are not well enough informed about an issue outside their own specialist area of science to take a firm view. Second, there is the sheer number of issues. Can we really prepare young people to hold an informed view on genetic engineering, embryo research, nuclear power, disposal of toxic substances, the health risks of saturated or unsaturated fats in the diet, the possible dangers of living close to high tension power lines, and so on?

Even if we could, can we anticipate the new issues that will arise during their lifetime? As the answer is surely no, are we then claiming that there is something transferable that students can learn by studying some of these issues, which will better equip them to deal with others in the future? If so, then we should try to spell out what this transferable core is.

The democratic argument points, I think, not to rather vague and ill-defined aims about developing 'decision-making skills' or 'increasing awareness of science in society', but rather to the need to give curriculum priority to *fundamental understanding* on which the more detailed knowledge needed to grasp particular issues can be built, if and when it is needed. We will return later to the question of what these 'fundamental understandings' might be.

The cultural and social arguments

The cultural argument is that science is a major achievement of our culture which all young people should therefore be helped to understand and to appreciate. The curriculum justification for science then becomes similar to that for literature, art or music. It might be argued that the cultural argument for science is stronger than for these; science is not just a major cultural achievement – it is *the* defining product of our culture, the thing which we can most confidently expect the historians and even archaeologists of the future to identify as characteristic of our time. And, as Midgley argues:

> Any system of thought playing the huge part that science now plays in our lives must also shape our guiding myths and colour our imaginations profoundly. It is not just a useful tool.
>
> (Midgley 1992: 1)

It would surely be a strange culture indeed that did not wish to pass on its most prominent thought-system to new generations. The problem for science educators is that we have not really thought out, I would suggest, what it would mean to teach, say, Newton's law of universal gravitation, or Lavoisier's discovery of oxygen, or the discovery of microbes by the early microscopists as cultural landmarks, rather than as useful knowledge or as illustration of scientific enquiry methods.

The social argument is closely related to the cultural one. It is that it is important for social cohesion to maintain links between science and the wider culture. Science has become increasingly remote and technical, and difficult for the layman to understand. The gulf between science and the rest of the culture threatens the health of both. Whilst we may agree that this is a concern, it does not lead very obviously to any specific criteria for science curriculum design. We might, though, note that 'reading-about-science' has never been regarded as an important part of the curriculum, We may be neglecting a powerful educational resource in constructing a model of the science curriculum which gives little or no role to the writings of authors like Stephen Jay Gould, Paul Davies, Richard Dawkins or Primo Levi.

Towards a science curriculum for public understanding

To summarize the discussion in the preceding section, I have argued that the utility argument points to a more technological emphasis in the science curriculum, that the democratic argument implies a need to focus on fundamental understandings which provide a basis for the learning of specific details when these are required, and that the cultural importance of science provides a strong argument for introducing all students to some of the major advances in our understanding of the world, seen as significant cultural events and achievements to be celebrated.

I now want to consider the form of science curriculum to which this might lead, looking in turn at each of three aspects of an understanding of science:

- understanding of *science content* (or substantive scientific knowledge);
- understanding of the *methods of enquiry* used in science;
- understanding of *science as a social enterprise.*

Understanding science content

What substantive science knowledge should be included in a science curriculum for public understanding? Whilst it is fashionable to scorn a simple 'deficit model' of public understanding – the idea that the 'problem' is simply that people don't have enough substantive science knowledge – it is surely the case that no one could be regarded as scientifically literate without some understanding of some science content. But what content?

Given the evidence of students' lack of understanding in so many basic areas, the guiding principle as regards curriculum content must surely be: do less but do it better. It is almost commonplace to observe that the science curriculum is overloaded. As a result, it is unclear about its priorities; students (and perhaps also teachers) are unable to see the wood for the trees. The plethora of textbooks, curriculum packages and syllabuses conveys an impression of lack of consensus about priorities, and about structure. What is central? What really matters?

I would suggest that the science curriculum from 5–16 should have two aims as regards science content:

- to help students become more capable in their interactions with the material world, by emphasizing a practically useful, technological way-of-knowing;
- gradually to develop students' understandings of a small number of powerful 'mental models' (or 'stories') about the behaviour of the natural world.

There is not space in this article to develop either of these ideas thoroughly, but I will try to use a few examples to illustrate what I have in mind.

A more technological emphasis

Take energy as an example – a concept which is rightly regarded as one of the great achievements of science. The problem is that the scientific energy concept is simply too abstract and difficult for most students up to 16. We might do better if we based our curriculum treatment on the everyday meaning of energy, which is essentially synonymous with 'fuel' – something which is used up in processes, makes things happen, is valuable and in limited supply, and so should be used sparingly. The curriculum would focus on useful ideas like fuel use and fuel efficiency. Ideas about insulation could be based on a simple 'caloric' model of energy, which is useful (and widely used by engineers) in this context.

Similarly, many students can cope admirably with a technological way-of-knowing about simple electric circuits, using ideas about closed loops to make circuits to switch things on and off as required, and variable resistors to control brightness of bulbs or speed of motors. But they quickly become lost in the theoretical model of current, voltage and resistance. Even practising electricians and repair men rarely use the formal model, but base their understanding on more pragmatic models and rules of thumb. In mechanics, a technological approach might include the uses of levers, gears and pulleys, and could explore friction and air-resistance in relation to real practical problems, without introducing the difficult and counter-intuitive idea of inertia.

These ideas are far from exhaustive. They are intended only as illustrations of topics where a significantly different approach might be adopted. There are other topics and perhaps also some new topics, such as information, where a technological way-of-knowing might be a more appropriate curriculum aim than an abstract theoretical understanding.

This may also be the place to acknowledge that there is a place, perhaps even a need, in the science curriculum for a small amount of what might be termed 'scientific general knowledge'. For example, it may be important for students to know that metals come from ores which are mined from the earth's crust, and that plastics are made (largely) from oil – without necessarily knowing much about the processes or chemical reactions involved.

Powerful models

Models are important because they are at the heart of science as an intellectual endeavour. The central aim of science is to provide explanations for natural phenomena; the form these explanations take is of a 'story', or 'mental model', which provides a means of thinking about what is going on, accounting for the things we have observed, and imagining how things might turn out in new situations.

Models of this sort are, however, rarely directly applicable to everyday situations. Their inclusion in the curriculum cannot be justified by a simple appeal to the utility argument, though they may, of course, provide the understanding for actions we carry out on the basis of trust, for example, when we follow medical advice about a course of treatment, or about changing our diet. Some models also provide the basic understanding which is essential for getting to grips with many key issues involving the application of science. They do not, of themselves, provide all we need to know to reach an informed view on the issue; but without the basic understanding they provide, it is hard to see how any rational understanding is possible. So, for example, Andersson (1990) shows how an understanding of the possible effects of pollution from vehicle exhausts depends on an understanding of the scientific model of a chemical reaction.

Therefore, he argues:

> The concepts used here – atom, molecule, chemical reaction – should be part of the mental equipment of every pupil by the time he or she leaves school. They are key concepts that help build a rough model of various situations, for examples, one's own working environment. These concepts enable us to form a general picture and provide a basis for further enquiry about the details.
>
> (Andersson 1990: 53–4)

Some models, on the other hand, like the scientific model of the solar system, have little practical utility, nor do they underpin an understanding of issues. But the idea that the earth goes round the sun (rather than vice versa) and rotates on its axis, and the way this can account for the seasons and for day and night, is surely something everyone should be helped to understand as part of their general education. It is part of coming to understand who we are and the sort of universe we inhabit. So too, in a different way, is an understanding of genetics and inheritance, and of evolution. The claim of these models to be included in the curriculum is largely cultural – that these ideas are cultural products of significance and beauty, and that a knowledge and understanding of them is life-enhancing.

The criteria, then, for choosing which models to include in the school science curriculum are their cultural significance and their role in underpinning an understanding, in broad terms, of issues which may enter the public domain or that of personal actions. The models I would nominate, in no particular order, are:

- the atomic/molecular model of matter (emphasizing the scientific understanding of chemical reactions as rearrangements of matter)
- models of the earth–moon and earth–sun systems, of the solar system, and of the universe
- the source–radiation–receiver model of interactions at a distance (leading to a ray model of light and of vision)
- the field model of interactions at a distance (gravitation, magnetism, electric fields)
- the 'germ' theory of disease
- the gene model of inheritance
- Darwin's theory of evolution of species
- models of the evolution of the earth's surface (rock formation, plate tectonics)

The first two of these should be used, in part, to develop ideas about size, scale and distance, from the very large to the very small. The 'germ' theory is also valuable in this regard, in introducing ideas about entities at a scale between the visible and the atomic/molecular. The last two in the list should be used, in part, to develop ideas about timescales.

Some other elaborations and applications are also important. It is, for instance, important to make explicit the application of the idea of a chemical reaction to biological processes so that students appreciate, for instance, that digestion of food provides building blocks for new tissue, or that plants make additional bulk by chemical reactions which use raw materials from the plant's environment. The cycling of some key chemicals (for example, of oxygen and carbon dioxide in the atmosphere) is also an important idea, which depends on a certain level of understanding of the atomic/molecular processes within closed (eco)systems.

If we are really to 'do less but do it better', then some long-established content will inevitably have to go. Some notable omissions from the content sketched above are the Newtonian model of motion, the scientific models of energy and change (entropy), a lot of detailed chemistry, waves and the scientific understanding of electric circuits, though several of these might remain, with a more technological emphasis, as discussed above.

Understanding the methods of science

A second aspect of understanding science involves knowing about the methods of scientific enquiry. A major difficulty, however, is that there is not universal agreement about what these methods are. Many of the ideas which have been (and still are) communicated, both implicitly and explicitly, by the science curriculum about the methods of science are naive, and counterproductive, from a public understanding of science point of view. 'Process science' and the 1991 version of the National Curriculum Sc1 (DES/Welsh Office 1991) are cases in point. The idea that the method of science is to begin with unprejudiced observations, to look for patterns in these, then to form hypotheses from which specific predictions can be made and tested experimentally is a caricature of the way scientists work; and, in the hands of learners, it does not lead to scientific knowledge or understanding. Children come to science, at age five, already able to observe, classify, hypothesize, predict, compare 'fairly', and so on, with high levels of skill in contexts where they see the purpose in doing so. There is no need to spend lesson time 'developing' these capabilities.

It is, of course, easier to criticize the teaching of science method than to make detailed and realistic proposals about how to improve it. One critical issue to resolve at the outset, I think, is whether we consider an understanding of science method valuable because it provides a generally useful method of enquiry which people should be encouraged to use more widely (a transferable skills argument), or because it is important for everyone to know something about the way scientific knowledge has been, and continues to be, obtained. The former is based on the utility argument, the latter on the democratic, social and cultural arguments.

There is little evidence to support the former argument: not only can no one describe the scientific method in detail, but it is also far from clear that a scientific approach is useful or appropriate in most situations of practical decision-making. There is no universal algorithm for 'finding out', or even for 'weighing up the pros and cons'. On the other hand, knowing (as opposed to merely assenting to) the scientific explanation of a phenomenon involves being able to give grounds for holding ideas and propositions to be true. So, an understanding of science content necessarily involves knowing something about how these ideas came to be held, and about the warrants for accepting them as useful and valid.

If our aim in the science curriculum, then, is to develop students' understanding of the ways in which scientific knowledge is obtained, it is useful to separate out two distinct strands:

- One has to do with the collection of empirical data which can serve as evidence in making or supporting a case. This involves an understanding of some procedural concepts, such as accuracy, reliability and validity. It has to do with understanding the relationship between a measurement or observation, and the 'truth'. It also includes the very notion of a measurement itself (the idea of a standard unit and a method of counting), of modelling behaviour in terms of relationships between variables, and of logical reasoning in situations involving several variables. Many of these ideas apply generally to systematic enquiry, not only in the sciences, and centre around the notion of evidence and the quality (or persuasiveness) of evidence. The curriculum implications, perhaps, are that practical work needs to give greater emphasis to uncertainty and error. Estimations of accuracy, reliability (the need to repeat measurements) and validity (are you measuring what you think you are measuring?) need to become much more commonplace, from an early age. We should try to avoid any suggestion that there is an infallible method, or algorithm, for gaining the sort of knowledge which can convince other people. This need not involve tasks with a high level of conceptual demand: convincing others that insulator A really is better than insulator B, or that shoe soles X really do grip better than soles Y could, in principle, do the job. And the use of evidence for persuading may need an audience, real or specifically created in the classroom, if it is to succeed.
- A second separate strand has to do with the role of theory in science. It involves understanding that the purpose of science is to generate explanations of the physical world which account for observed phenomena, and may predict others, or suggest phenomena to look for or create. The theories we put forward as explanations do not simply restate the data in different terms. They are conjectures, made on the basis of available evidence and data, but never completely entailed by that evidence. Theories do not emerge from the evidence; there is always an element of creative speculation. They do not report the data, but propose explanations of it. Theorizing involves imagination and guesswork, and risks being wrong. Understanding this strand of science method involves recognizing theory as separate from data, and being

able to relate theory and data appropriately – to say, for example, whether given data agrees or disagrees with a given theory (or with several) and to draw logical conclusions from this.

Understanding science as a social enterprise

Of the three aspects of an understanding of science, this is perhaps the hardest to relate to a curriculum specification. Many science educators (those associated with the STS movement (Solomon 1993), for example) agree that this third dimension is important, but it is often unclear what it is 'about science' that they want students to know. From a curriculum point of view, a key issue is to clarify what, exactly, this third dimension amounts to. What, precisely, do we want young people to understand about the social structure and relations of science?

I would pick out two key ideas (whilst acknowledging that there may be others):

- That scientific knowledge is the product of sustained social work. It is developed through a struggle to understand, make sense and communicate and share ideas. Ideas emerge from acting on the world, not just talking about it.
- That there are crucial differences between science in the laboratory and in the real-world. In the laboratory, situations are simplified, so that one entity in the situation can be isolated from the interference of others, and hence understood. Real-world situations, however, are invariably messy and complex. So there is always some uncertainty about how (or even whether) the laboratory findings apply; and about what weighting to give to different pieces of evidence. And, in most cases of dispute, forms of knowledge other than scientific knowledge, and including values, are relevant to the decision-making process.

A science curriculum for public understanding should aim to help students develop their awareness of both of these. As regards the first, the curriculum would provide opportunities for students to get to know more about real scientific work, by looking at some examples in detail. These should range from the routine scientific work of a hospital laboratory histologist or water board analyst, to the 'normal' science of much industrial and university research, to the mould-breaking, revolutionary developments in science. This might be provided through readings or video, but also surely by visits to places where science is done. And students should also, I think, learn something of the processes by which new scientific knowledge is produced: the sharing of new ideas and results at conferences and through papers in journals, the processes of refereeing and peer-review, the replication and checking of unexpected findings.

If we are thinking of the curriculum from 5–16, then we need a model of progression in this area, to guide the choice of examples used. Students might, over the period, study a number of specific examples of scientific work in some depth, chosen to illustrate, progressively, scientific ways of working such as:

- systematic, careful data collection (for example), in environmental monitoring or weather forecasting;
- 'inductive' pattern seeking (as, for example, in some epidemiology, or public health work);
- checking an idea by testing it (or a prediction based on it);
- proposing a new view of an area (such as Lavoisier's discovery of oxygen, or Pasteur's work on disease, or the continental drift and plate tectonic hypotheses).

One of the key messages from this sort of work should be that there is no single way in which science works to obtain new knowledge, and no guarantee of success in solving a problem. Looking at the 5–16 curriculum as a whole, the aim should be gradually to develop ideas about the need for a base of reliable data, the role of imagination in generating explanations, the reception of novel ideas, the causes of disputes and their eventual resolution.

Alongside these ideas about the development of scientific understandings of the world, there should also be some case studies of disputed applications of science, with the principal aim of highlighting the range of considerations (scientific and non-scientific) involved in reaching any practical decision. Here there are also clear links with understanding scientific methods of enquiry – in particular, ideas about reliability of data and the difference between data and explanation. Students should have experience of some extended studies, perhaps one each school year, in which they work in groups on a practical issue requiring them, as a group, to make and defend a decision with practical consequences. This sort of work would have to be supported by an extensive pack of background information and data.

Some conclusions

In the introduction to this chapter, I outlined some areas of concern about the current science curriculum: the evidence that little is learned, the sense that what is on offer may miss students' interests and needs, and the dulling uniformity of pace. How would the curriculum for public understanding sketched above address these concerns?

First, I think, by identifying clearly a small number of key models as the core content to be taught, and by providing a framework which enables clear goals to be set for a developing understanding of scientific methods and of science as a social enterprise, it provides a better basis for improving understanding of key ideas and for monitoring the extent of understanding.

For many of the key models, there is a considerable body of research data on children's ideas, learning difficulties and strategies for addressing these. Where there is not, clarity about aims would help us identify priority areas for further research and development of approaches.

Second, I think that a more technological emphasis, together with a focus on a small number of key models, would stand a better chance, if imaginatively presented, of catching and holding the interest of more students, than a curriculum whose structure and rationale is often unclear to teachers and must appear even less clear to learners.

Third, I would suggest that we need to include case studies of the historical development of ideas, of actual scientific work (either contemporary or historical), of disputes about the application of science, as well as more extended, practical investigations with a focus on assembling persuasive evidence to support a conclusion. These provide appropriate contexts for students to voice their own views and opinions, and to defend these, and also a means of varying the pace of science lessons – with groups of lessons devoted to more intensive development of key ideas, followed by others in which students undertake work which makes use of their developing understanding of these ideas, and so consolidates and reinforces it.

The science curriculum outline proposed above is no more than an outline sketch. It is not worked through in any detail. Issues of sequence and timing have not even been considered. Others may identify, and wish to argue for, different priorities. Hard questions need to be asked, and conventional answers challenged, if we are to move towards a science curriculum which is more suited to the task required of it, as a core element of the curriculum for all young people.

First we need to decide *why* we want to teach science to all our young people; from that we can perhaps work out *what* we want to teach them. Then research, linked closely to the development and evaluation of teaching materials and approaches, may be able to help us discover *how* best to teach these ideas. That, I think, is the project on which the science education community now needs to embark as a matter of some urgency.

References

Andersson, B. (1990) 'Pupils' conceptions of matter and its transformations age 12–16', *Studies in Science Education* 1990(18): 53–85.

Chapman, B. (1991) 'The overselling of science education in the 1980s', *School Science Review* 72(260): 47–63.

Claxton, G. (1991) *Educating the Inquiring Mind. The Challenge for School Science*, Harvester Wheatsheaf.

DES/Welsh Office (1991), *Science in the National Curriculum (1991)*, HMSO.

Driver, R., Squires, A., Rushworth, P. and Wood-Robinson, V. (1994) *Making Sense of Secondary Science. Research into Children's Ideas*, Routledge.

Durant, J., Evans, G. and Thomas, G. (1989) 'The public understanding of science', *Nature*, 6 July, 340: 11–14.

Gamble, R., Davey, A., Gott, R. and Welford, G. (1985) *Science at Age 15. Assessment of Performance Unit. Science Report for Teachers: 5*, DES/WO/DENI.

Jenkins, S. (1994) 'Misappliance of science', *The Times* 27 August: 14.

Layton, D. (1993) *Technology's Challenge to Science Education*, Open University Press.

Layton, D., Jenkins, E., Macgill, S. and Davey, A. (1993) *Inarticulate Science?*, Studies in Education Ltd.

Midgley, M. (1992) *Science as Salvation. A Modern Myth and its Meaning*, Routledge.

Millar, R. (1989) 'What is the scientific method and can it be taught?', in J. J. Wellington (ed.) *Skills and Processes in Science Education. A Critical Analysis*, Routledge.

Millar, R. and Driver, R. (1987) 'Beyond processes', *Studies in Science Education* 14: 33–62.

Milner, B. (1986) 'Why teach science and why to all?' in J. Nellist and B. Nicholl (eds) *The ASE Science Teachers' Handbook*, Hutchinson, pp. 1–10.

Solomon, J. (1993) *Teaching Science Technology and Society*, Open University Press.

Thomas, G. and Durant, J. (1987) 'Why should we promote the public understanding of science?' *Scientific Literacy Papers 1*, University of Oxford, Department of External Studies, pp. 1–14.

Wolpert, L. (1992) *The Unnatural Nature of Science*, Faber.

Section 4

Learners

Introduction

Scientific theories do not emerge directly from mere observation of the world, and neither do children's ideas. There is now a wealth of evidence that children construct their own understandings, which may be very different from accepted scientific ideas. One of the most influential figures in science education in the 1980s and 1990s was the late Rosalind Diver. The first chapter in this section is taken from her book *The Pupil as Scientist?*, published in 1983, when there was a growing interest in research into children's 'alternative ideas'. She gives some striking examples of how pupils' responses to situations and their subsequent learning are influenced by their prior knowledge. Pupils construct their own meanings from their experiences in science lessons which may be different from the ones intended, so teachers need to pay attention to what pupils already know.

Two complementary aspects of learning science are discussed in the following two chapters – developing conceptual understanding and developing thinking skills. John Leach and Philip Scott are concerned with conceptual learning. Learners make sense of new ideas in terms of what they already know, and children have a great deal of everyday knowledge about the world. However, scientific explanation is very different from everyday explanation. So, Leach and Scott argue that developing scientific knowledge is not about building on this everyday knowledge, but rather breaking away from it. To be able to support learners, teachers need to be able to identify where the differences between scientific and everyday ways of knowing lie. In contrast, Philip Adey is concerned not with domain-specific understanding but with developing general thinking skills. As children get older, they become more capable of processing information, for example by handing problems with greater numbers of variables. However, this happens not simply as a result of maturation, but also through the nature of the child's experiences. Adey describes an intervention programme in which pupils' cognitive abilities may be 'accelerated' through the use of appropriate strategies. Joan Bliss brings together a number of psychological perspectives, discussing theories about general schemes used in reasoning and about the learning of scientific knowledge. She offers a critique of these positions, and argues that, in learning science, more attention should be paid to reasoning with 'mental models' – helping pupils to manipulate these imagined representations of the world. An understanding of science does not come directly from the real world; it is 'about making sense of how scientists have made sense of the world'.

What are the consequences of a view of learning in which pupils are seen as individually constructing their own knowledge, and from experiences in the social as well as physical world? Clive Sutton argues that there should be a shift from 'doing' to 'puzzling' – from practical work to the interpretation of expressed ideas – and he emphasizes the role of communication and language. The principal object of study should be ideas as represented in the *words of people*, so that for a pupil, learning science is about sorting out another person's meaning and re-creating it in their own mind. As a consequence, teachers need to develop a greater range of teaching strategies than those often encountered in science classrooms. In recent years, there has been increasing interest in the role of informal learning in science, that is, the science which is learnt outside the classroom from television, newspapers, museums, and so on. Janette Griffin offers a framework that can facilitate learning in museums. Many teachers tend to impose formal learning structures on informal learning situations, but she argues that pupils can achieve more in a museum if they are treated as individuals and are given control over their own learning. By choosing their own areas of enquiry, and by being free to explore, she reports that not only were there gains in pupils' learning, but the *motivation* of students also increased. Perhaps this raises important issues about the way pupils learn in formal situations, too.

Paying attention to how different pupils respond differently to science has been a particular issue in the case of gender. In the past, there has been much concern about the under-achievement of girls. Patricia Murphy reviews the research in this area, which suggests that during the period of compulsory education, the achievement of girls and boys in science is rather similar; however, there are marked differences in attitudes and interests. The contexts within which science is studied affect boys and girls differently, and gender differences in learning styles mean that boys and girls respond differently to the same situation. Of course, gender is just one factor and pupils are different in many ways; understanding pupils as individual learners is at the heart of good teaching. By interacting with pupils, teachers are constantly assessing their pupils informally and giving them feedback. But it is through systematic, formative assessment that teachers can come to know their pupils better and provide them with individual guidance. Paul Black reviews the research on formative assessment, and concludes that it offers the potential for a very significant improvement in learning, in particular for low-attainers. However, the evidence suggests that the current emphasis on grades and the managerial role of assessment militate against the role of assessment to support learning. Good assessment is more than just adding tests to a teaching programme; it needs to be planned alongside all of the other components so that it becomes an integral part of teaching.

10 The fallacy of induction in science teaching

Rosalind Driver

Science is not just a collection of laws, a catalogue of facts, it is a creation of the human mind with its freely invented ideas and concepts. Physical theories try to form a picture of reality and to establish its connections with the wide world of sense impressions.

Einstein, A. and Infield, L. (1938) *The Evolution of Physics*

In our everyday life as adults we operate with a very complex set of beliefs and expectations about events. An egg rolls across the counter top in the kitchen and we know where to make a grasp for it before it falls over the edge and smashes to the floor. The fact that so many of us can drive around on our roads without more accidents occurring is possible because of the sets of expectations we have developed enabling us to predict the speed and movement of other vehicles on the road and the probable behaviour of pedestrians. Such sets of expectations mean we can live our daily lives without being constantly in a state of disorientation and shock. Similarly, children construct sets of expectations or beliefs about a range of natural phenomena in their efforts to make sense of everyday experiences.

A 10-year-old switched off the radio, noticed with surprise that it took over a second for the sound to fade away and commented: 'What a long length of electric wire there must be in that radio when you think how fast electricity travels.' Without any formal instruction, this child had already developed certain ideas about electricity, notably that it travels down wires, and that it travels very fast.

From the very earliest days in its life, a child develops beliefs about the things that happen in its surroundings. The baby lets go of a rattle and it falls to the ground; it does it again and the pattern repeats itself. It pushes a ball and it goes on rolling across the floor. In this way, sets of expectations are established which enable the child to begin to make predictions. Initially, these are isolated and independent of one another. However, as the child grows older, all its experiences of pushing, pulling, lifting, throwing, feeling and seeing things stimulate the development of more generalized sets of expectations and the ability to make predictions about a progressively wider range of experiences. By the time the child receives formal teaching in science it has already constructed a set of beliefs about a range of natural phenomena. In some cases, these beliefs or intuitions are strongly held and may differ from the accepted theories which science teaching aims to communicate.

One of the features of the science teaching schemes which have been developed over the last twenty or thirty years is a rejection of science as a catalogue of facts. Instead, teaching schemes have been produced which present science as a coherent system of ideas. Focus is on the integrating concepts or big ideas such as atomic theory in chemistry or kinetic theory in physics. Apart from doing justice to the nature of scientific theory itself, one of the important arguments for such an approach suggested by Bruner (1963) is that it helps pupils to apply ideas to new situations if the connections between those ideas are made explicit in teaching. Put in psychologists' jargon, it encourages 'transfer'.

One of the problems with this argument is that the connections that are apparent to a scientist may be far from obvious to a pupil. It is, after all, the coherence as perceived by the pupil that matters in learning. In developing science teaching material little attention has yet been paid to the ideas which children themselves bring to the learning task, yet these may have a significant influence on what children can and do learn from their science lessons. Over a decade ago, the psychologist David Ausubel commented on the importance of considering what he called children's preconceptions, suggesting that they are 'amazingly tenacious and resistant to extinction' and that 'unlearning of preconceptions might well prove to be the most determinative single factor in the acquisition and retention of subject matter knowledge' (Ausubel 1968).

This perspective on learning suggests that it is as important in teaching and curriculum development to consider and understand children's own ideas as it is to give a clear presentation of the conventional scientific theories. After all, if a visitor phones you up explaining he has got lost on the way to your home, your first reaction would probably be to ask 'Where are you now?'. You cannot start to give sensible directions without knowing where your visitor is starting from. Similarly, in teaching science it is important in designing teaching programmes to take into account both children's own ideas and those of the scientific community.

By the time children are taught science in school, their expectations or beliefs about natural phenomena may be well developed. In some cases these intuitions are in keeping with the ideas pupils will meet in their science lessons. They may be poorly articulated but they provide a base on which formal learning can build. However, in other cases the accepted theory may be counter-intuitive, with pupils' own beliefs and expectations differing in significant ways from those to be taught. Such beliefs I shall refer to as 'alternative frameworks'.

Another characteristic of the science curriculum development of the last few decades has been an emphasis on the heuristic method. This was prompted by the admirable concern to allow children to experience something of the excitement of science – 'to be a scientist for a day' (Nuffield Physics 1966). We are now recognizing the pitfalls of putting this approach into practice in classrooms and laboratories. Secondary school pupils are quick to recognize the rules of the game when they ask 'Is this what was supposed to happen?' or 'Have I got the right answer?' (Driver

1975, Wellington 1981). The intellectual dishonesty of the approach derives from expecting two outcomes from pupils' laboratory activities which are possibly incompatible. On the one hand, pupils are expected to explore a phenomenon for themselves, collect data and make inferences based on it; on the other hand, this process is intended to lead to the currently accepted scientific law or principle.

Some insight into this problem can be gained by considering different views of the nature of science. The most simplistic view of the scientific enterprise is, perhaps, the empiricist's view, which holds that all knowledge is based on observation. Scientific laws are reached by a process of induction from the 'facts' of sense data. Taking this view of science, observations are objective and facts immutable. Also, such a position asserts that science will produce a steady growth in knowledge: like some international game of 'pass the parcel', the truth about the natural world will be unwrapped and gradually, more will be revealed.

This inductivist position was criticized when it was first suggested by Bacon nearly 400 years ago, yet it has reasserted itself early in this century in the heuristic movement and later in some of the more naive interpretations of the discovery method adopted by the Nuffield science schemes.

For a long time, philosophers of science and scientists themselves have recognized the limitations of the inductivist position and have acknowledged the important role that imagination plays in the construction of scientific theories. In this alternative constructivist or hypothetico-deductive view, theories are not related by induction to sense data, but are constructions of the human mind whose link with the world of experience comes through the processes by which they are tested and evaluated.

Currently there are different views about the criteria for acceptance or rejection of scientific theories. The philosopher Popper (1972) asserts that, in addition to the individual's mental world, there exists a world of objective knowledge which has properties which can be assessed by logical principles without regard to the person or group of people who generated that knowledge. Others subscribe to a more subjective position. Polanyi (1958), for example, in his writings, indicates the importance of the commitment of an individual to a theory, a commitment which may be influenced by factors other than logic, with aesthetic criteria playing an important part. Science as a cooperative exercise, as opposed to an individual venture, is emphasized in the writings of Kuhn (1963) and Lakatos (1974). Viewed from a sociological perspective, such writers suggest that the criterion for acceptance of a scientific theory is that it is scrutinized and approved by the community of scientists.

Although there are these differences of view on the objectivity of scientific knowledge and the criteria for assessing theories, there is general agreement on two matters of importance to school science. The first is the recognition of pluralism in scientific theories. Following from this is acceptance of the revolutionary nature of science; that progress in scientific knowledge comes about through major changes in scientists' theories (or paradigms). This gives science educators the task of 'teaching consensus without turning it into an orthodoxy' (Ziman 1968). The second point of agreement is about the nature of observations:

these are no longer seen as objective but influenced by the theoretical perspective of the observer (Hanson 1958). As Popper (1970) said, 'we are prisoners caught in the framework of our theories'. This, too, has implications for school science, for children, too, can be imprisoned in this way by their preconceptions, observing the world through their own particular 'conceptual spectacles'.

I will illustrate some main points with a couple of classroom examples. The first example illustrates the hypothetico-deductive nature of science enquiries. It shows an investigation taking place, not from observation to generalization, but being initiated by a hypothesis which, in this case, derives from a pupil's alternative framework.

Two 11-year-old boys, Tim and Ricky, are doing simple experiments on the extension of springs when loaded. They have made their own spring by winding wire round a length of dowel. One end of the spring is supported in a clamp and a polystyrene cup is hanging from the other end (see figure below). Following instructions, they investigate the extension of the spring as they add ball bearings to the polystyrene cup. Ricky is adding the ball bearings one at a time and measuring the new length of the spring after each addition. Tim is watching him, then interrupts:

> How far is that off the ground? Pull it up and see if the spring does not move any.

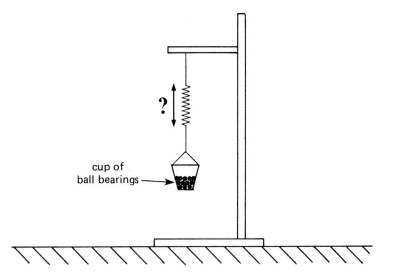

He unclamps the spring, raises it higher up the stand, and again measures its length. Apparently satisfied that the length is the same, he continues with the experiment. Later, when he was asked the reason for doing this, he explained that he thought the weight of the cup of ball bearings would increase if it were raised. To explain his reasoning, he picked up two marbles and held one up higher than the other:

This is farther up and gravity is pulling it down harder – I mean the gravity is still the same but it turns out it is pulling harder the farther away. The higher it gets the more effect gravity will have on it because, like if you just stood over there and someone dropped a pebble on him, it would just sting him, it wouldn't hurt him. But like if I dropped it from an aeroplane it would be accelerating faster and faster and when it hit someone on the head it would kill him.

It appears that Tim's idea of weight encompasses the notion of potential energy and leads him to predict a greater extension of the spring when it is further from the ground. He uses the same framework when considering the force required to hold a trolley at different positions on an inclined board, predicting that it will be harder to hold when it is higher up than when it is lower down the slope.

Not only does this example indicate how pupils' alternative frameworks can intrude into their activities in science lessons, it illustrates how, in some cases, alternative frameworks are more than an idiosyncratic response to a particular task; they may be general notions applied to a range of situations.

There is evidence from a number of investigations that pupils have common alternative frameworks in a range of areas including physical phenomena such as the propagation of light, simple electrical circuits, ideas about force and motion and chemical change, also biological ideas concerned with growth and adaptation.

It follows from a constructivist philosophy of science that theory is not related in a deductive, and hence unique, way to observations; there can be multiple explanations of events which each account for the data. In the example of Tim's idea of weight we see how he had developed an idea based on common experiences with falling objects, yet he had explained them to himself in a way that differed from the accepted physicist's view. The possibility of multiple interpretations of an event is also illustrated in the following example of work done in a science class of 12-year-old pupils. A pair of girls was doing an experiment in which an immersion heater was placed in blocks of different metals, each of the same weight (see figure overleaf). The pupils had been instructed on a worksheet to draw a temperature–time graph for each block as it was heated. The purpose of the experiment was to illustrate variation in specific heat capacities of different metals. The girls had chosen blocks of iron and aluminium, and towards the end of the lesson they were instructed to look at their graphs, compare them and suggest explanations for any differences. Here are their comments:

Pupil 1:   We've got to do a graph for the aluminium.
Pupil 2:   Good. Aluminium isn't so – um – it – .
Pupil 1:   Don't forget it has to go through, doesn't it? Through the thickness to reach there – the thermometer.
Pupil 2:   That was only thin to get to that.
Pupil 1:   Come on, we've got to put it away now.
                  The teacher enters the discussion.
Teacher: What has your experiment shown you?

Pupil 2:	That different – um – that different materials and that see how heat could travel through them.
Teacher:	What did you find out?
Pupil 1:	Well – er – that heat went through the – the iron more easier than it did through the – er – .
Pupil 2:	Aluminium.

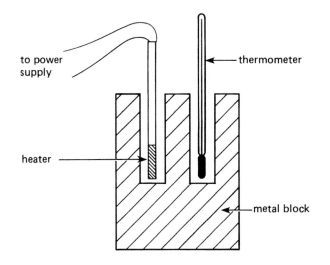

Here, pupils had performed the experiment and had collected their data, yet it appears from their comments that they interpreted the difference between the graphs for the two metal blocks, not in terms of the amount of heat required to raise the temperature of each by a certain amount, but in terms of the comparative conductivity of metals.

The more simplistic interpretations of the discovery approach in science suggest that we only need to give pupils the opportunity to explore events and phenomena at first hand and they will be able to induce the generalizations and principles themselves. The position suggested here is that children do make generalizations from their firsthand experiences, but these may not be the ones the teacher has in mind. Explanations do not spring clearly or uniquely from data.

Through the eyes of those initiated in the currently accepted theories of science, common school demonstrations, such as trolleys and ticker tapes, experiments with batteries and bulbs, or work with ray boxes, mirrors and prisms, appear to offer self-sufficient support for the underlying principles they are designed to demonstrate, whether it is Newton's Laws of Motion or the Laws of Reflection of Light. If children fail to abstract and understand these principles from their experiments, it may be seen as the children's error, either for not observing accurately or not thinking logically about the pattern in the results.

The constructivist view of science, on the other hand, indicates the fallacy here. If we wish children to develop an understanding of the conventional concepts and principles of science, more is required than simply providing practical experiences. The theoretical models and scientific conventions will not be 'discovered' by children through their practical work. They need to be presented. Guidance is then needed to help children assimilate their practical experiences into what is possibly a new way of thinking about them.

The slogan 'I do and I understand' is commonly used in support of practical work in science teaching. We have classrooms where activity plays a central part. Pupils can spend a major portion of their time pushing trolleys up runways, gathering, cutting and sticking tangling metres of ticker tape; marbles are rattled around in trays simulating solids, liquids and gases, batteries and bulbs are clicked in and out of specially designed circuit boards. To what end? In many classrooms, I suspect, 'I do and I am even more confused'.

This process of 'making sense' takes on even greater significance when considering children's alternative frameworks. Not only do children have to comprehend the new model or principle being presented to them, but they have to make the intellectual leap of possibly abandoning an alternative framework which, until that time, had worked well for them.

To use the language of philosophy of science, children sometimes need to undergo paradigm shifts in their thinking. Max Planck suggested that new theories do not convert people, it is just that old men die. If scientists have this difficulty in reformulating their conceptions of the world, is it a wonder that children sometimes have a struggle to do so?

References

Ausubel, D. P. (1968) *Educational Psychology: A Cognitive View*, Holt, Reinhart.

Bruner, J. S. (1963) *The Process of Education*, Random House.

Driver, R. (1975) 'The name of the game', *School Science Review* 56: 800–5.

Hanson, N. R. (1958) *Patterns of Discovery*, Cambridge University Press.

Kuhn, T. (1963) *The Structure of Scientific Revolutions*, Chicago University Press.

Lakatos, I. (1974) *Criticism and the Growth of Knowledge*, Cambridge University Press.

Nuffield Physics Teachers' Guide, No. 1, (1966) Longmans/Penguin.

Polanyi, M. (1958) *Personal Knowledge*, Routledge.

Popper, K. R. (1972) *Objective Knowledge*, Oxford University Press.

Popper, K. (1970) 'Normal science and its dangers', in I. Lakatos and A. Musgrave (eds) *Criticism and the Growth of Knowledge*, Cambridge University Press.

Wellington, J. J. (1981) '"What's supposed to happen, Sir?": Some problems with discovery learning', *School Science Review* 63: 163–73.

Ziman, J. (1968) *Public Knowledge*, Cambridge University Press.

11 The demands of learning science concepts

Issues of theory and practice

John Leach and Philip Scott

A Key Stage 3 science class is starting work on states of matter (CLIS 1987). The teacher has set them the task of identifying a range of objects as being either solid, liquid or gas. The objects include a block of iron, a beaker of water, a pile of sand, the air in the room, a piece of cloth, and so on. For most of the objects, the classification is not problematic. Some items do, however, generate interesting responses, as is shown by one student's diary comment after the lesson:

> In today's lesson we got twenty-eight different things and we had to find out if they were solid, liquid or gas. Myself, I thought it was very interesting but very easy the way I worked it out the ones I was not sure about like a cloth, *it didn't seem solid* but it wasn't gas and it wasn't liquid so it must have been solid. I don't see how people can get them wrong if they work them out like I do but still very interesting.
>
> (Darren)

This kind of response was not unusual (Johnston and Driver 1991), in that solids are frequently conceived as being hard, rigid objects. The block of iron is a prototypical example of 'solid' in everyday reasoning; non-rigid objects such as cloth and paper are not. Nevertheless, virtually all of the pupils were able to classify all of the objects correctly, some, like Darren, reasoning by a process of elimination. The next part of the exercise proved to be much more problematic. Here, the teacher asked the students to make explicit the criteria that they had used in making their classification. 'What is it about solids which allows you to identify them as being solid? What is it about liquids…?' Many of the students struggled to generate any criteria at all. As one student observed:

> I suppose knowing what a thing is is taken for granted because explaining this was very difficult. We were only able to write a few about each (solid, liquid and gas).

An interesting situation has arisen here. The students were able to classify the objects as solids, liquids or gases in a fairly straightforward way, but when asked to identify the criteria used they were unable to do so. The teacher had not anticipated that the students would experience such difficulties in generating criteria; there was a clear mismatch between what the teacher had expected the students to be capable of and what they were actually able to do. Mismatches of expectation such as this are not uncommon in science classrooms: a task seen as unproblematic by the teacher may create significant difficulties for students. If we, as teachers, are able to understand the reasons for some of these mismatches then we are in a better position to anticipate them in our planning and thus to address them in teaching.

In this chapter we wish to probe the reasons why mismatches, such as the one described above, develop as students learn science concepts. We believe that the science education research literature has important messages on this issue for practising science teachers, and this chapter sets out a theoretical perspective to *describe* what is involved in teaching and learning science concepts. In this theoretical perspective, we shall consider basic issues about the nature of scientific knowledge, and examine closely the cognitive demands made on pupils in coming to understand scientific concepts. Although the focus of the chapter is on describing and analysing the processes involved in science learning, we shall also briefly consider the implications of this perspective for planning teaching. The idea of 'Learning Demand' is introduced as a useful tool for thinking about the planning of teaching.

The social construction of scientific knowledge

The first point that we wish to make is that scientific knowledge is a social product. The theories of science that are taught in school have been debated and deliberated upon by groups of scientists (often over extended periods of time), rather than 'read from the book of nature' by individuals doing careful experiments. This is not to say that 'anything goes' in developing theories – scientists always face the challenge of convincing their peers that their theories are consistent with the available empirical evidence. In the context of the school science laboratory, it is clear that students cannot develop an understanding of the theories of science through their own observations, as the theoretical entities of science are simply not there to be seen. For example in learning about simple DC circuits, no amount of experience with batteries, bulbs and circuit boards will enable the pupil to develop an understanding of the theoretical entities of charge, current and voltage. These theoretical entities must be introduced to the learner, along with an understanding of how to use them in constructing explanations and why such explanations are more useful to scientists than everyday ones in talking about circuits. A further stage in the teaching and learning process might involve using batteries and bulbs to see if predictions from newly-acquired theoretical frames can be related to practical observations. From this perspective, learning science might better be characterized as a process of enculturation into a particular 'way of knowing', rather than the individual 'making sense' of the natural world in their own terms.

'Everyday' and 'scientific' ways of knowing

In many cases, the natural phenomena that are explained by the theories of science are familiar to us in our everyday lives, and are frequently talked about using similar words. In the episode described at the beginning of this article, students were familiar with talking about solids as hard, rigid objects in everyday contexts, but were less familiar with the broader, more rigorously defined notion of 'solid' used in science. It is certainly the case that many students have 'everyday' notions about natural phenomena which are perfectly adequate for the purposes of everyday life, but which are different from scientific theories. Learning science thus involves developing 'new ways of knowing about' familiar phenomena. It involves internalizing the perspective of a different culture and, in this respect, might be conceptualized as 'breaking away from', rather than 'building upon', everyday ways of knowing (Garrison and Bentley 1990). Not only must the learner develop an understanding of the new ways of knowing but also an appreciation of differences between alternative ways of knowing and the contexts in which it is appropriate to use each (Solomon 1987).

Differences between 'everyday' and 'scientific' ways of knowing include a range of features. As argued earlier, the actual entities from which explanations are constructed are likely to differ for the different ways of knowing. The scientific world is 'populated with entities such as atoms, electrons, ions, fields and fluxes, genes and chromosomes' (Driver *et al.* 1994). These are theoretical entities which might be referred to in everyday discussion but which are rarely used, with scientific meanings, as part of everyday explanations. In addition, scientific explanations not only draw on different conceptual entities but may also appear counterintuitive from an 'everyday' perspective. An example of this would be the scientific explanation for 'sucking through a straw', based on the action of the atmosphere – *the air around us* forces liquid into the mouth due to a difference in pressure! That the air should have any part at all to play in the process of sucking through a straw is likely to be very strange indeed for the learner (Scott 1993). In cases such as this, the *implausibility* of the scientific explanation can act as a barrier to learning.

Differences between everyday and scientific ways of knowing also exist in terms of the *nature* of the knowledge and the explanations used: epistemological differences exist between the different ways of knowing. For example, everyday explanations are often context-specific whereas scientific explanations are intended to be generalizable across as wide a range of contexts as possible. A further example would be that everyday explanations are often tautologous – a generally unacceptable mode of explanation for scientists. This can be seen in the case of a typical everyday explanation for liquid going into the mouth through the straw: the liquid goes in because I am sucking!

Learning demand

The point that we are making is that there are fundamental differences between everyday and scientific ways of knowing (both in terms of the content and nature of the knowledge used), which may not be apparent to students as they are engaged in learning science. The challenge for the science teacher involves helping students to make sense of scientific ways of knowing in terms of their existing knowledge, and then to differentiate these two ways of knowing.

The subtlety of this challenge is emphasized by the fact that learning concepts in different areas of the science curriculum necessarily involves different kinds of intellectual demand for the learner. These *'learning demands'* (Asoko *et al.* 1993) are determined by the differences between everyday and science ways of knowing. As argued earlier in this chapter, these differences may be in terms of the theoretical entities used or of the nature of the knowledge used. In different topic areas, the relationships between everyday and scientific views generate different kinds of learning demand. In some cases the scientific model, or explanation, closely mirrors everyday understandings. For example, the concept of speed as a ratio of distance travelled to time taken, often appears 'obvious' to pupils: how fast depends upon how far and time taken. These ideas are part of everyday understanding. By way of contrast, learning about Newton's First Law of Motion frequently proves to be problematic for the student. The scientific view, that steady velocity is achieved under conditions of *no* resultant force, is quite contrary to the everyday view of people (living in a world subject to frictional forces) that a *constant* force is needed to maintain steady motion. Here, the scientific view is quite different from everyday understandings and the learning demand is therefore substantial: the scientific view appears contrary to the ways in which people normally talk about events ('keep it going, keep pushing') and the evidence provided by one's own muscles in taking part in those events.

The notion of 'learning demand' is one which will be recognized by experienced science teachers who *know* that some topics are notoriously difficult to teach and learn, but perhaps are less clear about why that should be. Traditionally, analysis of learning about particular scientific concepts has tended to focus on the logic, structure and inter-relatedness of those scientific concepts which are the declared learning objectives of the teaching. Analysis in terms of 'learning demand' reminds us that such an approach addresses only half of the problem and that it is the *differences* between existing and scientific ways of knowing which need to be focused upon.

Implications for teaching and learning

With this perspective on learning science in mind, we now return to the case outlined earlier in which students were able to classify matter as solid, liquid or gas but found great difficulty in making explicit the criteria underpinning their classifications. Why should this be? In attempting to answer this question, it is instructive to return to Darren's diary entry:

> it didn't seem solid but it wasn't gas and it wasn't liquid.

This statement suggests that the student's interpretation of 'solid' was not based on the application of particular criteria. Rather, Darren appears to be comparing the objects under consideration to 'prototypical' solids, liquids and gases and making decisions on the basis of these comparisons. In everyday reasoning, solids are hard, rigid objects – hence, the problem for the student in conceptualizing a piece of cloth as a solid. By contrast, the view of 'solid' used in science might involve the application of criteria about a range of properties, and even consideration of atomic structure. This process of classifying materials into three mutually exclusive groups is a tool of school science, constructed for particular purposes. Materials in the real world do not fall neatly into solids, liquids and gases: they may be classified in many different ways. If students are to use a particular classification, then they need to be introduced to the socially-agreed purposes and rules of application of that classification. It is interesting to note that, although both teacher and students are using the terms 'solid', 'liquid' and 'gas' about the same objects, the underlying basis of classification used by each is quite different.

In this episode, the teacher is attempting to elicit the criteria which students use for classifying matter. We believe that, rather than working from criteria, students use simple prototypical examples in classifying matter and that it is this difference in ways of reasoning which has led to the difficulties experienced by the students and the mismatch of expectations generated for the teacher. Furthermore, it is precisely this *difference* in the ways of reasoning which determines the learning demand in this particular area of science.

It is tempting to think that, in accurately identifying the 'learning demands' for students in particular topic areas, the teacher might develop strategies to address those demands and enculture students into the science view, in an unproblematic way. Would that it were so! Learning science always involves students in making *personal* sense of the scientific ideas introduced in terms of their *existing* ways of knowing. As argued earlier, this often involves investing familiar terms with new meanings. The challenge for the learner in coming to understand that scientific concepts should not be underestimated, a point which is illustrated below.

After the lessons on states of matter, the students in the initial lesson were introduced to the particle model of matter. Many of those students had previously thought of matter as continuous, and this view was highly influential in their interpretations of the particle model. For example, many students suggested that air lies *in between* the particles in gases, being unable to reconcile their continuous model of gases with a particle model in which there is *nothing* in between the particles (Johnston and Driver 1991). Here, the science way of knowing (that there is nothing between the particles) is contrary to the existing view (that there is air) and furthermore, the science view contravenes a fundamental belief held by many of the students, that 'air fills all of space'. Once again, we have a situation where personally-held beliefs present a barrier to making personal sense of the science view; the elements of the scientific explanation are *intelligible* but simply not *plausible* (Hewson and Hewson 1991) from an everyday perspective.

Conclusion

In summary, we draw together the following points relating to teaching and learning about science concepts:

- Scientific knowledge is constructed rather than discovered, and is socially validated.
- As such, learning science concepts involves the introduction of new ways of knowing through the social process of teaching, rather than making sense of the natural world through personal observation and thought.
- Individuals often have existing 'ways of knowing' about the natural phenomena that are explained by the theories of science; although the terms used may be the same, the underlying patterns of reasoning are usually different.
- Differences between everyday and scientific ways of knowing determine the Learning Demand, for students, in particular areas of science.
- Learning science involves making personal sense of new ways of knowing, in terms of existing knowledge, and as such may be problematic.

These points about the nature of scientific knowledge and the nature of science learning do not lead to an algorithm for teaching (Millar 1989). We would, however, maintain that, just as this perspective on learning can be useful in interpreting teaching and learning, it can also provide a fundamental perspective in planning teaching. Central to this perspective is the notion of Learning Demand. In the case of classifying matter, the learning demand on students involved coming to understand a different basis for a familiar classification. In the case of introducing a particulate view of matter, the learning demand involved coming to understand a model of matter which challenges existing beliefs. As argued earlier, prediction of the learning demand associated with particular areas of science must be based on insights into differences between students' existing ways of knowing and the science view. Teaching can then be planned to address these differences in ways of knowing.

It could be argued that what is described here is no more than what good science teachers already do intuitively. We have some sympathy with that point of view. Good science teachers do have deep understandings of both their students' ways of thinking and the scientific perspective, and it is these insights which enable them to be sensitive to the varying intellectual demands of the school science curriculum, and to support their students in learning science. These understandings are usually implicit, however, and experienced teachers often have difficulty in explaining their insights on learning to less experienced colleagues. We believe that in developing the skills to identify and talk about learning demands in different parts of the science curriculum, then all science teachers can become better equipped to plan teaching approaches which create and sustain the meaningful dialogues which are fundamental to good teaching and effective learning.

References

Asoko, H., Leach, J. and Scott, P. (1993) 'Learning science', in R. Hull (ed.) *ASE Secondary Science Teacher's Handbook*, Hatfield: Association for Science Education.

CLIS (1987) *CLIS in the Classroom: Approaches to Teaching*, University of Leeds: Children's Learning in Science Research Group, CSSME.

Driver, R., Asoko, H., Leach, J. Mortimer, E. and Scott, P. (1994) 'Constructing scientific knowledge in the classroom', *Educational Researcher* 23(7): 5–12.

Garrison, J. W. and Bentley, M. L. (1990) 'Science education, conceptual change and breaking with everyday experience', *Studies in Philosophy and Education* 10: 19–35.

Hewson, P. W. and Hewson, M. G. A. B. (1991) 'The status of students' conceptions', in R. Duit and H. Niedderer, *Research in Physics Learning: Theoretical Issues and Empirical Studies*, Proceedings of an International Workshop, IPN, Keil.

Johnston, K. and Driver, R. (1991) *A Case Study of Teaching and Learning about Particle Theory: A Constructivist Scheme in Action*, University of Leeds: Children's Learning Science Research Group, CSSME.

Millar, R. (1989) 'Constructive criticisms', *International Journal of Science Education* 11(5): 587–96.

Scott, P. (1993) 'Overtures and obstacles: teaching and learning about air pressure in a high school classroom', in *Proceedings of the Third International Symposium on Misconceptions in Science and Mathematics Education*, Ithaca, NY: Cornell University.

Solomon, J. (1987) 'Social influences on the construction of pupils' understanding of science', *Studies in Science Education* 14: 63–82.

12 Children's thinking and science learning

Philip Adey

Children's ability to learn depends to an important extent on their ability to process new information. This chapter discusses how children's information-processing capability can be enhanced by a carefully constructed intervention programme which sets challenges and encourages pupils to become conscious of their own thinking. Science provides an excellent context in which such challenging problems can be set, but adopting such an intervention programme requires stepping back from a 'delivery' view of teaching, and recognizing that time spent in the early years of secondary schooling to the development of higher-level thinking repays itself later in significantly-enhanced learning capability.

How children process information

Passing information from one person to another is a lot more complicated than it may seem. People outside education sometimes believe that if a teacher knows something, and a child does not, then all the teacher has to do is to tell the child what they know. Anyone who has been a teacher knows that information does not get transferred that easily. And, in fact, if anyone were to reflect for a few minutes, they could gain an inkling of what the problem is.

'Daddy, where does rain come from?'

'Well, water from the sea gets evaporated by the sun's heat, it goes into the atmosphere, but when the air is blown over high ground it gets colder, and cold air can hold less water than warm air, so the water condenses, forms drops, and rain falls.'

Terrific, ninety-nine out of one hundred children switch off at this point. The one-hundredth says, 'What's evaporation? What's condensation? Why does the air get colder? Why doesn't cold air hold water?' Either way, not a lot of information has been transferred.

Knowledge is a funny thing. Where is knowledge? In people's heads? In books? In the collective unconscious? Knowledge is in all of these places but, unlike water, it cannot simply be poured from one place to another. This is because knowledge actually consists of an incredibly complex network of understandings, deeply embedded in social and cultural assumptions. Knowledge is never a set of isolated items or 'facts' which one person or book can pass to a learner. Even apparently trivial bits of knowledge, such as the correct number bus to get from Harrods to

Buckingham Palace, cannot simply be 'given'. The tourist in London who asks the question may be told, 'Number 14 goes nearest'. But in which direction? Is there a single fare? Where do I buy the ticket and how do I know when I am there? Only, the Londoner who takes all these peripheral pieces of information *for granted* can use the simple answer '14' to any effect.

All information needs to be processed by the receiver. The effectiveness of this information processing depends on a) the existing network of understandings that the receiver already has, and b) the power of their information-processing capability. If these are the two main controlling factors, there are four possibilities, summarized in Figure 12.1.

Our ability to process information develops with age and experience. It involves a qualitative shift in the type of thinking available; a growth in the number of variables that can be held in the mind at once and acted upon. This is the basis of the stages of cognitive development described by Jean Piaget. Children using what he describes as concrete operations are able to understand relationships between two variables, and simple cause–effect relationships. But it requires a higher level of thinking – formal operations – to be able to handle fluently problems with three or four variables. This is what is needed to understand how to control variables. If you cannot hold in mind at one time the possible values of the variables length, mass, and angle of swing of a pendulum, you cannot understand why it is necessary to hold two constant while you change the third. Likewise, proportional thinking requires that a ratio (two variables) be multiplied by a third variable to increase or decrease it by a given proportion. All three variables have to be held in the mind at once and manipulated independently, and such a demand on working memory is what characterizes formal operations.

Demand for such formal thinking starts to be made about levels 5 and 6 in the National Curriculum. These form something of a natural barrier of difficulty for progression through the curriculum.

But what exactly is the status of these different levels at which children process information? Do they form some sort of staircase up which all children ascend under the control of pre-determined maturational development of the central nervous system? No, they do not. Although there certainly is an element in the process which depends on maturation, progress is importantly influenced by the child's experiences. In other words, as teachers and as parents, we can have a real influence on the process of cognitive development.

We need to distinguish here between the ideas of *instruction* and of *intervention*. The meaning of instruction is unproblematic: it is the provision of knowledge and understanding through appropriate activities. Instruction can be categorized by topic and by domain and the end product of instruction can be specified in terms of learning objectives.

Intervention here is used in the sense of intervention in the process of cognitive development, that is in manipulating experiences aimed at maximizing the rate of progression through the different levels of thinking. Both instruction and intervention are necessary to an effective educational system, but instruction has been emphasized to the neglect of intervention. It could be claimed that intervention

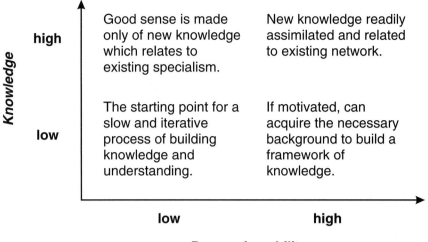

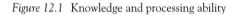

Figure 12.1 Knowledge and processing ability

actually offers the only route for the further substantial raising of standards in an educational world which has spent the last forty years concentrating on improved instructional methods.

How much does it matter?

For at least fifteen years, there has been a national campaign under successive governments to 'raise standards' of education. Whilst politicians tend to focus on assessment, goal-setting, inspection, and other essentially external pressures on schools, education professionals are more interested in the mechanisms of learning and teaching. We believe that if we can better understand how children learn, then we can certainly raise academic achievement by improving our professional practice. This is an approach which owes more to research, to theoretical models of learning, and to the professional expertise of teachers than it does to external controls. Here I want to focus on models and research which, over the last twenty years, have led to a fuller understanding of how children's ability to process information can be enhanced.

The theory and practice of increasing pupils' ability

To address directly the development of pupils' ability to process data does not mean trying to teach thinking skills like a set of rules. What we have to do is to provide the conditions under which the complex process of high-level thinking is most likely to develop. The term 'constructivism' is now well known in science education circles, meaning the need for pupils to construct their own knowledge and understanding. In cognitive intervention theory, we also depend on constructivism, but we broaden its meaning to include the pupil's construction of their own higher-level thinking abilities.

Here are some of the principles which are features of intellectually stimulating activities:

- *Challenge,* and the management of support to children in their problem-solving
- *Reflection:* encouraging pupils to become conscious of their own thinking strategies
- Questioning which aids children in the *construction of* 'reasoning patterns' – ways of thinking which have broad application
- *Bridging* the use of reasoning patterns from special contexts to science in general, and to life in general.

I will illustrate each of these principles with specific activities.

Take the idea of *challenge,* otherwise known as 'cognitive conflict'. Presented with a bunch of tubes varying in length, width, and material, and asked to find which variable affects the pitch of the note you get when you blow across the tube, a typical 11-year-old will choose a short, wide one and a long, narrow one. He may come to you and say, 'I've found that narrow tubes give lower notes than wide tubes'. This statement needs to be challenged, but the method of challenge is critical. It should be designed so that the pupil has the best possible chance of constructing the control of variables strategy for himself. Which of the two dialogues shown (Figure 12.2) do you think is most likely to achieve this?

Let us look now at *reflection,* known in the trade as 'metacognition'. A pupil has been investigating the load and lift forces in a 'wheelbarrow' made of a notched stick, with one end resting on a table edge, and a load hung from one of the notches (Figure 12.3). A force meter is hung from the other end to measure the lift. They have recorded the lift as successive loads are added and calculated the ratio of load to lift for each. With quite a bit of help and discussion, and comparing results from other groups they have established that the ratio is approximately constant, and have gone so far as to predict what the lift would be for a load that is too heavy to actually try.

The child is being encouraged to unpack their own thinking, to put on the table the process by which they reached an answer. This makes working explicit, so it becomes available for use again, and it emphasizes that the reasoning process is as important as the answer, although there may be many legitimate reasoning pathways to the same correct answer.

Our third principle was *construction.* Teaching for cognitive acceleration involves, above all else, putting the pupil in the position where they have to construct for themselves – slowly and often painfully – the type of thinking needed to tackle all sorts of scientific problems and investigations.

Bridging is the process of drawing attention to the many other contexts in which a reasoning pattern, developed in one particular context, can be applied. So, from the examples above, the bridging phase of a cognitive intervention lesson might involve a discussion of other times when the control of variables or proportionality 'ways of thinking' might come in useful.

Dialogue 1	Dialogue 2
T: How do you know the width affects the note?	T: How do you know the width affects the note?
P: The wide one gives a deeper note.	P: The wide one gives a deeper note.
T: But look at the tubes, they have different lengths as well as different widths.	T: Look at the tubes. How are they different?
P: Oh yes.	P: They are different widths.
T: How can you tell whether it is length or width, or both?	T: Anything else?
P: ???	P: Different lengths.
T: You can't, can you? If you change two things, you don't know which is having the effect, do you?	T: How do you know it is not the length that affects the note?
P: I suppose not.	P: Both the length and the width affect the note.
T: OK, go away and choose two tubes which have the same length, but different widths, and try those.	T: Maybe. But maybe it is just the width, or just the length. How could you tell whether it is length or width, or both?
	P: ???
	T: Go away and think about it, and try to find a pair of tubes that will prove whether it really is just the width that affects the note.

Figure 12.2 Two dialogues

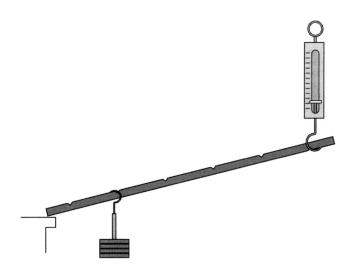

Figure 12.3 The wheelbarrow

CASE

All of these principles have been incorporated into the methods of 'Cognitive Acceleration' developed at King's College London, with demonstrable effects on their pupils' academic achievement. CASE (Cognitive Acceleration through Science Education) has introduced a method of teaching which focuses not so much on good instruction leading to the development of content knowledge, but rather on intervention in children's ability to process information. In other words, CASE is a programme designed to help children to think more effectively. When they think better, they learn better, because they are better equipped to make better sense of their regular science instruction.

The CASE programme consists of a set of thirty-two activities (called *Thinking Science*) designed to be used at the rate of one every two weeks instead of a regular science lesson, during the early secondary years. They are quite specifically signalled to pupils as 'special' lessons. It may seem that setting aside a special lesson once every two weeks for Thinking, when direct attention to covering curriculum content is set aside, makes it even more difficult to deliver the National Curriculum. But reflect for a moment on those words 'covering' and 'deliver' in the last sentence. What view of knowledge do such words imply? They imply that knowledge is a packet which can be delivered, or a set of topics and material which can be covered in the sense of going over it. This is precisely the view of knowledge against which I argue and which has been discredited by the constructivists. Pupils who process information more efficiently will learn more efficiently. Time spent in encouraging the development of the general processing mechanism may immediately be lost from 'covering' the curriculum, but it provides learners with the tools with which they can learn more effectively in the future.

Does it work?

In a word, yes, it does. In our original research, we asked ten schools to try CASE teaching in just one or two early secondary classes for two years, and to identify one or two matched 'control' classes who would follow their normal science curriculum. The CASE pupils made significantly greater gains in cognitive development over the two years of the experiment. More importantly, they demonstrated long-term effects on their ability to learn. Overall, pupils who had experienced CASE teaching in the early years of their secondary education gained higher grades in GCSE than matched control children who had not had CASE.

We published this data in 1991, and it attracted many schools who wished to find out how they could adopt the methods. At that time, we started to run two-year professional development courses for CASE, and also to train CASE Trainers who have been working in many parts of the UK ever since. In 1996, we got the first GCSE data from these schools with whom we started to work in 1991. This confirmed the original research results: CASE schools produced significantly higher 'value added' effects. After taking account of the intake level of their pupils, CASE schools get much higher proportions of pupils with level 6 or above at Key

Stage 3, and of pupils with grades A–C at GCSE, than non-CASE schools. And this is not only in science, but in mathematics and English as well. It seems that the pupils' enhanced processing ability is general, and can be applied across the curriculum.

CASE is not a 'silver bullet'. There is nothing magic about the particular set of activities published as *Thinking Science*. What is magic is the use that teachers make of them, and learning how to do this is not a straightforward matter. Teaching for cognitive stimulation requires an unusual amount of concentration on questioning skills, managing group and whole-class discussions, and provoking reflective thinking in pupils, but these are strategies that can be learned by any teacher prepared to commit some time and energy to developing the new skills.

Further reading

Adey, P. S. (1993) *The King's–BP CASE INSET Pack,* London: BP Educational Services.

Adey, P. S. and Shayer, M. (1994) *Really Raising Standards: Cognitive Intervention and Academic Achievement,* London: Routledge.

Adey, P. S., Shayer, M. and Yates, C. (1995) *Thinking Science: The Curriculum Materials of the CASE Project* (second edition), London: Nelson.

13 Learning science
Piaget and after

Joan Bliss

Background

The past forty years have seen worldwide investment in changes in the teaching of science. The 1960s saw large-scale secondary school curriculum development in the USA in the sciences, in physics (PSSC), chemistry (CBA and CHEM study) and biology (BSCS), followed in England by more than a dozen projects sponsored by the Nuffield Foundation. Many other countries followed, adapting these ideas or developing their own.

Primary education also underwent significant changes, very much influenced by the work of Piaget. Many new curriculum projects were generated amongst which were: a project at Berkeley directed by Robert Karplus (SCIS), in Britain projects in science and mathematics for ages 5–13, sponsored either by Nuffield or the Schools Council, as well as the Australian Science Education Project (ASEP).

Despite all this work, and some say because of it, children still find learning science difficult. This chapter is about some of the reasons why they do. Understanding children's learning of science is important both for improving the teaching of science and, more generally, as a part of understanding learning and cognitive development.

During the 1960s and later, the work of Jean Piaget had a direct influence on thinking about children learning science. More recently, new ideas from cognitive psychology, social psychology, language, and science education have begun to complement, modify or change our view of learning and teaching. Having had the privilege of working with Piaget for nearly a decade, and since I believe that there are important connections between his work and aspects of the newer approaches, I shall use his ideas as a point of reference for the discussion. A more developed version of the whole theme can be found in Bliss (1995).

Piaget and the primary curriculum

Piaget's concern was philosophical, about how knowledge develops, and the laws that govern this development, illuminated by how children think about such knowledge as they grow up. Thus he provided a rich and detailed collection of data about children's thinking and reasoning. He showed how ideas about conservation of weight, volume, density, matter, number, length, perimeter and area developed. He also described the development of measurement, movement, distance, speed, time, space, geometry and chance. Those developing the primary school curriculum could use these ideas directly, and in consequence much of that curriculum (for example, children classifying objects) reflects Piaget's ideas, but with their origin often forgotten.

Piaget's stage theory

Piaget was not content just to describe the many different ways in which knowledge develops. He wanted to know what the development of different ideas, such as number and measurement, had in common. Thus he hypothesized that there are developmentally different structures to account for changes in the way knowledge develops and so how children think; he postulated a series of qualitatively different stages to describe children's intellectual development from birth to adolescence.

This gave educators a new way of thinking about teaching and learning. They used it as a tool to match the content of science curriculums to children's spontaneous development, planning science activities to have a basis in what was known about development. In *Match and Mismatch*, Harlen, Darwin and Murphy (1977) attempted matching primary school activities to development, so that their curriculum contains an ordering of concepts such as classification, weight, length, volume, and cause and effect, and of processes such as observing, problem-solving, raising questions, exploring and finding patterns in observations.

In secondary school science, Shayer, in the 1970s used Piagetian stages of intellectual development to assess the Nuffield Foundation's projects in biology, chemistry and physics. He claimed:

> First, the stages of the course ought to follow the same order of increasing logical complexity as are present in the pupils' own development. Secondly, the age range over which the course is taught should match the age range over which these stages develop.
>
> (Shayer 1971: 183)

Shayer distinguished two levels of matching:

- the minimum level the pupil must have attained for interest to be sustained;
- the level needed to gain what is expected by the project.

He was able to give reasons why, for example, the early use in chemistry of the concept of the mole as an integrating idea was bound to present difficulties, and recommended delaying its introduction. Such analyses were important in creating an awareness of the sources of difficulty of some science concepts. But they also created a tendency to say that one must not teach something until children are intellectually 'ready' for it, permitting the opting out of teaching 'difficult' ideas.

Bruner pointed out that 'readiness' is a mischievous half truth because, 'One teaches readiness or provides opportunities for its nurture; one does not simply wait for it' (Bruner 1968: 29).

Piaget never dealt with large numbers of subjects. His work was in-depth investigations, letting children tell him what they knew about certain areas of knowledge. For him, it was the fixed *order* of succession of cognitive stages that was crucial, not the *age* at which children reached a given stage, which he expected to depend on physical maturation, learning, social factors and motivation.

A large-scale survey of secondary pupils between the ages of 11 and 16 showed that less than 30 per cent of children in English comprehensive schools were in Piaget's formal operational stage at 16 (Shayer *et al.* 1976). At much the same time, similar work in the USA by Lawson, Renner and Rowell found that many American undergraduates reasoned concretely rather than abstractly.

Formal operations and scientific reasoning

Piaget saw the stage of formal reasoning as using *general* operational schemes such as isolating and controlling variables, combinatorial, correlational, probabilistic and proportional thinking, and not in terms of reasoning *specific* to a domain.

This led to attempts both to investigate and to improve pupils' use of formal and scientific patterns of reasoning. In the USA in the 1970s, reasonably effective teaching materials were created to promote 13-year-olds' understanding of the idea of a controlled experiment. Also, science programmes were designed which attempted to enhance the acquisition of scientific reasoning.

Proportional reasoning, vital for science and mathematics, has attracted particular interest. Initially, proportional reasoning was seen as a general cognitive structure. However, much American work was able to show that adolescents' proportional reasoning is very much tied to the nature of the task. Mellar and Bliss (1993) argued that proportional reasoning is more a collection of strategies than a unitary cognitive structure.

More recently, Shayer and Adey developed a two-year intervention programme with 11- and 12-year-olds designed to accelerate formal thinking and promote general thinking skills (Shayer and Adey 1992a; 1992b). They got possible effects in some cases on public examination results some three years after the intervention without very clear positive effects on more immediate post-tests. Alternative explanations of these effects remain to be investigated.

Constructivism and the science curriculum

In the sense in which constructivism has been mainly understood in science education, Piaget was one of its early proponents, seeing children as constructing their own knowledge through their own activity. But while he followed this through in detail for younger children, accounts of older pupils' construction of ideas about science were lacking. Andersson diagnosed the difficulty as follows:

Although Piaget and others have described the development of reasoning in such a comprehensive manner, the model does not tell us, for instance, about what conceptions the pupils have of electricity, heat, light, matter, etc. before they begin science lessons. ... We must therefore to a large extent find out about the pupil's initial position by focusing on research activities on this problem.

(Andersson 1984)

It would be more correct to say that Piaget was interested in the knowledge which children could acquire without going to school, and his interest in the development of reasoning, in general, only came later. Piaget's main contribution to science education was an exploration of ideas about cause and effect, but this work was only published in a summary account in 1974.

From the 1970s, a worldwide trend in science education developed, describing pupils' ideas in science. It became clear that pupils' ideas were often very different from those of their teachers, or from the science specified in the curriculum. Some suggested that this trend resulted from dissatisfaction with the results of curriculum development. 70 per cent or more of research in science education in Germany and France was mainly focused on physics, e.g. electricity, light, temperature, heat, combustion, pressure, force and energy. If science is difficult, physics appears especially so.

Such work often took a constructivist view of learning, in which learners are seen as taking an active role in the development of their own ideas. Children's idiosyncratic ideas were no longer seen as 'wrong', but merely as different from those of their teachers (see Driver *et al.* 1985 for accounts of children's ideas).

The more that was found out about the surprising ways in which pupils construe the world, the more urgent became the desire to find ways of changing what they thought, especially in the face of the evidence that some of these intuitive ideas strongly resist change, even at university level. For example, the Children's Learning in Science Project (CLISP) tried conceptual change strategies for energy, the particle theory of matter and plant nutrition. Overall, although strategies have varied widely, successes have, on the whole, been modest.

Soon computers entered the fray. The Conceptual Change in Science project (Hennessy *et al.* 1995) had limited success in getting young secondary students to reason in a Newtonian way about force and motion, using computer simulations of Newtonian and non-Newtonian 'realities', with pupils themselves able to give the rules governing motion. Some important pre-conceptions even increased. Newton, it seems, *is* difficult.

Ideas about how to effect change include cognitive conflict and the specification of conditions for conceptual change (Posner *et al.* 1982). There are several things one can do with conflict: try something else, think about it, or block it. It is important to realize that learning from contradictions requires more than simply being made aware of conflict; the need to present alternatives (try something else) is crucial. Another important point to stress is that conceptual change can come from practical success, after which one tries to understand how that success was achieved.

Critique of constructivism?

Constructivism says that knowledge is constructed; beyond that it is a many-headed beast. For Piaget or for Kelly, knowledge is constructed by the individual by individual means; for (say) Vygotsky (1978), it is constructed by the individual through social means. Thus 'constructivism' gives different answers to the questions of: 'Who makes knowledge?', 'How this is done?', and 'On what basis it is held to be knowledge?'.

Although constructivism is a heterogeneous movement, many constructivists in science education derive their positions either from Piaget or from Kelly. These two origins lead to quite distinct and different views of 'what knowledge is' and thus have very different implications for research and classroom practice (Bliss 1993).

In science education, Pope and Gilbert (1983) drew inspiration from Kelly's personal construct theory (Kelly 1955), using it to lend support to teachers concerned with investigating student views. Their focus is on the uniqueness of each person's construction. One crucial difficulty with this approach is that it requires the teacher to diagnose each individual's constructs. In fact, however, most such research describes 'typical' constructs, not individual ones.

Such individual constructivism does not attribute a sufficient role to the teacher, the parent or the peer, and this has rightly led to attention being given to ideas from Vygotsky and others about the role of the adult or teacher in the pupil's learning.

Other constructivists draw inspiration from re-interpretations of Piaget. However, Piaget has nothing to say about individual differences, so although his philosophical ideas about the development of knowledge can be recruited, they leave open how one should think about the development of individuals.

A different objection to constructivism is that it sees the child just as learning about the world through experience. But science teaching can be seen as the way in which pupils are introduced into the communal world of science concepts and techniques, and communal standards of argument and evidence. Matthews (1992) gives an example: how Galileo changed not the facts but the arguments. Galileo did not see the real objects of science any differently from anyone else. But he did describe them differently and it is these descriptions, the theoretical objects of science, with which pupils have grapple. Constructivism rarely distinguishes between making personal sense of the real world, and understanding the socially constructed world of scientific ideas.

Challenges to Piaget

Three challenges to Piaget are particularly relevant to science education. They are:

- questioning the existence of 'formal operations';

- questioning the existence of general, non-domain specific abilities and of stages;
- insisting on the importance of the social, cultural and contextual dimension.

Many doubts about formal thinking stem from work which shows how even highly-educated adults perform badly on tasks involving abstract hypothetical thinking. The tasks get much easier when they are translated into concrete contexts. Piaget conceded that people would differ in their formal reasoning according to aptitude and personal specialization. But this defence denies the essential context-free nature of formal reasoning.

A kind of 'formal' thinking, which operates on symbols and signs rather than on representations of objects and events, certainly exists. The question is whether it should be regarded as a special way of thinking used on some occasions for some purposes, rather than being universalized as a highly-developed form of reasoning. There is little reason to suppose that it is much used in everyday life. Piaget may have made formal reasoning into a false God.

More generally, Keil (1986) and Carey (1985) see adults as different from children mainly by knowing more, not by possessing general cognitive structures. Carey argues that much of the evidence given to support stage-like development of cognitive structures could, in fact, reflect domain-specific re-organizations of knowledge.

Finally, there is the socio-cultural challenge, which sees context and cultural practice as the fundamental units within which thought has to be analysed. Human mental functioning is seen as emerging from, and located in, social practices. Such a theory of culture and cognition resists the separation of the individual from the environment of daily life (Rogoff and Lave 1984). A consequence of this new focus is to cast doubt on the very notion of the transfer of knowledge from one context to another. In these theories, development reduces to learning the culture.

Mental models

In the last decade, much attention has been given to seeing human thinking and reasoning as the manipulation of imagined entities, or as using 'mental models'. This view stands against 'formal reasoning' and accords better with what Piaget described as 'concrete operational reasoning'. There is a good case for saying that Piaget undervalued his account of concrete reasoning too much, seeing it only as a step towards formal reasoning. In fact, Piaget's formulation of how we think describes 'what you use to think with'; these are the mental 'tools for thought', which he called 'operations' or, more generally, 'schemes'.

Within the mental models research, two strands developed. In the first, 'mental models' are used to describe the 'content of thinking' and come from an area known as qualitative or naive physics; the second is concerned with mental models as more general 'tools for thought'. Illustrations of this first strand, focusing, for example on constructing systems which reason 'naturally', are found in the book *Mental Models* by Gentner and Stevens (1983). The second strand is that of the work of Johnson-Laird (1983). Here, a mental model is more like a set of mental tokens which are manipulated to form a structure, which might correspond with a structure in reality, while not representing it directly. In this case, the notion of a mental model is an attempt to describe 'tools for thought' – as was Piaget's.

Piaget never used the term 'mental model', but he can often be seen as speaking a similar language. Thus, leaving the sensori–motor stage (the first developmental stage) requires the child to construct a new plane of reality, *representing* the world in place of *acting directly* on it. Similarly, concrete operational thinking operates on imagined entities; that is, young children think about the world in terms of imagined objects and events. What Piaget rarely does is to discuss the nature of these representations.

Focus on ontology – a new way forward

Much past work on learning has drawn its ideas from *epistemology*, that is, the study of the *grounds of knowledge*. For example 'direct experience' has been seen as basic, both to learning and to the foundations of knowledge. The mental models position points in a new direction, namely an *ontological* focus on studying what people take to be the *nature of the things* in the world around them. What *is* comes before what is the case.

The work of Keil (1986) and Carey (1985), mentioned earlier, is in this mould. They suggest that the conceptual system is articulated by a core of ontologically basic categories, such as *physical object* and *event*. Basic ontological categories are few, but they provide the core organizational system for other concepts.

Piaget, too, made such a shift, but very late in his work. Throughout his work, Piaget saw knowledge as derived from two kinds of activity: logico–mathematical and physical activity. Through *logico–mathematical activity*, actions turn inward to become *mental* actions. It is the structure of the actions which is essential, not what the actions act upon. *Physical activity*, on the other hand, is about acting on *objects* and *physical situations*, learning about their size, colour, shape, weight, etc. But Piaget was less interested in the outcome of physical activity, so although he created this valuable concept, he then largely proceeded to neglect it. However, in work published posthumously (Piaget and Garcia 1987), Piaget began to address the development of meanings of physical entities, formulated with deceptive simplicity as understood through 'what can be done to them', 'what they can do' and 'what parts they are made of'.

Research done by a group in London with whom I was associated for ten years, focuses on common-sense everyday reasoning: taking ontology to be fundamental. Ogborn (1992) characterizes commonsense reasoning as, 'Ordinary, everyday, unreflective, practical reasoning about things which are mostly seen as obvious'. A first series of studies elicits underlying commonsense categories of pupils which organize thinking about such things as the sun, matter, stars, space, water, etc. Another extended series of studies has tried to get at ideas underlying people's thinking about force and motion. More recent research focused on human reasoning about the physical world, for example, about how electricity flows along a wire, an astronaut 'floats' in space or what keeps an aeroplane up.

For learning science, it seems to me that we should pay much more attention to physical rather than logical reasoning. Physical reasoning would not appear to be context free, indeed it would have to do with the creation of contexts. Contrary to some received wisdom related to the desirability of transfer, it is cognitively rather sensible to be very cautious about generalizing across different contexts. So, we might expect a slow, rather conservative process of noticing salient features of new contexts, which abstracts some of the features common to many physical situations, but which also contain the constraints of particular situations.

Conclusions

Piaget took epistemology seriously. For him the psycho-genesis of knowledge is necessary to it, asking how it comes about that people generally come to see the world as they do. He showed us that children brought to school a whole wealth of personal knowledge and ways of thinking about the world.

To understand something is more than seeing why it might be true (epistemology). The mental models position, which tries to understand what people take to be the nature of the things in the world around them (ontology), has, I think, much to offer a better understanding of the problems of learning science. For instance, the Newtonian view of force and motion involves a complete imaginative reconstruction of causes of motion. Science teaching consists, in part, of educating the intuitions.

We need to know where other areas of science involve similar re-constructions. It is also crucial to understand the processes by which children's ideas about the world may change or resist change. More work needs to go into an analysis of the origins of children's informal ideas across other science topics, to see how far they relate to deep-rooted intuitive thinking, and to see to what extent the scientific account itself challenges that thinking. We need to understand the gap, when there is one, between the everyday common-sense ontology which children are using and the scientific ontology. We should focus more than we have on the role of the teacher. All of these problems are particularly important to science.

Learning science is not about making sense of the real world purely for oneself; it is about making sense of how scientists have made sense of the world. The pupils' task in school is to come to terms with the scientific account of the world. But while scientists can see how the different ideas interrelate and fit into more general theories, pupils meet these different ideas in isolated, separate contexts which may or may not relate to their own experiences.

Teaching science is a matter of conveying a mental model. And teaching *about* science is a matter of conveying that science consists of stories which have been made up in the hope of describing essential bits of the nature of things. Both need the exercise of imagination through analogy and metaphor, together with plenty of first-hand knowledge of phenomena, so that physical reasoning has a chance to get built up and be applied to new things.

References

Andersson, B. (1984) 'A framework for discussing approaches and methods in Science Education', in F. Adams *Science and Computers in Primary Education: A Report of the Education Research Workshop held in Edinburgh (Scotland), 3–6 September 1984*, Edinburgh: Scottish Council for Research in Education.

Bliss, J. (1993) 'The relevance of Piaget to research into children's conceptions', in P. Black and A. Lucas (eds) *Childrens' Informal Ideas about Science*, London: Routledge, pp. 20–44.

Bliss, J. (1995) 'Piaget and after: the case of learning science', *Studies in Science Education* 25: 139–72.

Bruner, J. S. (1968) *Towards a Theory of Instruction*, New York: W. W. Norton and Co.

Carey, S. (1985) *Conceptual Change in Childhood*, Cambridge, MA: MIT Press.

Driver, R., Guesne, E. and Tiberghien, A. (eds) (1985) *Children's Ideas in Science*, Milton Keynes: Open University Press.

Gentner, D. and Stephens, A. L. (1983) *Mental Models*, Hillsdale, NJ and London: Lawrence Erlbaum Associates.

Harlen, W., Darwin, A. and Murphy, P. (1977) *Match and Mismatch. Raising Questions*, Edinburgh: Oliver and Boyd.

Hennessy, S., Twigger, D., Driver, R., O'Shea, T., Draper, S., Hartley, R., Mohamed, R. and Scanlon, E. (1995) 'A classroom intervention using a computer-augmented curriculum for mechanics', *International Journal of Science Education* 17(2): 189–206.

Johnson-Laird, P. (1983) *Mental Models*, Cambridge: Cambridge University Press.

Keil, F. (1986) 'On the structure-dependent nature of stages of cognitive development', in I. Levin (ed.) *Stage and Structure – Reopening the Debate*, Norwood, NJ: Ablex.

Kelly, G. A. (1955) *The Psychology of Personal Constructs*. Vols. 1 and 2, New York: Norton.

Matthews, M. (1992) 'Constructivism and empiricism: an incomplete divorce' (personal communication).

Mellar, H. and Bliss, J. (1993) 'Expressing the student's concepts versus exploring the teacher's: issues in the design of microworlds for teaching', *Journal of Educational Computing Research* 9(1): 89–113.

Ogborn, J. (1992) 'Fundamental dimensions of thought about reality', in *Teaching About Reference Frames: From Copernicus to Einstein*, Proceedings of GIREP Conference, Torun, Poland, August 1991, Torun: Nicholas Copernicus University Press.

Pope, M. and Gilbert, J. (1983) 'Personal experience and the construction of knowledge in science', *Science Education* 67: 193–203.

Piaget, J. (1974) *Understanding Causality*, New York: Norton.

Piaget, J. and Garcia, R. (1987) *Vers une Logique des Significations*, Geneva: Murionde.

Posner, G. J., Strike, K. A., Hewson, P. W. and Gertzog, W. A. (1982) 'Accommodation of a scientific conception: toward a theory of conceptual change', *Science Education* 66(2): 211–27.

Rogoff, B. and Lave, J. (1984) (eds) *Everyday Cognition: Its Development in Social Context*, Cambridge, MA: Harvard University Press.

Shayer, M. (1971) 'How to assess science courses', *Education in Chemistry* 7: 182–6.

Shayer, M., Kucheman, D. and Wylam, D. (1976) 'The distribution of Piagetian stages of thinking in British middle and secondary school children', *British Journal of Educational Psychology* 46: 164–73.

Shayer, M. and Adey, P. (1992a) 'Accelerating the development of formal thinking in middle and high school students II: postproject effects on science achievement', *Journal of Research in Science Teaching* 29(1): 81–92.

Shayer, M. and Adey, P. (1992b) 'Accelerating the development of formal thinking in middle and high school students III: testing the permanency of effects', *Journal of Research in Science Teaching* 29(10): 1101–15.

Vygotsky, L. S. (1978) *Mind in Society, The Development of Higher Psychological Processes*, Cambridge MA: Harvard University Press.

14 Well, Mary, what are they saying here?

Clive Sutton

The prospect of *adding* anything to an already crowded agenda for science is something I would want to resist, so in seeking to outline the day-to-day implications of my position I am also considering how the modern goals of school science might be achieved more effectively, more efficiently, and with greater satisfaction to pupils and teachers. I therefore want to explore the balance amongst the various activities that can go on in science lessons. How much telling? How much 'doing'? How much puzzling and problem solving? As I see it, good telling and good puzzling can both gain greater prominence, while 'doing' should be derived from these and made more purposeful by that connection, and less time-consuming.

I am sure that if learners are to get a feel for language as an interpretive system, they must have experience of using it that way themselves. They should also regularly meet scientific ideas which are presented as expressions of thought rather than definite information, so that there is some point in puzzling over them. Most important, a reasonable proportion of the lesson time should be devoted to comparing different people's understanding. The phrasing in the title of this chapter is meant to point in that direction. There is an explanation of some scientific idea, probably on paper. The teacher signals that there is room for doubt about it, provides space for the pupil to make an interpretation, and tries to maintain a relationship which can carry discussion. Many teachers work this way intuitively in their informal interactions with pupils, but my contention is that the established routines of science lessons do not make adequate provision for it in the formal business of the lesson.

Puzzling and telling are complementary. A clear exposition by the teacher, or in the pages of a book, is one component, but the pupils' learning is in making sense of what is said or written. Lessons organized with this in mind should therefore include time for puzzling, and for pupils to restate what they understand to be the key ideas. Although this sometimes occurs informally in discussion, it will normally require some structure, and some formal means of public report about what they have made of the topic.

In practice, tasks of that kind are not given substantial periods of time, however much their use has been urged. There is something in the traditions of science teaching which marginalizes them, and can even make them unsuccessful when first tried. It is partly the pupils' own expectations of language – i.e. of *not* using it to explore and interpret ideas, or at least not doing so in science. It is also an over-confidence in practical work. Teachers and pupils together have started to believe that handling things at the bench is the main source of understanding, that science lessons are a direct study of nature. My case in this chapter is that the principal object of study should be not nature itself but *sets of ideas*, as represented in the written or spoken words of *people*. Telling about these ideas, and puzzling over them, should be the core of lessons. Apart from improving the quality of learning, I believe this would immediately reinstate the human dimension, and overcome the criticism that science seems dehumanized. It would, of course, retain the importance of practical work, but place it in a very different light.

Practical work revisited

It has often seemed that the ideal science lesson is one in which pupils are actively engaged in bench work for a lot of their time. We expect to see them busily wiring a circuit with different numbers of bulbs, washing inks across absorbent paper, timing the fall of little parachutes, or soaking wrinkled raisins to see them swell. As teachers, we have taken a pride in organizing such events, because the pupils handle real materials and we believe that they 'learn by doing' rather than just by being told. We have seen ourselves as 'managers of learning' rather than as didactic dispensers of information. It seems quite odd therefore to question the system, particularly as I do not wish to imply that hands-on experience is not important. Nevertheless, there is a problem.

Practical work seems to offer many opportunities for interpretive activity, as we can say: 'What is going on here? What do you think is happening? Write down what happened'. Unfortunately, that kind of invitation places the pupil not in the reasonable role of interpreting what someone is trying to say, but in the *more difficult* role of interpreting nature. It is a tall order, when thoughtful minds have struggled for decades over the same phenomena! No wonder the experience sometimes fails to boost the self-esteem of the learners, and their confidence in the value of their own ideas.

The solution is to stop thinking of science lessons as the study of nature. Science itself may be a study of nature, but science lessons should be the study of what people have said and thought about nature. The main object of interpretive activity should be not the circuit itself, but *what someone has said about the circuit*, not the events in the test tube alone but *someone's way of talking about them*, not the raisin, but *a written account* of the de-wrinkling, with its words about 'concentrations', 'membranes' and 'permeability', and behind the words an *author*, clearly envisaged as a *human being*. This person, who told the 'story' we are considering: what was he or she trying to say? Science lessons should be the study of systems of meaning which human beings have built up. Practical work is necessary in order to get a feel for those systems, and to give an understanding of what the evidence is which supports the scientific view, but it should not be thought of as the source that ideas come from.

'Word work' for the extraction of ideas

Let me try to represent this recommendation diagramatically, with two kinds of activity – Task A and Task B. If the main object of study is *someone's words*, then the lesson will be planned around those words and not around the circuit board or the test tube. Equipment will be needed, but it will not dominate the time available for study, and there will be time for a proper interplay of tangible experience on the one hand, and interpretive talk and writing on the other. We will have something like the arrangement below.

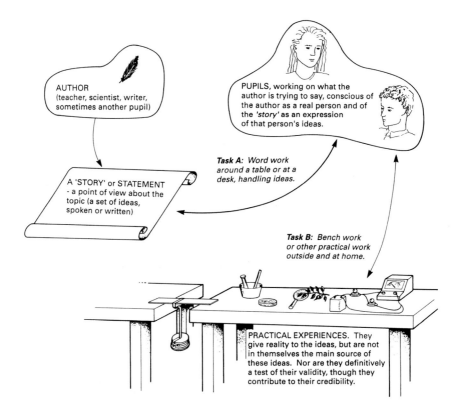

AUTHOR
(teacher, scientist, writer,
sometimes another pupil)

PUPILS, working on what the author is trying to say, conscious of the author as a real person and of the *'story'* as an expression of that person's ideas.

A 'STORY' or STATEMENT
- a point of view about the topic (a set of ideas, spoken or written)

Task A: Word work around a table or at a desk, handling ideas.

Task B: Bench work or other practical work outside and at home.

PRACTICAL EXPERIENCES. They give reality to the ideas, but are not in themselves the main source of these ideas. Nor are they definitively a test of their validity, though they contribute to their credibility.

Within such a pattern, the total time devoted to Word Work (within and between lessons) should exceed that spent on Bench Work. Well-chosen, appropriate resource materials are required, as well as lots of good ideas for organizing the work with them. In the past, most of the creativity of science teachers was channelled into organizing Task B. The need now is for a corresponding inventiveness in relation to Task A.

Science lessons as appreciation of ideas

It is important that what I have called a 'Story' or Statement in the diagram is not seen as an account of fact, but as an expression of thought by some *person* who can be identified or at least envisaged. It offers a point of view, a kind of explanation, a way of talking about the topic. It forms the principal material of the lesson. It does not have to be written, though having something on paper can make it easier to argue about. To cater for a wide range of abilities, it will need to take many different forms on different occasions, for example:

- something the teacher says, briefly, or writes on the board
- a snippet from a text book
- a newspaper cutting
- two slightly different explanations written by pupils in last year's class
- a snatch of videotape
- a food package label.

Sometimes the words of actual scientists may be used. The art of selecting suitable items is one of considerable subtlety, as they must be capable of leading in to the key talk-system of the topic, and also of engaging the pupils. Usually they must be short, so that there is opportunity to go over the material several times, to comment, interpret, query, and go back to it, as well as to experience the relevant phenomena practically.

The type of science lesson I am describing bears some resemblance to a literature lesson in which the object of appreciation – be it a poem or a prose paragraph – is presented quite quickly, leaving time and scope for reflection, for talk, and for each participant to move towards a considered restatement of their own. Certainly an academic proposition in science, such as $P_1V_1 = P_2V_2$ requires at least as much time and effort to make sense of it, as might be given to a literary one like 'All the world's a stage'. What did the writer mean, and how do we re-create that meaning for ourselves? We could call this 'appreciation of scientific ideas' or even 'meaning extraction'.

Actually, there are many classes in which it would not be the best strategy to start with anything like such an academic message as P_1V_1 and all that, but the topic of Boyle's Law has been so long established in science syllabuses that I will stay with it for the moment in a form suitable for an academic group, and use it to illustrate how practical experiences can be short and purposeful, leaving more time for the meaning–extraction activities. Here, then, are some components for a couple of lessons on the squashability of gases:

1   A very short *experience* of 'the spring of the air', for everyone individually, squeezing a scaled syringe full of air or another gas.
2   A passage such as *Statement 1*, to be read and puzzled over in pairs and trios, leading to some agreed re-statement of what they think the writer was trying to say.
3   A short *presentation by the teacher*, with demonstration apparatus, but not using large sections of lesson time to collect experimental results.
4   *Practical desk-work* – plotting a graph using second-hand data (included in

Statement 1   L'étude quantitative de la compressibilité des gaz

This is what it says in a French school book, in the section about compressing gases. What are the main points that the writer of the book is trying to make?

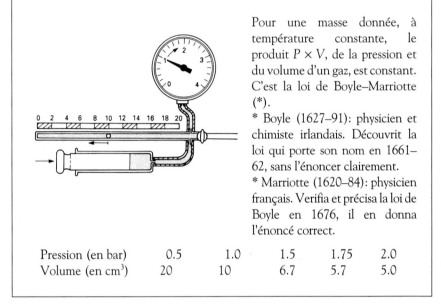

Pour une masse donnée, à température constante, le produit $P \times V$, de la pression et du volume d'un gaz, est constant. C'est la loi de Boyle–Marriotte (*).

* Boyle (1627–91): physicien et chimiste irlandais. Découvrit la loi qui porte son nom en 1661–62, sans l'énoncer clairement.
* Marriotte (1620–84): physicien français. Verifia et précisa la loi de Boyle en 1676, il en donna l'énoncé correct.

Pression (en bar)	0.5	1.0	1.5	1.75	2.0
Volume (en cm³)	20	10	6.7	5.7	5.0

Statement 1), and then a re-statement of what the graph says – made by pupils, with support as necessary.

5   For an extension, or homework with a high ability group, one could add a further passage such as that in Statement 2, in which we can hear Boyle himself speculating about how to account for the spring of the air.[1]

The teacher must be confident of winning the involvement of the pupils in both kinds of task, and there are situations in which it would be easy to take the pessimistic view that only active benchwork will hold the attention of those pupils whose minds seem not so readily drawn to collective thought. That is not an adequate justification for practical work, and anyway, such an estimate of pupils' abilities is too pessimistic; it indicates the need for a different task and a changed social relationship, not for abandoning the strategy. In this case, I draw some confidence myself from the human interest of Boyle's identification of what he so interestingly called 'the spring of the air'.

For English-speaking pupils, a passage for Statement 1 would more usually be in English, and when I use the word 'interpret' I am not thinking primarily of that special subsection of interpretive activity which we associate with foreign languages. However, in this case a school book from France does give an added

Statement 2   Boyle's speculations about the reasons for the spring of the air

Robert Boyle published his most famous account of the air in 1660, and called it *New Experiments Physico-Mechanical, Touching the Spring of the Air and its Effects; Made, for the most Part, in a New Pneumatical Engine.* Some years later he wrote more speculatively about what might account for its springiness:

> Of the structure of the elastical particles of the air, divers conceptions may be framed, according to the several contrivances men may devise to answer the phaenomena: for one may think them to be like the springs of watches, coiled up, and still endeavouring to fly abroad. One may also fancy a portion of air to be like a lock or parcel of curled hairs of wool; which being compressed… may have a continual endeavour to stretch themselves out, and thrust away the neighbouring particles…
>
> I remember too, that I have, among other comparisons of this kind, represented the springy particles of the air like the very thin shavings of wood, that carpenters and joiners are wont to take off with their planers… And perhaps you may the rather prefer this comparison, because… these shavings are producible out of bodies, that did not appear, nor were suspected, to be elastical in their bulk, as beams and blocks, almost any of which may afford springy shavings… which may perhaps illustrate what I tried, that divers solid… bodies, not suspected of elasticity, being put into corrosive menstruums,… there will, upon the… reaction that passes between them in the dissolution,… emerge a pretty quantity of permanently elastical air.
>
> But possibly you will think, that these are but extravagant conjectures; and therefore… I shall… willingly grant, that one may fancy several other shapes… for these springy corpuscles, about whose structure I shall not now particularly discourse… Only I shall here intimate, that though the elastical air seem to continue such, rather upon the score of its structure, than any external agitation; yet heat, that is a kind of motion, may make the agitated particles strive to recede further and further… and to beat off those, that would hinder the freedom of their gyrations, and so very much add to the endeavour of such air to expand itself.
>
> And I will allow you to suspect, that there may be sometimes mingled with the particles, that are springy,… some others, that owe their elasticity, not so much to their structure, as their motion, which variously brandishing them and whirling them about, may make them beat off the neighbouring particles, and thereby promote an expansive endeavour in the air, whereof they are parts.

How many distinctly different ideas does Boyle try out? What impression do you get about which, if any, of them he prefers, and what is your evidence?

human dimension. What are they saying about this in Paris? Why do they say that?... and so on. The technical meaning of the passage hardly differs at all from that in a British book, but its historical and social significance to the French author was different, and there is an opening here for some discussion of the nature of scientific ideas. Data in a foreign language may seem daunting for pupils (and teachers) at first, more so than later experience justifies. Nevertheless, the teacher must judge the match of such a task to the age, experience and confidence of the pupils, and decide whether the task can be 'sold' to them as a worthwhile one, and how much support they may need in order to gain a feeling of success from it.

Statement 2 contains some very difficult language, but I think it is not appropriate to simplify it and replace it by teachers' words on paper. The result would too easily seem like something to be learned rather than something to be puzzled over. I would feel the same if the data page were part of a modern technical manual on car engine compression ratios. The place for simplification is in the *speech* of both pupils and teachers, where difficult expressions can be taken alongside their more everyday equivalents.[2]

Many lessons on Boyle's Law have no doubt been intended to have a structure of the kind I have described, dwelling on the appreciation of the idea. I think, however, that unless interpretation of meaning of the written word is advertised and proclaimed as the main purpose of the lesson, too much of the available time can be used in collecting figures from experimental equipment. The impact of the lesson then, is not of engaging the learners' minds with great scientific thoughts, but just of passing on authoritative knowledge.

Returning to the comparison of a science lesson and a literature lesson, probably there should be no fundamental difference, because in each case some person's meaning has to be sorted out and re-created in the minds of the learners. In a science lesson it is an advantage that we have access to tangible experience, but this cannot replace the interpretive work that must be done. Bench work should be primarily an aid to extracting the meaning from the words, and checking one's own interpretation of them. Pupils may seem to be checking Boyle's Law, but what they should be checking is their own idea of what Boyle meant, and how he came to that view.

Types of interpretive activity

In British schools, over-reliance on bench work may have passed its peak in the 1970s, when published schemes were characterized by long sequences of practical worksheet after practical worksheet. Moves to diversify learning activities are found in the more recent curriculum projects, and there is much talk of 'flexible learning and a *range* of teaching and learning strategies'. One guide for writers of new material for publication gives a list, of which the following is an abbreviated version.

In adult education or other sectors of the secondary school, such a list would not look at all strange, but for science teachers these activities are not so obviously right and necessary. 'Discussing ideas in small groups' surely lends itself to waffle,

Ways of learning: a checklist of (overlapping) approaches[3]

- by watching and listening
- by doing bench or field work, to a plan which someone else made for you
- by practical investigations which *you* plan, or help to plan
- by interpreting and evaluating data from charts, tables, graphs, etc.
- by tackling a technological problem, where you *try to design a solution*
- by *discussing ideas in a small group*
- *by writing – putting ideas together for an audience other than the teacher*
- by close, reflective reading
- by teaching: *presenting a short talk or a poster to explain ideas to other students*
- by *devising maps, diagrams and charts* to express and communicate ideas
- by *taking part in role-plays*, simulations, and games
- by manipulating ideas and information with a computer
- by searching through audio-tapes, slides and video resource materials
- by careful analysis of 'case-studies' of events outside school

and 'writing for an audience other than the teacher' sounds a bit peripheral, and not what pupils expect to do in science. As for drama and role-play, that might be nice for a change, but is it really learning science? And if someone suggests that pupils should prepare speeches for a debate, it definitely seems like an extra rather than a crucial part of the learning. Debates are associated with opinions rather than with the consolidation of factual knowledge – more suitable for current affairs than for a science lesson.

The non-bench activities, therefore, have a somewhat uncertain status, not quite accepted by pupils or teachers as part of the real learning of science, and for that reason they may not be exploited to the full. Sometimes they are recommended on the common-sense view that variety is a good thing, and the best way to avoid the boredom of repetitive routines. Although we do need variety, it would be a pity if these activities were seen only in that way. Part of my purpose in this chapter has been to express a rationale within which they can be seen to be more central to the learning. If pupils and their parents, as well as teachers, understand the need for interpretive effort, then the writing or the role-play will be used more positively for that purpose. To design a carefully thought-out flow chart on a poster, or to get ready to speak about it to the class, or to work out on paper how to explain to a younger child what (say) 'pasteurization' is – these are exactly the tasks which make an appropriately high level of demand on the pupils, and require interpretive effort of them. With care, they also enable teachers to provide a supportive environment in which to encourage that effort. Diversified activities are not luxuries and extras, but necessary to the process of getting pupils to grapple with the ideas of science. Without them, I suggest that the bench work will continue to alienate as many pupils as it excites, and to leave others quite untouched by these ideas.

There is, however, the question of professional skills. A science teacher who can get an oscilloscope to work does not necessarily feel confident in organizing a role-play, or in motivating pupils to set out their written reports for a non-scientific audience. Such skills were formerly outside the province of the science teacher, and although they are now being learned, it is not in any systematic way. They are self-taught by enthusiasts and passed on slowly to others.[4] There are many helpful techniques which will either have to be assimilated into the repertoire of science teachers' skills, or else we shall need more differentiation of teachers' roles, with some members of the team specializing more in preparing pupils to work over ideas while others provide the back-up of well-organized practical experience.

Kinds of resource material

In Britain, the most extensive collection of resources to stimulate alternative activities is found in the SATIS units – *Science and Technology in Society*.[5] They offer a great diversity of activity and place in the hands of pupils data which are both more problematic than commonly found in a science textbook, and of much greater human interest. Using them generally involves much more talking, discussing and interpreting, relative to the standard bench work. Does such material automatically switch teachers and learners into a different style of language use, or does the rationale have to be made explicit? Many SATIS activities can be justified on several different grounds, not the least of which is that they are fun, but often the gains might be greater if parents and pupils were quite clear that (say) a technological problem is being set in order for the pupils to clarify their understanding of the relevant scientific concepts in their own words. A few examples of activities are listed in Table 14.1.

Most of these units provide material which requires the readers to get at the writer's intention, and to re-express it for themselves. They are a direct stimulus to word work as I have described it, and they make it legitimate for the learner to have a point of view based on a clear understanding of relevant science, in a way which textbooks and instruction sheets do not. This is one of the reasons why a technological problem is sometimes a better starting point for learning some science than is direct study of the science itself. Technological problems are not closed-ended, and it is usually clear that more than one solution is acceptable, so it is easier for a learner to put forward an idea which draws on scientific knowledge, without fear of looking foolish. It is also easier for the teacher to be open to varied suggestions, whereas when direct discussion of a scientific problem is attempted it is hard for a teacher to avoid the trap of searching the class for the 'expected' answer, and greeting others with such faint praise that genuine discussion dies out.

SATIS-type activities will not automatically lead into the clarification of the full vocabulary and network of concepts in the related scientific topics, unless pupils and teacher approach them with that intention in mind. They are, however, a way

Table 14.1 Examples of SATIS activities

Title of SATIS unit	Activities
The limestone enquiry	Analysing technical data, identifying by discussion the relevant facts and issues for consideration at a Planning Enquiry about a quarry extension discussion of briefing papers for groups making representations at the enquiry, presenting ideas in a role-play of it.
X-rays and patients	Analysing technical documents; selecting and presenting information in a form suitable for patients in a waiting room.
The label at the back	A survey at home of fabrics and their uses; collating the information and presenting a summary, with explanation.
The re-trial of Galileo	Studying role-description cards, identifying ideas important to original participants; discussing each role, then playing them in a dramatised re-enactment of the trial.

of engaging the minds of the learners, placing them in positions of initiative in relation to ideas, and giving them a different concept of the part played by their own use of language in their learning.

Maintaining the learner's freedom

Freedom of interpretation is a key feature of good resource materials. There should be enough doubt in them to set the pupil's mind moving, and keep it moving, and also it should be legitimate for the doubt to lead to more than one acceptable conclusion, so that anyone may make reasoned estimates of the meaning without fear of being totally wrong. Under those circumstances, language will naturally be used to explore what is meant, what was intended, and what we now understand. Teaching and learning will involve a degree of negotiation of the meaning: 'This is what I think is meant; how do you and other people understand it?' Some activities designed to support inexperienced readers work by artificially increasing the amount of uncertainty about what is being said.[6] In this connection, the power of narrative material about science seems to have been neglected. We know that a story can hold average readers much more easily than other kinds of writing, and Bruner[7] points out that narrative prose exerts its effect by recruiting the reader's imagination and triggering presupposition about what may be coming next, or what underlies what has already been said. The reader's mind is working on what is *not* present on the page, as well as what is there. The lack of explicit spelling out of every aspect is the feature which makes it possible for the reader to enter into and engage with the story. It offers freedom to do that, whereas explicitness would reduce the freedom, and hence the degree of involvement with the text. Perhaps one reason why a factual account of a scientific topic in a textbook often fails to hold attention is that it does not leave enough doubt, or lead the reader to fill it out from his or her own thought. There are not enough cues to uncertain possibilities to keep the average reader thinking ahead. Of course, scientific books make a virtue of spelling things out, and leaving no doubt. Here is one of several places where features appropriate to science itself are not so appropriate for education.

For the future we may need two types of reading material – one to encourage the exploration of scientific ideas, the other to form a reliable quick guide to their structure. The traditional textbook is the latter only. There is also a case for making a clear division between two different kinds of lesson – one called 'Exploring scientific ideas' and the other 'Learning the systematics of science'. In the first of these, the freedom of the learner could be preserved absolutely, with a rule that there are no assumptions about 'right answers'; we are just exploring what people have thought and said about scientific matters. The teacher's role could be unambiguously one of encouraging and supporting speech and writing by the pupils, and the resources for these lessons would be of the types already discussed. In the second kind of lesson it would then be more legitimate to present the currently-accepted structures of thought through clear exposition, without encroaching on the freedom of the learner to think. A relatively old-fashioned style of textbook, as a grammar of the subject, would also have its rightful place in that second kind of lesson, so avoiding the confusions of recent years when so-called 'textbooks' have attempted to do too many things at once.

Support for the interpretive writer

What happens to pupils' writing is of crucial importance if the habit of using language interpretively is to be established. The individual learner's idea of what writing is for can be extensively shaped by the attitudes of the teacher, and what the teacher explicitly or implicitly encourages. Teachers therefore need to be aware of the power of their taken-for-granted routines. For pupils to make full use of writing for the purpose of sorting out meaning probably requires the system of intermittent dialogue between teacher and pupil about what they write, a system which has been fully described elsewhere.[8]

Factors which matter include:

1   What the teacher does with pupils' writing when it has been completed.
2   The amount of time spent beforehand on discussing the purpose of the writing, its possible form and content, expectations in terms of style, and reasons for these.
3   The writer's sense of audience while attempting to set down ideas.
4   The extent to which the teacher allows and encourages a variety of styles.

These are all deeply affected by the teacher's beliefs about what the writing is for. An extended account of these beliefs has been published by Douglas Barnes.[8]

Social and emotional climate

None of what I have described in this chapter can occur unless appropriate social relationships are established between teacher and pupils and amongst the pupils themselves. Much of this chapter has been about the cognitive functions of language, and I had better acknowledge therefore, that in the classroom it is the emotional functions which have priority. What, for example is happening in the following exchanges?

Teacher: Gather round here please… One at a time now… Listen to Vijav… I think you can make a good job of the graph, can't you?

Pupils: Do we have to do it now?… I'm no good at graphs… [and later] Hey, Miss, it really works!

It would be silly to seek the importance of what is said here just in terms of the instruction or information that seems to pass. Questions of feeling, of a learner's self-concept, and of organization and social control, are threaded through the words; they remind us that language has many functions in addition to the interpretation of ideas.[9] At the simplest level, there is often a direct clash in the classroom between using language to encourage thought, and using it for social control. For example, when teachers are helping pupils to elaborate their first thoughts, and to gain confidence in reasoning out an idea, they use long attentive pauses,[10] yet a common and successful technique for the management of large groups involves a kind of dominance strategy with very short pauses in the teacher's delivery!

To adopt an interpretive view of language requires a certain kind of social relationship between teacher and taught which we could describe as one of enhanced respect for the learner and the learner's ideas, so the only possible strategy is to accompany him or her on a journey in thought. As a teacher, one needs to have rather less confidence in the obviousness and rightness of one's own way, or the textbook way of explaining the phenomenon under discussion. And of course, the first task in teaching is not to arrange the subject matter, but to gather the minds of the learners, to a point where one can say:

Well, Vijay, and Alan, and Mary, what do you think these people had in mind when they put it that way?

Notes

1 Boyle's speculations: See Marie Boas Hall (1965) *Robert Boyle on Natural Philosophy – An Essay with Selections from his Writings,* Bloomington: Indiana University Press.

2 Is simplification of language desirable in science education? My view is that 'the language problem' of the science classroom is not adequately solved by adjusting 'readability levels' downwards, or by trying to avoid technical terms. It is more to do with an absence of encouragement for flexibility of expression, for putting the same idea in more than one way. Ideally this flexibility should be shown first in speech, and then not discouraged in writing. A word like 'elastic' means more when 'squashable', 'stretchable', 'resilient' and 'compressible' are used alongside it, rather than as a replacement for it, and of course they show that there is something about the material which we

are trying to interpret, not just to label. Teachers can show the value of this flexibility first by practising for themselves the habit of using both technical and less technical phrasing, and then by accepting and understanding the learner's struggles in the same direction.

Some degree of difficulty in the material to be read is actually a help in providing incentive for the learners to 'decode' it and make a restatement in their own words. To translate everything into simpler language also carries a risk of being condescending. Pupils are entitled to expect that they will be taught how to cope with technical, and even abstruse, language, and we should get them into the habit of doing so. Where pupils are very unconfident readers, the best strategy seems to me not to re-write ideas for them, but to select more suitable written materials from real life, which are just a little above their present level of coping. If the label on the new shoe says '100 per cent synthetic materials' or even 'polybutadiene' that is something to be grappled with, not avoided.

3   Ways of learning: Andrew Hunt (1991), personal communication. The list on which I have drawn was prepared for writers of learning episodes within the publication programme of the Nuffield Modular Science Project.

4   Professional skills for the management of interpretive activities: a programme of professional development in this field would involve workshops on the management of writing, reading, role-play, etc. The manner of focusing thought and feeling on the occasions where these activities are to work well is not the same as getting the class ready for practical work at the bench. Professional development for this work would also have to provide background in the history of ideas, which many science teachers have not got from their own higher education.

5   SATIS units are published by the Association for Science Education, Hatfield. (i) John Holman (ed.) (1986) *Science and Technology in Society: Teaching Units and Teacher's Guide.* ASE, Hatfield; (ii) Andrew Hunt (ed.) (1990) *SATIS 16–19,* from the same source.

6   Structured reading activities: increasing uncertainty in order to engage the reader's active search for meaning. Two of the best-known activities which exaggerate the uncertainty to a level which will give readers' minds a more direct task to work on are:

- Sequencing a scrambled text and arguing the reasons for that sequence, and
- reconstructing missing portions – not just odd words, but larger sections as when (say) the edge of the paper has been destroyed or 'lost'.

These and other such activities have become more widely known since the work of the Reading for Learning Project and they are called DARTs (Directed Activities Related to Text). See Davies, F. and Greene, T. (1979) *Reading for Learning in Science,* University of Nottingham School of Education. Both the quoted methods offer the interest of a detective hunt, and both can be powerful because they require the reader *to build up a general idea of what is being said,* and from this to predict the missing parts, or argue what the order of presentation must have been. Such devices must be used sensitively, and the reconstruction game should not be confused with the very different process of asking pupils to fill in missing words here and there, which frequently stimulates hardly any general interpretive effort. Also, because the modified passages are artificially contrived, they could quickly pall in over-use. A better long-term support to active engagement with reading would be to break the monopoly now held by informative non-fiction, and offer more science books and booklets which have a strong narrative thread, as well as more reading materials of the SATIS type which come from sources other than books.

7   Narrative prose and its effect on the reader's freedom of interpretation: See Jerome Bruner (1986) *Actual Minds, Possible Worlds,* Harvard University Press, e.g. p. 25, and also Chapter 9, 'The language of education'.

8   Support for the interpretive writer, dialogue marking, etc.: See Peter Benton (1981) 'Writing – how it is received' and Owen Watkins (1981) 'Writing – how it is set', both in C. R. Sutton (ed.) *Communicating in the Classroom,* Hodder and Stoughton, tenth impression, 1991.

Teachers' beliefs about the purposes of writing: See Yanina Sheeran and Douglas Barnes (1991) *School Writing,* Open University Press, especially Chapter 2, 'Scientific language'.

9   The many functions of language. See David Crystal in *The Cambridge Encyclopaedia of Language* (Cambridge University Press, 1987). He discusses a range of functions for language, amongst which are the following, in my order, not his: recording the facts; as an instrument of thought; as

an expression of identity; for control of reality; for social interaction; emotional expression; phonetic pleasure.

Scientific language is often seen as mainly for recording facts, whereas I have been giving more prominence to its use as an instrument of thought. Its role in developing a sense of social identity for members of the scientific community, and for pupils in a classroom, deserves much more attention.

10   Language for social control: For an account of the role of attentive pausing, see Mary Budd Rowe (1973) 'Science silence and sanctions' in *Teaching Science as Continuous Enquiry*, McGraw-Hill.

15 Look! No hands!

Practical science experiences in museums

Janette Griffin

If we wish [students] to develop their own judgement we should encourage them to use it. If we wish them to trust their senses and observe accurately, we cannot at the same time tell them 'what they should have seen'. If we wish them to be interested in finding answers to their own questions, we cannot hope to train them by working on our questions. ... The ability to see the relevance of something known to something new is not a matter of 'intelligence' or 'effort' or 'depth of understanding', but of experience, and of the specific strategies, born of experience, that a learner possesses for generalising and extending their knowledge modules into unknown territory.

(Claxton 1993: 206)

Introduction

School excursions to museums (and I use 'museum' as a generic term to include science museums, science centres, natural history museums, zoos and gardens) can form an integrated and innovative component of school practical learning in science. Museums are informal learning environments where teachers have limited control over the specific ideas or experiences with which the students are engaged. For school groups to make successful use of museums as learning resources, appropriate teaching and learning approaches and strategies involving a shift from task orientation to student-centred learning orientation, are required. By allowing student learning to happen in a natural way, that is, by allowing personal interest and curiosity to drive it, not only will students be gaining more from their excursion but they will also be practising scientific investigative processes. Incorporation of the excursion into school-based investigations renders the purposes for the visit clearly apparent, and gives students a goal to achieve back at school using the information gathered at the museum. This chapter explores how museum visits can be used to meet three major purposes for practical work, and introduces a framework to facilitate students' learning in museums.

Practical experience in school science

Practical work is an integral component of primary and secondary school science in many countries. The term 'practical work' has many manifestations, however it has often come to mean little more than hands-on activity which has something to do with science. The emphasis on the use of our hands and the insistence on the need for a laboratory, rather than emphasis on the learning processes, has curtailed opportunities for giving students a full range of experience with the practices of science and its vital role in our lives. School practical work is commonly teacher-directed busy work, poorly planned and with an unclear purpose. As several authors have suggested, it has too often become distant from scientific investigation (Claxton 1991; Hodson 1994; Klopfer 1990; Nott 1996; White 1996).

Good curriculum design may be assisted by regarding practical work as having three major purposes:

- to deepen understanding of scientific ideas;
- to experience scientific processes;
- to acquire scientific research skills.

Hodson (1996) refers to these three goals as: learning science; learning about science; and learning to do science. Underlying these purposes is a further set of goals including self-motivation, stimulation of creativity, recognition of the relevance of scientific understanding, and independent thought. Furthermore, as Woolnough and Allsop (1985) point out, practical work can be regarded as comprising *experiences, exercises* and *investigations*. By cross-matching these three 'styles' or strategies with the three main purposes, a useful mix of student activities can be achieved. One of many possible matches leads to a programme of practical work consisting of:

1   Having experiences, which facilitate understanding of scientific ideas.
2   Carrying out investigations using scientific processes.
3   Conducting exercises which lead to acquisition of scientific research skills.

This combination of programme components provides a platform for discussing the utilization of museum environments for practical work. This chapter addresses each in turn, following a brief look at the nature of learning in museums.

Learning in museums

Museums can be considered as informal settings for learning. They are non-directed, exploratory, voluntary and personal, and proceed through curiosity, observation, activity, a sense of wonder, speculation and theory testing (Ramey-Gassert *et al.* 1994). Museums are informal settings where visitors are invited to choose their experiences, where ideas may not necessarily be met in sequence, where learning may be fragmentary and unstructured, where learning is collaborative. Learning in informal settings is driven by curiosity and maintained by meeting a challenge and gaining satisfaction. Personal ownership of the learning is a fundamental component. The learning strategies that occur naturally in a museum setting reflect those described by a constructivist theory of learning.

> the constructivist view emphasises the active and imaginative dimensions of learning and discovery.
>
> (Russell 1995)

The active processes of constructing meaning from sensory input and curious observation are, at the same time, the essence of practical science (Hein 1996). Museums, places of *musing,* or of 'gazing meditatively or wonderingly' (Macquarie Dictionary 1981), are ideal settings for active, contemplative learning. While museums and science centres may not come readily to mind when thinking of school practical science, I would like to explore their potential for meeting the three components of the practical work programme described above. In the following section, I shall discuss how an understanding of the features of museums and museum learning can be used to extend students' experiences with the components of practical work.

Learning through practical experience in museums

Having experiences which deepen understanding of scientific ideas

Practical work may provide students with experiences that reinforce theoretical ideas they encounter, and may help them to make sense of their world. Hodson (1994) reminds us that the first step towards making sense of our world is familiarization with that world. Sense-making is determined by our experiences, specifically experiences which are not merely events which happen, but events which connect with other experiences to make things meaningful (Dewey 1958). The unique and vital contribution that a museum makes is the opportunity to confront the 'real thing', and in many cases to experience the range and variety of 'real things' through sensory interaction. Thus, visitors can use museum objects to extend their perceived realities and pre-existing mental constructs (Dierking 1996). However, since visitors *select* their experiences and encounters, they are likely to develop a wide range of perceptions and understandings of the world (Bentley and Watts 1994).

Learning is a very individual process and museums provide good opportunities for people to learn independently and by choice. While exhibits are generally structured and sequenced, few visitors use the displays in this way (Falk and Dierking 1992). Although visitors may be aware of the structure and this may form a background to their viewing, they generally select what they view based on attraction to particular displays. This attraction may be related to size, colour or activity level, or it may be a much more personal matter, where the exhibit has some elements to which the visitor personally relates, or in which they have a particular interest. For whatever reason, it arouses their curiosity. Museums incorporate a range of opportunities to accommodate a variety of learning styles and strategies. For example, most museums and science centres include a mix of static displays, demonstrations, hands-on exhibits, interactive exhibits, videos and multi-media interactives, so that visitors can choose the styles of displays as well as the content with which they wish to engage. In this way, they can readily accommodate to personal learning styles and interests.

Finally, the understanding of scientific ideas can involve two levels of learning, which Golley (1988) terms the analytical or microscopic and the synthetic or macroscopic. On the one hand, museums provide unique opportunities to examine objects or specimens closely to understand detail such as animals' claw shapes or other adaptations. On the other hand, museums allow appreciation of the big picture by providing a wide range of specimens or objects to allow comparisons, trends and patterns to be appraised. More importantly, museum exhibits are generally the results of dialogue between practising scientists, communication and learning experts providing a deep and considered approach to the topic. The days of simply displaying a set of objects with little context are largely past, and most exhibits have a major and important message to deliver. So the detail is set within a physical and an intellectual context.

Carrying out investigations using scientific processes

As argued above, emphasis on the use of our hands and the perceived need for a laboratory have narrowed opportunities to give students experience with the processes of science. To help students gain experience and understanding of scientific processes they need time to play and experiment both with ideas and with their hands, to ask their own questions and then seek answers. Genuine investigation demands time for contemplation and synthesis of prior experiences with newly-encountered evidence. Time is needed for students to consider whether results 'add up, make sense and feel right' (Siu 1975) and, if they don't, to investigate why. Students also need the opportunity to recognize that scientific investigation can incorporate a variety of data sources, both first- and second-hand, and that consideration and incorporation of existing views in the development of one's own ideas is not only a basis of learning, but is an integral part of the scientific process. Museums are reference sources that go beyond normal classroom resources. Museums can present the progression of scientific ideas through comparisons between real objects, such as the development of knowledge in astronomy through examination of instruments used. Current scientific research techniques and processes, in areas such as genetics, are exhibited through case studies of practising scientists. The tentative and changing nature of scientific understanding can be grasped through displays of changing views on human evolution. Providing students with access to the processes by which scientists have generated new knowledge equips them to further their personal investigative learning endeavours (Hodson 1994; 1996).

Museums provide insights into 'ideas related to the collection, validation, representation and interpretation of evidence' (Gott and Duggan 1996: 793). The displays themselves offer opportunities for students to gather data in a way different from that in the laboratory. They foster close and detailed observations, comparisons and deciphering of patterns in data. They allow the testing of theories and predictions through direct observation. Natural learning processes in museums incorporate sharing and communicating ideas and the constant raising of questions. Museums can encourage the creative aspects of science, such as hypothesis construction and experimental design using the breadth of data presented (Bloom and Powell 1984).

The opportunity to explore using our hands and our minds is provided by museums in numerous and varied ways. In some museums, this is done by placing interactive exhibits in the context of theoretical or historical displays such as, perhaps, a maritime theme. Other institutions present a range of interactive displays with a strong central theme that lends itself to manipulation, for example transport, or some biological themes. Some museums have developed exhibits that concentrate on particular scientific processes such as observation. Still others have incorporated environmental studies in laboratory, display and field contexts.

One of the criticisms levelled at science centres has been the apparently unstructured play that takes place. Yet learning, and particularly science learning, is itself a playful process. Semper elaborates:

> play is rarely considered a significant part of learning. ... But play is a serious matter in science education. It leads to the development of skills in observation and experimentation and the testing of ideas, and it provides an opportunity to independently discover order in nature.
>
> (Semper 1990: 54)

Learning involves toying with ideas in an attempt to reduce complexities until simple and elegant generalizations emerge. It involves time to explore and become thoroughly familiar with objects and ideas (Duckworth 1992). Playing with our minds and playing with our hands are not mutually exclusive activities. One can, and often does, lead to the other. In developing the Exploratorium in San Francisco, Oppenheimer (1968: 174) considered that science museums provide 'an environment in which people can ask questions and answer them by their own experimentation'. They offer an opportunity for students to adventure, take risks and learn through failure (Hodgkin 1985).

Conducting exercises which lead to acquisition of scientific research skills

Several authors (Harlen 1985; 1992; Sheppard 1993) describe skills involved in scientific inquiry which are directly applicable to learning in a museum: observing and exploring, raising questions, proposing ways to answer questions, examining, comparing, analysing, finding patterns in observation, evaluating, classifying, applying ideas in new situations, gathering information, recording observations systematically, using evidence critically and logically, communicating information in various and appropriate ways.

In museums, students can develop perceptual skills that teach them how to gather information from objects and experiences. They can have meaningful learning experiences by allowing the objects to be the primary means of communication (Sheppard,1993). Duncan Cameron, quoted in Voris *et al.* (1986), adds:

> Surely the goal [of museum visits] is to open up the world of sight and sound and touch for each child, by sharpening his perceptual skills, and to make him [sic] sensitive to new sources of data in the world around him. It is to develop each child's inductive skills so that he can form more meaningful relationships with his environment.

The skill of selecting and recording relevant information in a useful manner can be practised particularly effectively in a museum setting. Museums offer a large range of information, which may seem overwhelming to students. Helping students to recognize the way in which this information is classified or displayed will in turn help them to learn how to select, sort, classify, code, synthesize and analyse information and, finally, how to communicate it. Tasks involving these skills will teach students that classification and recording of data can be based on clear and stated criteria, and that the methods will be influenced by the purpose for which it will be used, such as to show relationships between animals, or chronological development of technologies.

Observations and data gathering in a museum can lead to further questions for investigation. In some instances, these questions may be answered through further examination of the objects and information available at the museum. Alternatively, these questions may be answered through experimental processes carried out back at school.

Facilitating learning in a museum

Successful management of museum experiences, which address these three components of practical learning programmes, will help students to recognize that science is not just a school subject occurring in a laboratory. For this to occur, teachers need to take an active role in facilitating appropriate learning strategies, which allow students to benefit from the full potential of museum resources. Previous research has shown that teachers in both primary and secondary schools in Sydney have a poor understanding of ways to facilitate learning during excursions to museums (Griffin 1996; 1998; Griffin and Symington 1997). Learning opportunities are hampered by over-use of a task-oriented approach in which teachers concentrate more on control and discipline than on student learning. In response, a framework has been developed for school–museum learning with a theoretical base in research into school visits to museums, family group behaviour in museums, and social constructivist approaches to teaching and learning. Following trials with teachers from a range of schools, and subsequent modifications, this framework was called School–Museum Integrated Learning Experiences in Science or SMILES.

SMILES involves students bringing their own chosen questions or 'areas of inquiry' to the museum, and ensures that students have considerable control over their learning, within parameters provided by the teacher. It ensures that the students and teachers have a clear, shared purpose for their visit. SMILES rests on three Guiding Principles for teachers:

- Integrate school and museum learning.
- Provide conditions for self-directed learning.
- Facilitate learning strategies appropriate to the setting.

The first Guiding Principle for creating effective conditions for learning is that the museum visit is embedded in a school-based learning unit. If students are conducting an ecological study of their local environment, for example, then a visit to a natural history museum is one part of the investigation. If the students are studying work and machines then a visit to a science museum or science centre is an integral component. By placing the museum visit firmly in a school-based learning unit, clear learning purposes for the visit can be established. In the first example, the students may wish to investigate the animals' adaptations for feeding, or the relative sizes of the prey and predators in their region, or gather data on the survival requirements of each of the animals they know to be in their environment. This information can then be placed back into the context of their local environment and used to help answer their investigation questions. For example, it will help students to build a food web for their environment, or answer questions about the relative numbers of different species found in the field investigations. In the second example, the students may find answers to questions about the applications of different simple machines in everyday equipment. They may be able to make comparisons between the use of these principles in present and past times and then consider why there have been changes. If there are hands-on exhibits, they may be able to experience the different effort required to lift a very heavy object using a range of pulleys; or examine a cut-away of a complex machine to determine the use of a range of simple machine principles. Further questions can be raised which may spark investigations back at school. Can they design a better version of the machine they have seen?

The importance of a clear purpose shared by teachers and students is also discussed by Hart *et al.* (2000) with reference to school-based practical work. In both their research and that described here, teachers were not always aware of the importance of this aspect and the strong, positive impact that clearly articulating the intent or purpose for specific practical science activities has on student learning.

The second Guiding Principle is to give the students as much ownership of their learning as is possible, and this is can be achieved by providing conditions that allow for self-directed learning. Students are encouraged to develop their own areas of inquiry to take with them to the museum – perhaps selecting a particular group of animals to investigate for the ecological study example given above, or a particular set of machines for the 'work and machines' study. Alternatively, they may choose to investigate more widely – for example, protection from predators by *all* the animals they know to be in their environment, or investigation of the conditions under which one machine is more efficient than another. Allowing students to select their own area of investigation as the basis for their viewing provides personal incentive and ownership of learning.

Among the most common concerns expressed by students in the study of current practices was that they had little control over the length of time they could investigate a particular exhibit – they either were forced to stay too long, or they didn't have long enough to see what they wanted (Griffin 1998). Once students have seen what they want in a particular room, they naturally become restless and off-task behaviours may emerge. The learner-centred climate of SMILES allows students to move where and when they wish within constraints required for safety and supervision, and to use whatever form of learning they wish (e.g. watching a video, using hands-on displays, reading, drawing, writing, talking with classmates, and so on). This can be managed in several ways. A successful option is to have sufficient adults accompanying the group to allow small groups to operate independently.

The third Guiding Principle is to address the environmental needs of the students. A museum is an unfamiliar learning environment for most students. Discussing with students the purpose of the institution, the roles of people who work there, and the method of specimen and display preparation, will all reduce distractions on arrival and focus students' attention. In addition, physical orientation to the venue before and on arrival will help students quickly to locate the parts of the venue that they wish to visit, reduce the possibility of students becoming lost, and assist them in finding the restrooms and refreshment areas.

Research into family group behaviours in museums reveals that the majority of groups take a break after no more than an hour, they need to sit down when possible, and they talk to each other a great deal (Falk and Dierking 2000). These physical needs must be built in to school excursions as well.

Further, observations of school groups in my research, revealed 'waves of concentration' by the students (Griffin 1998). There was an apparent need for 'mental' rests, in addition to physical rests. Allowing students periods of superficial viewing appeared to facilitate a return to more focused and concentrated learning activity within a short time-period. This observation, coupled with those of family groups, suggests that teachers need to allow their students short physical and mental breaks, rather than cajoling them 'to keep working' and 'not to waste time'. It may be that by 'keeping on working' they will, in fact, waste more learning time, as their overall capacity to synthesize information may decline.

The learners' inquiry approach used in SMILES embodies the scientific process of inquiry and learning. It involves the four key steps of developing questions, gathering data, analysing data and synthesis of information (Allard 1994). One of the most significant outcomes of its application to school–museum visits, was clear recognition by the students of their own level of learning. Further, the majority of students interviewed talked not only about their learning, but also about their enjoyment of learning. Many commented that they enjoyed the excursion because they were learning *and* having fun. While laboratory-based practical work is often claimed to have motivational value, research support is somewhat ambiguous (White 1996). By contrast, the motivational value of experiences based on SMILES is clear.

Conclusion

There is a direct link between self-driven learning in museums and practical learning of science.

Like all learning, that which takes place in museums, whether we are looking for 'practical' learning or cognitive learning, is influenced by the learner's prior experience, current conceptual understanding, expectations, and attitudes. In the same way that providing students with a recipe to follow and then recording the correct result from the blackboard is anathema to scientific investigation, taking students to a museum without a clear, shared purpose, student ownership of the learning, and a goal to achieve with the gathered information, may be a waste of the time and money invested in school excursions.

By incorporating the three Guiding Principles of SMILES – integration of school and museum learning; provision of conditions for self-directed ownership of learning; and facilitation of learning strategies appropriate to the setting – the three key parameters of *purpose, ownership,* and *choice* will ensure that students will be learning science, learning about science and learning to do science on school excursions to museums. Moreover, if students can be encouraged to enjoy and to recognize resources like museums as interesting places for life-long learning, then we can help students to see science and practical science as something beyond a school subject.

References

Bentley, D. and Watts, M. (1994) *Primary Science and Technology*, Buckingham: Open University Press.

Bloom, J. N. and Powell, E. A. (1984) *Museums for a New Century*, Washington, DC: American Association of Museums.

Claxton, G. (1991) *Educating the Inquiring Mind*, London: Harvester Wheatsheaf.

Claxton, G. (1993) 'The interplay of values and research in science education', in P. J. Black and A. M. Lucas (eds) *Children's Informal Ideas in Science*, London: Routledge, pp. 190–207.

Dewey, J. (1958) *Experience and Nature*, New York: Dover Publications Inc.

Dierking, L. D. (1996) 'Contemporary theories of learning', in G. Durbin (ed.) *Developing Museum Exhibitions for Lifelong Learning*, London: Museums and Galleries Commission, pp. 25–9.

Duckworth, E. (1992) 'Museum visitors and the development of understanding', in S. K. Nichols (ed.) *Patterns and Practice: Selections from the Journal of Museum Education*, Washington, DC: Museum Education Roundtable, pp. 168–73.

Falk, J. H. and Dierking, L. (1992) *The Museum Experience*, Washington, DC: Whalesback Books.

Falk, J. H. and Dierking, L. (2000) *Learning from Museums*, Walnut Creek, CA: AltaMira Press.

Golley, F. (1988) 'Great ideas in science – the ecosystem', in P. Heltne and L. Marquardt (eds) *Science Learning in the Informal Setting*, Chicago: Chicago Academy of Sciences, pp. 99–108.

Gott, R. and Duggan, S. (1996) 'Practical work: its role in the understanding of evidence in science', *International Journal of Science Education* 18(7): 791–806.

Griffin J. M. (1996) 'Museums are educational institutions but are they always places of learning?' in M. Anderson, A. Delroy and D. Tout-Smith (eds) *Identity, Icons and*

Artefacts: Proceedings of the Inaugural Museums Australia Conference, Fremantle, November 1994, Perth: Museums Australia, pp. 99–102.

Griffin J. M. (1998) 'School–museum integrated learning experiences in science: a learning journey', unpublished Ph.D. thesis, University of Technology, Sydney.

Griffin, J. M. and Symington, D. J. (1997) 'Moving from task-oriented to learning-oriented strategies on school excursions to museums', *Science Education* 81(6): 763–79.

Harlen, W. (1985) *Teaching and Learning Primary Science*, London: Harper and Row.

Harlen, W. (1992) *The Teaching of Science*, London: David Fulton Publishers.

Hart, C., Mulhall, P., Berry, A., Loughean, J., and Gunstone, R. (2000) 'What is the purpose of this experiment? Or can students learn something from doing experiments?', *Journal of Research in Science Teaching* 37(7).

Hein, G. E. (1996) 'Constructivist learning theory', in G. Durbin (ed.) *Developing Museum Exhibitions for Lifelong Learning*, London: Museums and Galleries Commission, pp. 30–4.

Hodgkin, R. A. (1985) *Playing and Exploring: Education Through the Discovery of Order*, London: Methuen.

Hodson, D. (1994) 'Redefining and reorienting practical work in school science', in R. Levinson (ed.) *Teaching Science*, London: Routledge, pp. 159–63.

Hodson, D. (1996) 'Practical work in school science: exploring some directions for change', *International Journal of Science Education*, 18(7): 755–60.

Klopfer, L. E. (1990) 'Learning scientific enquiry in the student laboratory', in E. Hegarty-Hazel (ed.) *The Student Laboratory and the Science Curriculum*, London: Routledge, pp. 89–96.

Macquarie Dictionary (1981) Sydney: Macquarie Library.

Nott, M. (1996) 'When the black box springs open: practical work in schools and the nature of science', *International Journal of Science Education* 18(7): 807–18.

Oppenheimer, F. (1968) 'The role of science museums', in E. Larrabee (ed.) *Museums and Education*, Washington, DC: Smithsonian Institute Press, pp. 167–78.

Ramey-Gassert, L., Walberg, H. J. I. and Walberg, H. J. (1994) 'Re-examining connections: museums as science learning environments', *Science Education* 78(4): 345–63.

Russell, T. (1995) 'The enquiring visitor: useable learning theory for museum contexts', *Journal of Education in Museums* 16: 19–21.

Semper, R. J. (1990) 'Science museums as environments for learning', *Physics Today* 90(11): 50–6.

Sheppard, B. (1993) 'Aspects of a successful field trip', in B. Sheppard (ed.) *Building Museum and School Partnerships,* Washington: American Association of Museums.

Siu, R. G. H. (1975) 'The art of Chinese baseball and research management', *Research Management* 75(1): 15–18.

Voris, H., Sedzielarz, M. and Blackmon, C. (1986) *Teach the Mind, Touch the Spirit*, Chicago: Field Museum of Natural History.

White, R. T. (1996) 'The link between the laboratory and learning', *International Journal of Science Education* 18(7): 761–74.

Woolnough, B. and Allsop, T. (1985) *Practical Work in Science*, Cambridge: Cambridge University Press.

16 Science education

A gender perspective

Patricia Murphy

Introduction

The issue of gender and science education has been debated for over three decades. In the 1970s and 1980s the main concern was with females' access, participation and achievement in science. In the 1990s, the concern shifted to focus on male underachievement and the general decline in interest in science amongst pupils, post-16. A frequently cited quotation in writings about science learning is that of Ausubel's:

> If I had to reduce all of educational psychology to just one principle, I would say this: The most important single factor influencing learning is what the learner already knows. Ascertain this and teach him (sic) accordingly.
>
> (Ausubel 1968: iv)

Whilst this principle remains an important one in any constructivist approach to teaching and learning, it fails to take account of the relationship between the social world and the learner. As Rogoff puts it, learners 'are active participants in understanding their world, building on both genetic and socio-cultural constraints and resources' (Rogoff 1990: 37). If we take developments in understanding about learning seriously then we cannot understand individuals' thinking apart from the contexts in which it appears; contexts in which peoples' experiences and values are significantly shaped by their gender.

To consider the impact of gender on pupils' engagement and achievement in science it is essential to understand how gender mediates their thinking, both within and without school and the relationship between these two sources of learning. The evidence referred to in this chapter is concerned, in the main, with group differences. Whilst a focus on group differences fails to take account of the variation amongst girls and boys it helps to *illuminate* the nature of gender mediation and its impact. The chapter addresses three questions:

- do gender differences in uptake and achievement in science and technology-related courses exist?

- what are the sources of these differences and how do they mediate teaching and learning in schools?
- if there are existing and anticipated gender-related problems in science education what are these, which pupils are likely to be affected by them and how can they be addressed?

Achievement trends

International and national surveys

Evidence of a gender problem in science education came from surveys that compared performance across nations or across regions within a nation. Between the 1970s and 1980s, two IEA studies (International Association for the Evaluation of Educational Achievement) established a gender gap in favour of boys in all branches of science, and the gap was found to increase with age. The performance gap was greater in the tests of physical science. Boys also showed more positive attitudes towards science than girls and reported a higher level of interest in science-related activities. The overall gap in science performance was attributed to lower performance by girls on items which tested understanding rather than recall of science (Keeves 1986; 1992). The USA National Assessment of Educational Progress (NAEP) science surveys replicated the IEA pattern of performance (NAEP 1978). The British Columbia Science Surveys (BCSS) (Hobbs *et al.* 1979), however, found boys ahead of girls only on tests of physics and measurement skills.

The national surveys of science performance carried out in the 1980s in England, Wales and Northern Ireland for pupils aged 11, 13 and 15 years (Assessment of Performance Unit (APU)) also found that gender differences increased with age. These surveys, unlike others, included a broad range of test items that assessed scientific process skills and procedural understanding as well as concept application. The findings showed that, across the ages, the performance of boys and girls depended on the construct assessed, with girls outperforming boys on practical tests of making and interpreting observations, whilst boys showed superior performance in the application of physical science concepts (DES 1988a; 1998b; 1989). The attitude questionnaire showed girls' interests lying in biological and medical applications and boys' interests involving physics and technological applications.

The third International Mathematics and Science Study reported that for pupils aged 12–13 years and 14–15 years, there were no statistically significant differences except in chemistry, and then only for 12–13 year olds (Keys *et al.* 1996). A review of USA studies of science performance (Willingham and Cole 1997) also suggests that a decrease in the performance gap between girls and boys has occurred over the last three decades. The gap that does exist increases as pupils go through school.

General Certificate of Secondary Education (GCSE) – entry and performance in science

Another source of information is examination entry and performance at the end of compulsory schooling. Prior to the National Curriculum, far fewer girls than boys were entered for physics, chemistry and science examinations at 16–plus and far fewer boys were entered for biology. Boys outperformed girls in general science, chemistry and physics and girls outperformed boys in biology. In 1993, girls outperformed boys in the GCSE single award science and performed equally well in double award science. By 1997, there was a performance gap in favour of girls. The trend is for slightly more girls than boys to be entered for the single award and slightly more boys than girls for the double award. More boys than girls continued to take single sciences across the three subjects. There were small performance differences in favour of girls in physics and chemistry and a quite large gap in favour of boys in biology.

These overall sub-group comparisons need to be interpreted with care, particularly in the case of single sciences where the populations are selective and may reflect different ability spreads. The distribution of grades shows that boys and girls are represented across the full grade profile for these examinations. Gorard *et al.* (1999) report that there are no systematic differences at any age between the performance of boys and girls at the lowest level of any measure of attainment; the achievement gaps are at the highest level of attainment. A further factor is *how* grades are achieved in combined science when overall performance appears to be similar. Bell's analysis (1997) at question level revealed that boys were outperforming girls on questions requiring the application of physics concepts.

The problem of the incomparability of populations taking different examinations is further compounded by tiered entry. There is evidence from research in GCSE mathematics (Stobart *et al.* 1992) that more boys than girls are *not* entered for GCSE because pupil disaffection is increased in the lower tier. Disaffection is considered to be greater for boys than girls.

> Low ability girls are generally better motivated than low ability boys. Boys tend to feel that the foundation (lower) tier is not worth it. Girls are often more content to take a lower tier.
>
> (Stobart *et al.* 1992: 28)

Fewer girls than boys were placed in the higher tier because of their perceived lack of confidence and an assumption that girls are more adversely affected by examinations than boys. In both cases, the teachers' judgements were based on affective rather than cognitive characteristics of pupils.

National assessment in England

In science overall, at age 10–11, girls are found to slightly outperform boys. However, fewer girls than boys achieve the higher level of attainment and more girls than boys achieve the average levels (QCA 1998a). At age 13–14, Key Stage 3, there were no overall differences in the performance of girls and boys (QCA 1998b). There are two tiers of entry for this Key Stage. In the 1996 KS3 tests, fewer girls than boys were entered for the higher tier (32 per cent compared with 37 per cent). The study found that on the higher tier paper, males outperformed females on the great majority of question parts. Of the twenty question parts where a gender difference in performance was noted, sixteen were concerned with physics topics, three with chemistry/earth science and only one with biology.

Since 1990, the rates of entry into physics and chemistry A level examinations (age 18+) has declined significantly for both males and females, in spite of a marked increase in female entrants to A level. Research has shown that the entry patterns found at A level are maintained into higher education. Smithers (1997) reported that, in spite of the massive expansion in degree entry between 1986 and 1995, chemistry and physics numbers have remained on a plateau of around 3,000 in England. Head (1999) reports that 'men dominate the university intake in physics with 81 per cent of the cohort and with 62 per cent in chemistry. In biology, women are in the majority making up 55 per cent of the undergraduates'. In engineering in 1997, there were six times as many male as female graduates. The figures show little change in entry across the various engineering disciplines in the last ten years.

Performance trends show no overall differences between girls and boys. Males and females are represented across the range of achievements in national tests and examinations. Any gender-related issues in science education cannot, therefore, be attributed to innate differences between sex groups. A review of a range of entry and achievement patterns suggests that girls and boys are equally able to undertake and achieve in science and technology courses. Significant gender differences in pupils' options reveal traditional 'masculine' and 'feminine' subject and occupational stereotypes. These differences continue in post-compulsory education, in universities and in the workplace. What is more, these differences appear to withstand radical changes in curriculum and assessment policy and practice.

Gender differences in pupils' interests and expectations

The lack of evidence of cognitive differences between the sexes has led to an emphasis on psycho–social explanations for gender differences. In the early development of gender identities, Duveen emphasized the transition from 'external identities as children are incorporated into the social world through the actions of others, to internalised identities as children become independent actors in the field of gender' (Duveen 2000: 12). As a consequence, boys and girls engage in different hobbies and pastimes from an early age. They develop different ways of responding to the world and making sense of it. As Fivush observes, 'gender thus moves beyond knowing which behaviours are deemed appropriate for females and males to become a self-regulating system' (1998: 60). Browne and Ross (1991) studied a large sample of pre-school children and observed that, from a very young age, children develop clear ideas about what 'girls' do and what 'boys' do. The activities girls were observed to take part in by choice were labelled as *creative* and included drawing, creative activity, reading a book or talking to an adult. Boys, on the other hand, were observed to prefer *constructional* activities.

In another research study, Murphy (1997) noted that children's interests were either seen as unproblematic, and therefore not challenged, if they corresponded with pre-school activity, or were exploited to ensure engagement with particular learning goals. In other words, gender differences are built on in schooling as the following quotes from day care staff indicate:

> Getting them [the boys] to settle down to a story was really quite a task. What I resort to is any book that has a tractor, a dumper in it, any sort of machinery. I don't have a problem settling the girls. Girls are much more interested in drawing and as a result quite often are more forward than boys when it comes to using pencils and scissors. Girls seem to enjoy the colours and the process of drawing. Boys just aren't interested.
>
> (Murphy 1997: 97–8)

The self-regulating nature of gender development serves to shape pupils' views of their realms of competence in school which, in turn, affects their achievements in science. Across the hundreds of science tasks monitored by the APU, there were found to be systematic *content* effects, i.e. it was not the task itself but what the task was about that influenced performance, e.g. interpreting a table of information about flowering plants or about spare parts for cars. Across the ages, girls and boys as groups avoided certain contents, irrespective of what construct was being assessed or their understanding of it. Typically, questions that involved content related to health, reproduction, nutrition and domestic situations, showed girls performing at a higher level than boys. This performance difference arose because more girls than boys attempted the questions and reported that they felt confident in their ability to respond. In questions where the content was more overtly 'masculine', the converse occurred. 'Masculine' contents included cars, building sites, submarines, machinery, space travel, etc.

Interests and salience

The different experiences pupils acquire outside of school not only affect the skills and knowledge they develop but, crucially, their understandings of the situations and problems in which to apply them. Activities that are gender-typed vary in their *goals* and *purposes*. Thus, if girls are engaging more in creative, socially-orientated tasks and boys more in constructional, technical tasks, then what they learn to attend to will vary. When asked to observe phenomena, objects or events without any cues as to what was salient, girls more than boys took note of colours, sounds, smells and texture. Boys took note of structural details. When boys were directed in tasks to observe sounds, etc. they were perfectly capable of doing so (Murphy and Elwood 1998). However, without this direction, students' differing views of salience remain unchallenged and the potential constraints on their learning continue.

Research by Murphy (1991) found that the setting of tasks in science was treated differently by girls and boys. Girls tended to consider contextual features as an integral part of the tasks they formulated, unlike boys who tended to consider issues in isolation. One effect of this is that girls formulate more complex, multivariable investigations, which may be very difficult for them to address procedurally. Furthermore, their tasks are often not recognized by teachers, who judge them to be examples of girls' misunderstanding. Consequently, girls are often required to pursue other pupils' tasks or accept one imposed by the teacher. In a situation where pupils aged 9–10 were investigating the rate of dissolving, a teacher used a worksheet which suggested the 'problem' was a father who could not get his sugar to dissolve in his tea. The actual task specified on the same worksheet was to 'Find out how the time taken for sugar to dissolve depends on the temperature of the liquid'.

In previous activities, the teacher had been at pains to represent science as relevant to children's daily lives but had also, throughout his teaching, introduced pupils to the nature of scientific evidence and appropriate procedures to acquire it. In a mixed group of one girl and two boys, the children's different views of what the problem was emerged. For the boys, it was to carry out a science investigation, for the girl, to solve the father's dilemma. One boy suggested, therefore, that three temperature readings were essential – cold, warm and hot. For the girl, only warm and hot were necessary, as she commented, 'Nobody drinks cold tea'. Neither the boys nor the teacher could understand the girl's refusal to undertake the third reading as she was able to state the task as being to find out how temperature affects dissolving. Nor was the girl able to explain that the evidence she needed was for the father in the worksheet and *not* to establish a pattern in results which would allow her to describe a relationship between two variables. In the end, she was required to do what she saw as the boys' investigation.

Girl: Why should I have to do what the boy wants?
Teacher: But he's come up with a suggestion.
Girl: Yeah, a suggestion and you want me to do it. You think it's a good idea?
Teacher: I do think it's a good idea.
Girl: But if I don't, do I still have to do it?
Teacher: Is it going to tell you something? You give him a good reason why you shouldn't do it.
Girl: Right, the situation is that someone wants their sugar to dissolve quicker in their tea, right? So we, so nobody, but they still want warm tea or hot tea but they don't want exactly cold.
Teacher: You're too hung up on this rather than what it is you're trying to find out.

For the teacher and the boys, the everyday setting was irrelevant to the task. For the girl, the context was integral to the task. The problem she was trying to solve was the dilemma of the father's unsweetened tea and, as she said repeatedly, 'No one drinks cold tea'.

In school science, it is often assumed that students will focus on single variable effects and that, once pupils can do this, they will do it, irrespective of contextual issues. There is considerable evidence that extraction is an approach to thinking that males employ more than females (Head 1996). However, if extraction is a significant requirement for learning in science education, this needs to be made clear to pupils. Furthermore, more careful attention needs to be paid to how science is represented to pupils. Pupils could easily be shown how a relationship between temperature and rate of dissolving could be used to explain how best to dissolve sugar in tea. What is problematic is to represent science as *directly* engaged with solving everyday problems, rather than offering explanations for them. Teaching pupils how science acts in the world needs to be part of the specified curriculum, particularly any future curriculum concerned with scientific literacy.

Gendered styles of learning

The more pupils engage in gendered activities, the more they develop gender-related ways of being in the world. Two generalized aspects of these gendered ways are pupils' learned styles of communication, both written and oral.

Research has linked pupils' gendered choices of reading to the styles of written response they develop. At age 15, over half the boys surveyed by the APU, compared to one-third of the girls, said they preferred reading books which gave accurate facts. Twice as many girls than boys liked to read 'to help understand their own and other people's personal problems'. A 'girls' preferred written style is described as extended, reflective composition, and a 'boys' style as more often episodic, factual and focusing on commentary detail (Gorman *et al.* 1988).

Research in science suggests that a particular style of response is valued in subjects like physics and it is a style more consonant with boys' learned styles of writing. This is particularly the case at A level (Elwood and Comber 1996). Furthermore, attributes of style come to be associated with cognitive abilities. Hence, drawing on multiple perspectives, more typically seen in a female response, is interpreted by teachers as 'a lack of courage to discard irrelevant details', whereas male responses are described as more clinical, strongly arguing a point and are associated with risk-taking, flair and sparkle. One reason for the decrease in interest and participation of girls in science may be that their competence is questioned at the same time as their preferred and learned ways of responding to the world are devalued. Interventions which have made explicit the style of response expected, and extended the range valued, had a significant effect on the level of achievement in physics by females at age 18 (Hildebrand 1996).

Research has also established gender differences in the ways in which adults talk with girls and boys. Girls are both talked to more than boys and seek exchange with adults more often. Pre-school children's talk also reveals significant gender differences in the style of communication for girls and boys (Thompson 1994). The preference of girls for working collaboratively and through discussion with others was noted in the UK surveys of design and technology (Kimbell *et al.* 1991: 126). Girls were observed displaying an ability to take on a wide range of issues in discussion and acting as facilitators to the boys' ideas, 'being able to give them lots of support and to point out the strengths and weaknesses of their ideas'.

Research looking at talk in science classrooms and Design and Technology workshops (Murphy 1999) found that girls, more than boys, talked out loud about their work and actively sought each other's views and gave each other support. Consequently, girls were more likely to develop a shared reference to support their problem-solving. Boys' lack of shared talk was not seen as problematic. Indeed, the successful pupil at secondary level appeared to be the one who worked independently and quickly. Boys who needed help typically avoided asking teachers and waited for support when their male counterparts had finished their work. This had significant negative effects on their progress.

Teacher expectations and gender

The expectations of teachers have been found to have a direct impact on pupils' beliefs about their competence. Girls continue to rate their achievements in science lower than boys. This is a cross-cultural phenomenon. In the study into gender differences in examinations at 18+, physics teachers' assessment of female attitudes to the subject were much less positive than for males (Elwood and Comber 1996). The majority of teachers disagreed with suggestions that female students had the confidence to succeed at physics. Nor did teachers expect their female students to pursue a career that involved physics. Male students were, however, expected to continue with their studies beyond A level.

Teachers' beliefs about pupils do influence their self-concepts in relation to subjects. Head (1996) describes the way males tend to attribute success to their own efforts and failure to external factors. Girls, however, do the converse. An extensive review of research studies (Howe 1999) concluded that boys dominated class interactions, and that boys were selected more often by teachers than girls, in part because they attracted more attention. Boys also received more feedback from teachers, both positive and negative. Girls received less negative feedback, but what they received was focused on their work and influenced their expectations of themselves and their abilities negatively (Dweck *et al.* 1978). One issue that is rarely discussed is the effect of teachers' behaviours on boys' performance. If some boys hold an exaggerated view of their potential achievements and if they have learnt to attribute failure to external factors, their ability to reflect on their own learning is restricted. Furthermore, if some male students struggle in science because of a mismatch between their beliefs about their ability and reality, then disaffection and demotivation may be a consequence.

Discussion

The debate about gender differences has clarified that innate cognitive differences between girls and boys are not the issue. However, girls' increased participation and success in science only obtains when access is required, rather than being a matter of choice. Furthermore, performance results analysed at question level continue to show significant differences between the achievements of girls and boys on aspects of science. A further area that needs consideration is tiered entry in national and examination entry. There is evidence that ceiling and floor effects on pupils' achievements arise because of teachers' perceptions of gender differences related to affective rather than cognitive factors.

Such effects matter because of the impact they have on pupils' views of themselves in relation to science. Teachers evaluating KS3 assessment observed that it functions as 'a disincentive to further learning.' (ATL 1998: 28). Furthermore, the preponderance of physical science tasks in the higher tier paper was seen to discriminate against girls (ATL 1999). Assessment in science influences the development of pupils' self-esteem. A self-protective reaction to its influence, therefore, will lead pupils to turn away from science. If the subject, in its definition of achievement and ways of knowing, already marginalizes some pupils, formal assessments introduced throughout schooling could accelerate and increase the disaffection.

When choices remain traditional, stereotypical patterns emerge in course uptake. There is evidence of some change to this in girls' enhanced entry and performance at A level. However, the decline in uptake post-16 in physics and chemistry is a matter for concern. Some argue that, as there is no crisis in science and technology-related career recruitment, this concern is misplaced. This begs the question of the purpose and goal of education post-16 and raises the related question of the reasons behind pupils' choices. The increased uptake of mixed A levels to serve more wide-ranging career choices is one explanation. Another can be perceptions of subjects such as science post-16. Elwood and Comber (1996) reported that most teachers and students considered A level physics to be difficult and some teachers described it as boring, 'an issue-less, non-discursive subject leading to sterile teaching and teachers'. In response to this, there have been some major curriculum developments such as the Institute of Physics' A level project and the SLIP curriculum project (Whitelegg and Parry 1999). There is evidence that such initiatives work if there are accompanying shifts in the teaching and learning strategies to ensure pupils' experiences are valued and alternative ways of working are allowed. These alternative ways included co-operative group work, creative drawing and writing, role-play, problem-solving, brainstorming and modelling. The curriculum changes had also to be incorporated into the assessment procedures, i.e. assessment tasks set in real-world contexts to match students' interests and a range of ways of showing learning allowed, including the visual, student-designed investigations and process folios of students' changing ideas. All of these attributes can be related to developments in views about effective teaching and learning.

Such changes were implemented in the Australian State Victoria Certificate of Education Physics curriculum and examination for 18-year-olds and there was a 10 per cent increase in the pass level for all students. There were dramatic shifts in the number of females achieving 'A' grades, 44 per cent compared with 29 per cent for males. However, this was not the case for all girls. Both in enrolment and achievement levels, girls from low socio-economic areas were still disadvantaged (Hildebrand 1996). The extant social conditions that confront some pupils, particularly those from low socio-economic backgrounds, may reduce their ability to deal flexibly with gender stereotypes associated with roles and adult work. It is, there-fore, crucial that in implementing interventions to enhance access and achieve-ment, that differences within and between gender groups are considered.

Currently, any changes to reintroduce choice in the science curriculum for 14–16-year-olds will disadvantage pupils, girls more than boys, but also boys who already feel that science is too difficult or of less relevance to their lives. As the Equal Opportunities Commission (EOC) noted, 'without a renewed emphasis on developing gender equality in schools, opening up choice increases stereotyping, reinstates a gendered curriculum and reduces the potential for equality in the work place' (EOC 1999: 217).

Replacing a pedagogy for *boys* with a pedagogy and curriculum for *some girls* is not the answer. Providing initial teachers and practising teachers with evidence of pupils' different reactions to the same science content, set in difference contexts, will raise their awareness of the issue and of the options and possibilities available in the science curriculum. This evidence is increasingly available (Sjøberg 1999). A more radical and enduring change would emerge if models of learning environ-ments that enhance the interests of a range of pupils were developed and made available, including modifications of teaching material and strategies. It is not the choice of context that matters, but how that context is used to motivate and engage pupils and allow them to bridge between their past experiences and future learning in ways that make sense of them. Changes to learning environments make demands on pupils as well as teachers. Any pedagogic intervention, if it is to succeed, requires the reconstruction of the teaching contacts 'to counteract the habits (of mind) acquired by pupils' (Perrenoud 1998). Without such changes, our National Curriculum and assessment system may increasingly meet the needs of only some pupils and continue to fail the most vulnerable.

Gender differences in achievement and interest in science do exist but their sources are psycho–social rather than innate. To address these sources requires changes to the science curriculum, its assessment and teaching. This raises the following questions:

- How can the current initial teacher-training curriculum be altered to equip teachers with the understanding and practice to work with gender effects in the classroom?
- What changes to the organization of science teaching would be necessary to achieve learning environments that cater for individual differences?

The answers to these questions imply radical changes. If such change is not forthcoming we have to ask: are we content for science to become a subject only for some of our children?

References

ATL (1998) *An Evaluation of the 1998 Key Stage 3 tests in English, Mathematics and Science*, London: Association of Teachers and Lecturers.

ATL (1999) *An Evaluation of the 1999 Key Stage 3 Tests in English, Mathematics and Science*, London: Association of Teachers and Lecturers.

Ausubel, D. P. (1968) *Educational Psychology: A Cognitive View*, New York: Holt, Rinehart and Winston.

Bell, J. (1997) 'Sex differences in performance', in *Double Award Science GCSE*, paper presented at BERA Belfast, August 1997.

Browne, N. and Ross, C. (1991) 'Girls' stuff, boys' stuff: young children talking and playing', in N. Browne (ed.) *Science and Technology in the Early Years*, Buckingham: Open University Press.

Department of Education and Science (1988a) *'Science at age 11 – A Review of APU Survey Findings'*, London: HMSO.

Department of Education and Science (1988b) *'Science at age 15 – A Review of APU Survey Findings'*, London: HMSO.

Department of Education and Science (1989) *'Science at age 13 – A Review of APU Survey Findings'*, London: HMSO.

Duveen, G. (2000) 'Representations, Identities, Resistance', in K. Deaux and G. Philogene (eds) *Social Representations: Introductions and Explorations*, Oxford: Blackwell.

Dweck, C. S., Davidson, W., Nelson, S. and Enna, B. (1978) 'Sex differences in learned helplessness: the contingencies of evaluative feedback in the classroom', *Development Psychology* 14: 268–76.

Elwood, J. and Comber, C. (1996) *'Gender Differences in Examinations at 18+: Final Report'*, London: University of London Institute of Education.

Equal Opportunities Commission (1999) 'Gender issues in vocational education and training and workplace achievement of 14–19-year-olds: an EOC perspective', *The Curriculum Journal* 10(2): 209–29.

Fivush, R. (1998) 'Interest, gender and personal narrative: how children construct self-understanding', in L. Hoffman, A. Krapp, A. K. Penninger, and J. Baument (eds) *Interest and Learning*, Kiel: University of Kiel.

Gorard, S., Salisbury, J. and Rees, G. (1999) 'Reappraising the apparent underachievement of boys at school', *Gender and Education* 11: 3.

Gorman, T. P., White, J., Brook, G., Maclure, M. and Kispal, A. (1988) *Language Performance in Schools: Review of APU Language Monitoring 1979–1983*, London: HMSO.

Head, J. (1996) 'Gender identity and cognitive style', in P. Murphy and C. Gipps (eds) *Equity in the Classroom: Towards Effective Pedagogy for Girls and Boys*, London: Falmer Press/UNESCO Publishing.

Head, J. (1999) *Understanding the Boys: Issues of Behaviour and Achievement*, London, USA and Canada: Falmer Press.

Hildebrand, G. M. (1996) 'Assessment interacts with gender', in P. Murphy and C. Gipps (eds) *'Equity in the Classroom: Towards Effective Pedagogy for Girls and Boys'*, London: Falmer Press/UNESCO Publishing.

Hobbs, E. D., Bolt, W. B., Erickson, G., Quelch, T. P. and Sieban, B. A. (1979) *British Columbia Science Assessment 1978, General Report 1*, British Columbia: Ministry of Education.

Howe, C. (1999) *Gender and Classroom Interaction: A Research Review'*, Edinburgh: Scottish Council for Research in Education, Education and Industry Department.

Keeves, J. P. (1986) 'Science education: the contribution of IEA research to a world perspective', in N. T. Postlethwaite (ed.) *International Educational Research, Papers in Honor of Torsten Husén,* Oxford: Pergamon Press.

Keeves, J. P. (1992) *Learning Science in a Changing World, Cross-National Studies of Science Achievement: 1970 to 1984,* The Netherlands: International Association for the Evaluation of Educational Achievement.

Keys, W., Harris, S. and Fernandes, C. (1996) *Third International Mathematics and Science Study. First National Report Part 1,* Slough: NFER.

Kimbell, R., Stables, K., Wheeler, T., Wosniak, A. and Kelly, V. (1991) *The Assessment of Performance in Design and Technology,* London: School Examinations and Assessment Authority.

Murphy, P. (1991) 'Gender differences in pupils' reactions to practical work', in B. Woolnough (ed.) *Practical Science,* Milton Keynes: Open University Press.

Murphy, P. (1997) 'Gender differences – messages for science learning', in K. Harnqvist and A. Bergen (eds) *Growing up with Science: Developing Early Understanding of Science,* London: Jessica Kingsley.

National Assessment of Educational Progress (1978) *Science Achievement in the Schools. A Summary of Results from the 1976–77 National Assessment of Science,* Washington, DC: Education Commission of the States.

Perrenoud, P. (1998) 'From formative evaluation to a controlled regulation of learning processes towards a wider conceptual field', *Assessment in Education* 5(1): 85–102.

QCA (1998a) *Standards at Key Stage 2 English, Mathematics and Science,* London: Qualifications and Curriculum Authority

QCA (1998b) *Standards at Key Stage 3 Science,* London: Qualifications and Curriculum Authority.

Rogoff, B. (1990) *Apprenticeship in Thinking: Cognitive Development in a Social Context,* New York: Oxford University Press.

Sjøberg, S. (1999) *The SAS-study: Science And Scientists Cross-cultural Evidence and Perspectives on Pupil's Interests, Experiences and Perceptions,* Norway: Science Education, ILS, University of Oslo.

Smithers, A. (1997) *Students' Science Choices, Beyond 2000: Science Education for the Future,* paper presented at the Nuffield Seminar, January 1997.

Stobart, G., White, J., Elwood, J., Hayden, M. and Mason, K. (1992) *Differential Performance at 16+: English and Mathematics,* London: Schools Examination and Assessment Council.

Thompson, R. B. (1994) 'Gender differences in communicative style: possible consequences for their learning process' in H. Foot, C. Howe, A. Anderson, A. Tolmie and A. Warden (eds) *Group Tutoring,* Southampton: Computational Mechanics Publications.

Whitelegg, E. and Parry, M. (1999) Real-life contexts for learning physics: meanings, issues and practice, *Physics Education,* 34(2): 68–72.

Willingham, W. W. and Cole, N. S. (1997) *Gender and Fail Assessment,* London: Lawrence Erlbaum Associates.

17 Formative assessment
Raising standards inside the classroom

Paul Black

This chapter gives a brief overview of lessons about formative assessment that can be gleaned from a review of the literature. This is presented under three headings, dealing, respectively, with evidence about the learning gains that can accrue from improvement in formative assessment, with evidence about the present quality of formative assessment in classrooms, and with lessons about ways in which that quality could be improved.

The chapter concludes with two sections which look to future developments. The first discusses in outline the development of theory for formative assessment, so as to provide a firm basis for future research and development work. The other is concerned with changes in policy that are needed to support formative assessment so that its potential for raising standards can be fully realized.

Evidence – two examples

The evidence in these first three sections is based on an extensive survey of the research literature, which yielded a variety of types of evidence. The most directly striking were those with a careful evaluation of the effect of enhancing formative assessment within a piece of teaching. Two examples will serve to illustrate both the research studies and some of the typical results obtained.

First example

This involved work to develop an inquiry-based middle school science curriculum (Frederiksen and White 1997). An innovative teaching course was focused on a practical inquiry approach to learning about force and motion, and the work involved twelve classes of thirty pupils each in two schools. Each class was taught to a carefully constructed curriculum plan in which a sequence of conceptually-based issues was explored through experiments and computer simulations using an inquiry cycle model that was made explicit to the pupils. The experimental work was structured around pupils' use of tools of systematic and reasoned inquiry. There was emphasis on communication skills, and all of the work was carried out in peer groups. Each class was divided into two halves for one fraction only of their class time: in this fraction, a control group worked on a general discussion about improving the module, whilst an experimental group used these same times for discussion of their assessment, structured to promote reflective assessment, with both peer-assessment of presentations to the class, and self-assessment.

All pupils were given the same basic skills test at the outset. The outcome measures were of three types: a mean score on projects throughout the course; a score on two chosen projects which each pupil carried out independently; and a score on a test of the physics concepts involved. On the mean project scores, the experimental group showed a significantly better overall score than the control; however, when the pupils were divided into three groups according to low, medium or high scores on the initial basic skills test, the low scoring group showed a superiority, over their control group peers, of more than three standard deviations, the medium group just over two, and the high group just over one. A similar pattern, of a superiority of the experimental group over the control group which was more marked for pupils with low scores on the initial basic skills test, was also found for the other two outcomes. Amongst the pupils in the experimental group, those who showed the best understanding of the assessment process achieved the highest scores.

This science project worked with a version of formative assessment which was an intrinsic component of a more thorough-going innovation to change teaching and learning. The experimental control difference here lay in the addition of formative assessment, not by extra assessment work by teachers, but by the focus on self- and peer-assessment achieved by giving pupils opportunities to reflect on their learning. Two other distinctive features of this study are, first, the use of outcome measures of different types but all directly reflecting the aims of the teaching, and, second, the differential gains between pupils who would have been labelled 'low ability' and 'high ability' respectively.

Second example

In this example (Butler 1988), the work was grounded more narrowly in an explicit psychological theory, in this case about a link between intrinsic motivation and the type of evaluation that pupils have been taught to expect. The experiment involved forty-eight 11-year-old Israeli pupils selected from twelve classes across four schools, half of those selected being in the top quartile of their class on tests of mathematics and language and the other half being in the bottom quartile. They were taught material not directly related to their normal curriculum, and given written tasks to be tackled individually under supervision, with an oral introduction and explanation. Three sessions were held, with the same pair of tasks used in the first and third. Each pupil received one of three types of written feedback with returned work, both on the first session's work before the second, and on the second session's work before the third. The second and third sessions, including all of the receipt of, and reflection on, the feedback, occurred on the same day. For feedback, one-third of the group was given individually-composed comments on the match, or not, of their work with the criteria that had been explained to all beforehand. A second group was given only grades, derived from the scores on their session's work. The third group was given both grades and comments. Scores on the work done in each of the three sessions served as outcome measures.

For the 'comments only' group, scores increased by about one-third between the first and second sessions, for both types of task, and remained at this higher level for the third session. For the 'grades only' group, scores declined on both tasks between the first and last sessions, but showed a gain on the second session, on some types of task, which was not subsequently maintained. The 'comments with grade' group showed a significant decline in scores across the three sessions. Tests of pupils' interest also showed a similar pattern: however, the only significant difference between the high and low achieving groups was that interest was undermined for the low-achievers by either of the regimes involving a feedback of grades, whereas high-achievers in all three feedback groups maintained a high level of interest.

A significant feature here is that, even if feedback comments are in principle operationally helpful for a pupil's work, their effect can be undermined by the negative motivational effects of normative feedback, that is by giving grades. The results are consistent with other literature which indicates that 'task-involving' feedback is more effective than 'ego-involving' feedback, to the extent that even the giving of praise can have a negative effect with low-achievers. They also support the view that preoccupation with grade attainment can lower the quality of task performance. This study raises the possibility that, in normal classroom work, the effectiveness of formative feedback will depend upon several detailed features of its quality, and not on its mere existence or absence. It also suggests, like the first study, that there can be differential effects, between low- and high-achievers, of any type of feedback.

Evidence – the effectiveness of formative assessment

A review of the research evidence on formative assessment been published in the journal *Assessment in Education* (Black and Wiliam 1998a) together with seven short articles commenting on our work by leading educational experts from Australia, France, Hong Kong, Switzerland, and the USA. Two short versions of the review, with additional arguments about policy implications, have also been produced (Black and Wiliam 1998b; 1998c). The preparation of this review involved checking through many books, through the issues of over 160 journals for the past nine years, and through earlier reviews of research. This process yielded about 580 articles or chapters to study. Out of this emerged a 36,000-word article, which uses materials from 250 sources.

From the literature published since 1986, it is possible to select at least twenty studies – the number depends on how rigorous a set of selection criteria are applied – similar to the examples above in that the effects of formative assessment have been tested by quantitative experiment–control comparisons. All of these studies show that innovations that include strengthening the practice of formative assessment produce significant, and often substantial, learning gains. These studies range over ages (from 5-year-olds to university undergraduates), across several school subjects, and over several countries. The experimental outcomes are reported in terms of effect size, which is the ratio of the net mean learning gain to the standard deviation of the pupils' scores. Typical effect sizes for the experiments reviewed are between 0.4 and 0.7: such effect sizes are larger than most of those found for educational interventions. An effect size of 0.4 would mean that the average pupil involved in an innovation would record the same achievement as a pupil just in the top 35 per cent of those not so involved, whilst a gain effect size 0.7, if realized in the recent international comparative studies in mathematics (TIMSS – Beaton *et al.* 1996), would raise a country from the middle forty-one countries involved to being one of the top five.

Several of these studies exhibit another important feature, illustrated in the first example above, which is that improved formative assessment helps the (so-called) low-attainers more than the rest, and so reduces the spread of attainment whilst also raising it overall. One very recent study was entirely devoted to low-attaining pupils and pupils with learning disabilities, and showed that frequent assessment feedback helps both groups enhance their learning (Fuchs *et al.* 1997). Any gains for such pupils could be particularly important, for any 'tail' of low educational achievement is clearly a portent of wasted talent. Furthermore, pupils who come to see themselves as unable to learn usually cease to take school seriously – many of them will be disruptive within school, others will resort to truancy. Given the habits so developed, and the likelihood that they will leave school without adequate qualifications, such pupils are likely to be alienated from society and to become the sources and the victims of serious social problems.

So it seems clear that very significant learning gains could lie within our grasp. The fact that such gains have been achieved by a variety of methods which have, as a common feature, enhanced formative assessment, indicates that it is this feature which accounts, at least in part, for the successes. However, it does not follow that it would be an easy matter to achieve such gains on a wide scale in normal classrooms.

The reports we have studied bring out, between and across them, other features that seem to characterize many of the studies, namely:

- All such work involves new ways to enhance feedback between those taught and the teacher, ways that require new modes of pedagogy and will therefore call for significant changes in classroom practice.
- Underlying the various approaches are assumptions about what makes for effective learning, in particular that pupils have to be actively involved.
- For assessment to function formatively, the results have to be used to adjust teaching and learning, so a significant aspect of any programme will be the ways in which teachers do this.
- The ways in which assessment can affect the motivation and self-esteem of pupils, and the benefits of engaging pupils in self-assessment, both deserve careful attention (Butler 1987; 1988; Butler and Neuman 1995).

Evidence – the quality of teachers' classroom practices

There is a wealth of research evidence that the everyday practice of assessment in classrooms is beset with problems and shortcomings, as the following quotations, all from studies of classroom formative practice, indicate:

> Marking is usually conscientious but often fails to offer guidance on how work can be improved. In a significant minority of cases, marking reinforces under-achievement and under-expectation by being too generous or unfocused. Information about pupil performance received by the teacher is insufficiently used to inform subsequent work.
>
> (General report on secondary schools – OFSTED 1996: 40)

> Why is the extent and nature of formative assessment in science so impoverished?
>
> (UK secondary science teachers – Daws and Singh 1996: 99)

> The criteria used were 'virtually invalid by external standards'.
>
> (Belgian primary teachers – Grisay 1991: 104)

> Indeed they pay lip service to it but consider that its practice is unrealistic in the present educational context.
>
> (Canadian secondary teachers – Dassa *et al.* 1993: 116)

The most important difficulties, found in the UK but also elsewhere, may be briefly summarized in three groups as below.

Effective learning

- Teachers' tests encourage rote and superficial learning; this is seen even where teachers say they want to develop understanding, and many seem unaware of the inconsistency.
- The questions and other methods used are not discussed with or shared between teachers in the same school, and they are not critically reviewed in relation to what they actually assess.
- For primary teachers particularly, there is a tendency to emphasize quantity and presentation of work and to neglect its quality in relation to learning.

Negative impact

- The giving of marks and the grading functions are over-emphasized, while the giving of useful advice and the learning function are under-emphasized.
- It is common for teachers to use approaches in which pupils are compared with one another, the prime purpose of which appears to them to be competition rather than personal improvement. In consequence, assessment feedback

teaches pupils with low attainments that they lack 'ability', so they are demotivated, believing that they are not able to learn.

Managerial role of assessments

- Teachers' feedback to pupils often seems to serve social and managerial functions, often at the expense of the learning functions.
- Teachers are often able to predict pupils' results on external tests, because their own tests imitate them, but at the same time they know too little about their pupils' learning needs.
- The collection of marks to fill up records is given greater priority than the analysis of pupils' work to discern learning needs; furthermore, some teachers pay no attention to the assessment records of previous teachers of their pupils.

Of course, not all of these descriptions apply to all classrooms, and indeed there will be many schools and classrooms to which they do not apply at all. Nevertheless, these general conclusions have all been drawn by authors in several countries, including the UK, who have collected evidence by observation, interviews and questionnaires from many schools.

Evidence – important features of classroom assessment

The self-esteem of pupils

> A number of pupils ... are content to 'get by' ... . Every teacher who wants to practise formative assessment must reconstruct the teaching contracts so as to counteract the habits acquired by his pupils.
>
> (Perrenoud 1991: 92, talking of pupils in Switzerland)

The ultimate user of assessment information, which is elicited in order to improve learning, is the pupil. Here there are two aspects, one negative and one positive. The negative is illustrated by the above quotation. Where the classroom culture focuses on rewards, 'gold stars', grades or place-in-the-class ranking, then pupils look for the ways to obtain the best marks rather than at the needs of their learning which these marks ought to reflect. One reported consequence is that, where they have any choice, pupils avoid difficult tasks. They also spend time and energy looking for clues to the 'right answer'. Many are reluctant to ask questions out of fear of failure. Pupils who encounter difficulties and poor results are led to believe that they lack ability, and this belief leads them to attribute their difficulties to a defect in themselves about which they cannot do a great deal. So they 'retire hurt', avoid investing effort in learning which could only lead to disappointment, and try to build up their self-esteem in other ways. Whilst the high-achievers can do well in such a culture, the overall result is to enhance the frequency and the extent of under-achievement.

The positive aspect is that such outcomes are not inevitable. What is needed is a culture of success, backed by a belief that all can achieve. Feedback to any pupil should be about the particular qualities of his or her work, with advice on what he or she can do to improve, and should avoid comparisons with other pupils.

Self-assessment by pupils

However, there is a further dimension. Many of the successful innovations have developed self- and peer-assessment by pupils as ways of enhancing formative assessment, and such work has achieved some success with pupils from age 5 upwards. The main problem that those developing self-assessment encounter is not the problem of reliability and trustworthiness: it is found that pupils are generally honest and reliable in assessing both themselves and one another, and can be too hard on themselves as often as they are too kind. The main problem is different; it is that pupils can only assess themselves when they have a sufficiently clear picture of the targets that their learning is meant to attain. Surprisingly, and sadly, many pupils do not have such a picture, and appear to have become accustomed to receiving classroom teaching as an arbitrary sequence of exercises with no over-arching rationale. It requires hard and sustained work to overcome this pupils' culture of passive reception (Fairbrother 1995; Parkin and Richards 1995). For formative assessment to be productive, pupils should be trained in self-assessment so that they can understand the main purposes of their learning and thereby grasp what they need to do to achieve.

The involvement of pupils in their own assessment changes both the role of the pupil as learner and the nature of the relationship between teacher and pupil, making the latter shoulder more of the responsibility for learning and calling for a radical shift in pupils' own perspectives about learning. A science teacher in Spain reported on the difficulty in achieving this aim:

> The idea of self-evaluation is a difficult one, because the students don't fully comprehend the idea and only really think in terms of their exam mark. Generally speaking they don't reflect on their own learning process in an overall fashion. [They think] their assessment has more to do with the effort they made than with what they have actually learnt. In fact the main reason why students fail is their lack of study techniques, since they still tend to try to simply memorise things.
>
> (Black and Atkin 1996: 99)

This quotation shows that the expectations that pupils have built up from their experiences of assessment in school can constitute an obstacle to their taking a positive role in assessment. This is supported in an account of a study of primary pupils in the Geneva Canton (Perrin 1991). Here, it emerged that the pupils believed that the summative assessments of them were for the school's and their parents' benefit, not for themselves. The weak pupils believed the purpose was to make them work harder. Since the assessment was not used to tell them how to work differently, they saw it as a source of pressure, which made them anxious. As a consequence of such evidence, the Canton decided to reduce its summative tests and enhance the formative role of assessment.

Where formative assessment has been emphasized, it has been found that pupils bring to the work a fear of assessment from their experience of summative tests and it takes some time for them to become more positive about formative work. They share with teachers a difficulty in converting from norm-referenced to criterion-referenced ways of thinking This matters because, as long as pupils compare themselves with others, those with high attainment are too little challenged and those with low attainment are demotivated. The conversion happens more effectively if teachers can give time to setting targets for individual pupils: the self-referenced approach seems to be a key here.

The evolution of effective teaching

The research studies show very clearly that effective programmes of formative assessment involve far more than the addition of a few observations and tests to an existing programme. They require careful scrutiny of all of the main components of a teaching plan. As the argument develops it becomes clear that instruction and formative assessment are indivisible.

To begin at the beginning, the choice of tasks for class and homework is important. Tasks have to be justified in terms of the learning aims that they serve, and they can only work well if opportunities for pupils to communicate their evolving understanding are built into the planning. Discussion, observation of activities and marking of written work, can all be used to provide the opportunities.

Discussions, in which pupils are led to talk about their understanding in their own ways, provide the opportunity for the teacher to respond to and re-orient the pupils' thinking. However, teachers often respond, quite unconsciously, in ways that inhibit the learning of a pupil. Recordings commonly show that the teacher is looking for a particular response and, lacking the flexibility or the confidence to deal with the unexpected, tries to direct the pupil towards giving the expected answer (Filer 1993; 1995; Torrance and Pryor 1995; Pryor and Torrance 1996). Over time, the pupils get the message: they are not required to think out their own answers. The object of the exercise is to work out, or guess, what answer the teacher expects to see or hear, and then express it so that the teaching can proceed.

The posing of questions by the teacher is a natural and direct way of checking on learning, but is often unproductive. However, where, as often happens, a teacher answers their own question after only two or three seconds, and where a minute (say) of silent thought is not tolerable, there is no possibility that a pupil can think out what to say. There are then two consequences: because the only questions that can produce answers in such a short time are questions of fact, these predominat; pupils don't even try to think out a response – if you know that the answer, or another question, will come along in a few seconds, there is no point in trying. It is also common for only a few pupils in a class to answer teacher's questions. The teacher, by lowering the level of questions and by accepting answers from a few, can keep the lesson going but is actually out of touch with the understanding of most of the class – the question–answer dialogue becomes a ritual, one in which all connive, and thoughtful involvement suffers.

There are several ways to break this particular cycle. They involve giving pupils time to respond, asking them to discuss their thinking in pairs or in small groups so that a respondent is speaking on behalf of others, giving pupils a choice between different possible answers and asking them to vote on the options, asking all to write down an answer and then reading out a selected few, and so on. What is essential is that any dialogue should evoke thoughtful reflection in which all pupils can be encouraged to take part, for only then can the formative process start to work.

Class tests, and tests or other exercises set for homework, are also important means of promoting feedback. However, the quality of the test items, that is their relevance to the main learning aims and their clear communication to the pupil, needs scrutiny. Good questions are hard to generate and teachers should collaborate, and draw – critically – on outside sources, to collect such questions. Given questions of good quality, it is then essential to ensure the quality of the feedback. The research studies quoted above have shown that if pupils are given only marks or grades, they do not benefit from the feedback on their work. The worst scenario is one in which some pupils get low marks this time, they got low marks last time, they expect to get low marks next time, and this is accepted as part of a shared belief between them and their teacher that they are just not clever enough. Feedback has been shown to improve learning where it gives each pupil specific guidance on strengths and weaknesses, preferably without any overall marks. Thus, the way in which test results are reported back to pupils so that they can identify their own strengths and weaknesses is a critical feature. Pupils must be given the means and opportunities to work with evidence of their difficulties. Thus, for formative purposes, a test at the end of a block or module of teaching is pointless in that it is too late to work with the results.

All these points make clear that there is no one simple way to improve formative assessment. What is common to them is that a teacher's approach should start by being realistic, confronting the question 'Do I really know enough about the understanding of my pupils to be able to help each of them?'

Much of the work needed can give rise to difficulties. Some pupils will resist attempts to change accustomed routines, for any such change is threatening, and emphasis on the challenge to think for yourself (and not just work harder) can be disturbing to many. Pupils will find it hard to believe in the value of changes for their learning before they have experienced the benefits of such changes.

Many of the initiatives that are needed take more class time, particularly when a central purpose is to change the outlook on learning and the working methods of pupils. Thus, teachers have to take risks in the belief that such investment of time will yield rewards in the future, whilst 'delivery' and 'coverage' with poor understanding are pointless and even harmful.

Underlying such problems will be two basic issues. The one is the nature of each teacher's beliefs about learning. The other issue is the beliefs that teachers hold about the potential to learn of all of their pupils. To sharpen the contrast by overstating it, there is on the one hand the 'fixed IQ' view – a belief that each pupil has a fixed, inherited, intelligence, so that little can be done apart from accepting that some can learn quickly and others can hardly learn at all. On the other hand, there is the 'untapped potential' view, prevalent in some non-Western cultures, which starts from the assumption that so-called 'ability,' is a complex of skills that can be learnt. Here, the underlying belief is that all pupils can learn more effec-tively if one can clear away, by sensitive handling, the obstacles set up by previous difficulties, be they of cognitive failures never diagnosed, or of damage to personal confidence, or a combination of the two. Clearly, the truth lies between these two extremes, but the evidence is that ways of managing formative assessment that work with the assumptions of 'untapped potential' do help all pupils to learn and can give particular help to those who have previously fallen behind.

Towards a theoretical framework

The main components of a fully-developed theory of formative assessment would seem to be:

- A general learning theory with emphasis on constructivism, for no feedback to pupils can be effective unless it guides their learning in helpful directions.
- Models for the epistemology of each subject and hence of learning progress within each, for without this the goals for learning cannot be chosen and specified.
- A theory of the cognitive acts of learning through feedback: guidance to pupils, and their own self-assessment, must be based on a clear perception of the learning goal, understanding of their present state of knowledge, and some means to close any gap between these two – the desired and the present states (Sadler 1989).
- Analysis of self- and peer-assessment and of the particular learning processes and social interactions that these involve.
- Study of the effects of different styles of feedback on self-esteem, self-attribu-tion and readiness to learn.
- Student–teacher and pupil–peer interactions in learning as a case of social discourse.

However, this is a first sketch, not a definitive list, and there is certainly more to be done to sharpen the rationale and the coherence of these elements into a useful unifying scheme. Any theory has to be composed to serve a particular purpose: in the present case, what may be most useful is a theory for teachers' action, which can set out useful principles and guides. Such a theory might distinguish between, and interrelate:

- teachers' perceptions and responses to the social and educational context in which they have to work;
- their assumptions about learning;

- their assumptions about the nature of feedback, including cognitive and motivational aspects;
- the principles bearing on the immediate decision-taking and action to which they have to commit themselves, without time for reflection, throughout a teaching day.

What seems both obvious and problematic is that this whole area is at the heart of pedagogy and may have to be appraised and shaped further in terms of a theory of larger scope to encompass school learning comprehensively. One of the limitations of this chapter is that this has not been attempted, so that what is here needs the discipline of a broader context.

Policy development

The evidence presented above establishes that a clearly productive way to start implementing a classroom-focused policy for raising standards would be to improve formative assessment. This same evidence also establishes that to do this would not be to concentrate on some minor or idiosyncratic aspect of the whole business of teaching and learning. Rather it would be to concentrate on several essential elements, namely the quality of teacher–pupil interactions, the stimulus and help for pupils to take active responsibility for their own learning, the particular help needed to move pupils out of the 'low-attainment' trap, and the development thereby of the habits needed by all if they are to become capable of life-long learning. Improvements in formative assessment which are within reach can contribute substantially to raising standards in all of these aspects.

However, the improvement of formative assessment cannot be a simple matter. There is no 'quick fix' that can be added to existing practice with promise of rapid reward. On the contrary, if the substantial rewards of which the evidence holds out promise are to be secured, this will only come about if each teacher finds their own way of incorporating the lessons and ideas that are set out above into their own patterns of classroom work. This can only happen relatively slowly, and through sustained programmes of professional development and support (Black and Wiliam 1998b). This does not weaken the message here – indeed, it should be a sign of its authenticity, for lasting and fundamental improvements in teaching and learning can only happen in this way.

References

Beaton, A. E., Mullis, I. V. S., Martin, M. O., Gonzalez, E. J., Kelly, D. L. and Smith, T. A. (1996) *Mathematics Achievement in the Middle School Years*, Boston, MA: Boston College.

Black, P. J. and Atkin, J. M. (1996) *Changing the Subject: Innovations in Science, Mathematics and Technology Education*, London: Routledge (for OECD).

Black, P. and Wiliam, D. (1998a) 'Assessment and classroom learning', *Assessment in Education* 5(1): 7–71.

Black, P. and Wiliam, D. (1998b) *Inside the Black Box: Raising Standards through Classroom Assessment*, London: King's College.

Black, P. and Wiliam, D. (1998c) 'Inside the black box: raising standards through classroom assessment', *Phi Delta Kappan* 80(2): 139–48.

Butler, R. (1987) 'Task-involving and ego-involving properties of evaluation: effects of different feedback conditions on motivational perceptions, interest and performance', *Journal of Educational Psychology* 79(4): 474–82.

Butler, R. (1988) 'Enhancing and undermining intrinsic motivation: the effects of task-involving and ego-involving evaluation on interest and performance', *British Journal of Educational Psychology* 58: 1–14.

Butler, R. and Neuman, O. (1995) 'Effects of task and ego-achievement goals on help-seeking behaviours and attitudes', *Journal of Educational Psychology* 87(2): 261–71.

Dassa, C., Vazquez-Abad, J. and Ajar, D. (1993) 'Formative assessment in a classroom setting: from practice to computer innovations', *The Alberta Journal of Educational Research* 39(1): 111–25.

Daws, N. and Singh, B. (1996) 'Formative assessment: to what extent is its potential to enhance pupils' science being realized?', *School Science Review* 77(281): 93–100.

Fairbrother, B. (1995) 'Pupils as learners', in B. Fairbrother, P. J. Black and P. Gill (eds) *Teachers Assessing Pupils: Lessons from Science Classrooms*, Hatfield: Association for Science Education, pp. 105–24.

Filer, A. (1993) 'Contexts of assessment in a primary classroom', *British Educational Research Journal* 19(1): 95–107.

Filer, A. (1995) 'Teacher assessment: social process and social product', *Assessment in Education* 2(1): 23–38.

Frederiksen, J. R. and White, B. J. (1997) 'Reflective assessment of students' research within an inquiry-based middle school science curriculum', paper presented at the Annual Meeting of the AERA, Chicago.

Fuchs, L. S., Fuchs, D., Karns, K., Hamlett, C. L., Katzaroff, M. and Dutka, S. (1997) 'Effects of task focused goals on low achieving students with and without learning disabilities', *American Educational Research Journal* 34(3): 513–43.

Grisay, A. (1991) 'Improving assessment in primary schools: "APER" research reduces failure rates', in P. Weston (ed.) *Assessment of Pupils' Achievement: Motivation and School Success*, Amsterdam: Swets and Zeitlinger, pp. 103–18.

OFSTED (1996) *Subjects and Standards: Issues for School Development arising from OFSTED Inspection Findings 1994–5, Key Stages 3 and 4 and Post-6*, London: HMSO.

Parkin, C. and Richards, N. (1995) 'Introducing formative assessment at KS3: an attempt using pupil self-assessment', in B. Fairbrother, P. J. Black, and P. Gill (eds) *Teachers Assessing Pupils: Lessons from Science Classrooms*, Hatfield: Association for Science Education, pp. 13–28.

Perrenoud, P. (1991) 'Towards a pragmatic approach to formative evaluation', in P. Weston (ed.) *Assessment of Pupils' Achievement: Motivation and School Success*, Amsterdam: Swets and Zeitlinger, pp. 79–101.

Perrin, M. (1991) 'Summative evaluation and pupil motivation', in P. Weston (ed.) *Assessment of Pupils' Achievement: Motivation and School Success*, Amsterdam: Swets and Zeitlinger, pp. 169–73.

Pryor, J. and Torrance, H. (1996) 'Teacher-pupil interaction in formative assessment: assessing the work or protecting the child?', *The Curriculum Journal* 7(2): 205–26.

Sadler, R. (1989) 'Formative assessment and the design of instructional systems', *Instructional Science* 18: 119–44.

Torrance, H. and Pryor, J. (1995) 'Investigating, teacher assessment in infant classrooms: methodological problems and emerging issues', *Assessment in Education* 2(3): 305–20.

Section 5

Research

Introduction

The last two decades have seen considerable growth in science education research, and there now exists a substantial body of evidence about teaching and learning science. But what is the relationship between research and classroom practice, and how can it be developed? These issues are addressed in this section's first chapter by John Gilbert, editor of *International Journal of Science Education*, from which the three research papers in this section have been drawn. Gilbert outlines the key challenges that are currently facing science education worldwide, and ways in which research is addressing these. He argues that a diversity of approaches is essential both for the development of research and for encouraging its impact on practice.

A major part of science education research has been concerned with investigating children's understandings of scientific concepts, and the next three chapters have been chosen to reflect this work. The focus of this research has been not just to find out, but to explore pupils' incorrect responses, to try to characterize these and to consider how the ideas might have arisen. Because these ideas may often be common to many children and are not simply idiosyncratic responses, understanding how children understand and construct their knowledge of the world has importance for teaching. Initially, research tended to focus on the physical sciences, but subsequently, more attention has been paid to biological concepts. The three studies included here have drawn on topics across the sciences; each of them uses a variety of methods to probe understanding, and these methods are valuable not just as research instruments but as illustrations of some approaches to assessment which could be used in the classroom.

In the first study, undertaken in the early 1980s, David Shipstone's focus is on students' understanding of electricity, and from the results of a series of written questions, he proposes a number of models of electricity which may account for their responses. A very commonly held, and erroneous, idea about the flow of current is the 'sequence model', in which instead of thinking globally about the circuit as a whole, pupils reason locally about the behaviour of the current as it 'travels around' the circuit. The widespread prevalence of this view means that it is of particular importance to pay attention to it when teaching about electricity. Philip Johnson reports on a longitudinal study of a cohort of pupils, following the development of their understanding of particle theory. He argues that there are two dimensions to this development – the understanding that matter *consists* of particles and that properties derive from the *collective behaviour* of particles. This, he argues, has important consequences for the ways that ideas about particles are introduced to pupils. The third paper is one of a series by John Leach, Rosalind Driver, Philip Scott and Colin Wood-Robinson investigating children's ideas about ecology. The paper included here is concerned with the design of the study (the results being reported elsewhere) and includes details of the research probes used. Of particular importance in this paper is the discussion of some key issues about how to characterize and probe children's developing understanding, and how these informed the design of the probes.

Research such as that described in these chapters has, over the last two decades, profoundly influenced the way we see pupils' learning in science. To a certain extent, the results of this research have also influenced the design of the curriculum (though many would argue too little). However, while some teachers are aware of the findings and take account of them in their teaching, it would be fair to say that they have not had a significant impact on the day-to-day practice in most classrooms. The same applies to other areas of research. In the final chapter, Richard White addresses the question of why it is that research appears to have such little effect on classroom practice. Two of the key factors he identifies are teachers' perceptions of research, and the conditions and culture within which teachers work, and he discusses some projects which have overcome these problems through productive collaboration between teachers and researchers. Teachers' perceptions of research as being too removed from the realities of the classroom may have had some justification in the past, when a 'control of variables' approach meant that the effects of context were a nuisance to be eliminated rather than key factors to which teachers need to pay attention. Research has moved on, and its findings now have something of relevance to say. The conditions and culture within which teachers work, however, make it difficult for these findings to have influence. Teachers tend to be isolated in their classrooms; development can only occur within a culture in which teachers are able to observe and discuss each other's practice and to draw on evidence to inform their teaching.

18 Science education and research

John Gilbert

The nature of desirable and possible relationships between research in education and the practice of education continues to be widely debated. The tensions inherent in the various positions that can be taken are shown in the field of science education.

Challenges to science education

However science education takes place, whether formally or informally, whether for younger citizens or for older citizens, a number of goals are currently being pursued to a greater or lesser extent. The existence of major reviews of science education, e.g. Project 2061 in the USA, and the introduction of new or revised governmental prescriptions for science education, e.g. the National Curriculum for Science in the UK, suggest that these goals are perceived, at a political level, as not being met. The goals, and the problems in meeting them, are:

1   An understanding of the key concepts of science. Those concepts which are emphasized, both in formal curriculums and in informal provision, often seem to derive their importance from historical events in science rather than from an anticipation of future directions for scientific enquiry and achievement. Presenters, teachers or script writers are unclear how to put them forward to best effect. The evidence of tests, albeit often flawed, is that many, if not most, learners of all ages do not achieve a worthwhile understanding of them.
2   The use of scientific methods of enquiry. Whilst practical work is a significant part of formal science education in many, but by no means all, countries, its value has not been unequivocally established. Indeed, the reasons for that provision are often unclear to participants, both to the teachers and to the taught. The contention that there is no one way of conducting a scientific investigation suggests that efforts to teach such a way, which is what is presently done, are doomed to failure (Millar and Driver 1987).
3   An appreciation of the relationship between science and society. Whilst extensively advocated, and indeed included in syllabuses, this goal is given only a low priority in practice. It is not clear to many teachers what should be taught, why, or how. Even the relationship between science and technology is poorly articulated (Hurd 1991; Gilbert 1992).

4   The contribution of science to personal development. Science education seems to provide little with which students can come to understand the everyday world more effectively, e.g. in order to attain and retain good health, in order to predict real physical events in the environment.

5   An appreciation of the nature of scientific knowledge and explanation. The common understanding was effectively summed up by Kyle *et al.* (1991):

> [students] believe: (*a*) science is a collection of facts to be memorized; (*b*) all the information in the science textbook is true; (*c*) the total sum of scientific knowledge is known; and (*d*) science is a quantitative, value-free, empirical discipline. Moreover, students often fail to understand that: (*a*) science proceeds by fits and starts; (*b*) science is inherently open-ended and exploratory and that ideas based on evidence are still fallible; (*c*) scientific ideas are enhanced through a process of sharing, debating, and consensus building; and (*d*) continual enquiry is a fundamental attribute of the science enterprise.
>
> (Kyle *et al.* 1991: 414)

6   Access to careers which make use of science and technology. The ideas of science do seem to be playing an increasing part in an ever-larger proportion of jobs, even if not requiring the levels of understanding implied by the Science curriculum. Employers do complain, rightly or wrongly, about the level of scientific knowledge and skills amongst employees.

If science education is to retain the relatively high level of political, and hence financial, support that it enjoys in many countries, then these challenges have to be met effectively.

Challenges to research in science education

It might be expected, at first glance, that research into science education could, and indeed should, both directly address and resolve the challenges to practice identified above. A range of criticisms of the focus of address of research into science education have been put forward by Hurd (1991) and Rutherford (1993). These can be turned into the form of challenges. If research into science education is to have more impact on practice then:

1   research must directly address perceived and anticipated problems of practice;
2   the range of topics so addressed must be increased;
3   the customary tight constraints on studies must be relaxed, so that they correspond to the circumference of parameters of the context within which a problem is set;
4   studies of similar problems in different contexts must be brought together into a cohesive whole, such that the public debate of issues is facilitated;
5   studies must not be conducted by science educators in isolation, but by drawing on expertise in the social, behavioural and policy sciences;

6   a continuing review of the philosophy and methodology of much science education research is called for. As Hurd (1991) puts it:

> The physical science model, so widely used in educational research, with its emphasis on the experimental control of variables and statistical analysis, has limited value for investigating issues raised by the reform movement. The whole idea of trying to pinpoint answers to questions that are raised in advance of a study produces results of little consequence. Better would be a model derived from ecology that recognizes complexities and assumes broad patterns of interactive behaviour such as would be characteristic of a teacher and students in learning situations.

The qualitative/quantitative debate has been going on for more than twenty years. It would be more productive if the debate was now about the role of different methodologies in studies conducted for a range of purposes in different contexts.

In Shavelson's (1988) view, it is fallacy, for educational research in general, to assume that the direct applicability of research to practice can be achieved. For direct application to be possible:

> Research would have to be relevant to a particular issue and be available before a decision needed to be made; research would address the issue within the parameters of feasible action and provide clear, simple, and unambiguous results; research would be known and understood by the policy-maker or practitioner and not cross entrenched interests; recommendations from research would be implemented within existing resources; and research findings would lead to choices different from those that decision makers would otherwise have made.
>
> (Shavelson 1988: 5)

In frequent experience, the scope of research is unlikely to match exactly that of particular problems of practice, and research does not produce timeless truths because the context of practice is continually changing, so there is a 'sell by' date for all research. The issue, again, is how to change research so as to achieve the greatest potential impact on practice.

The greatest challenge to research and researchers is posed by the use, by many governments, of what Ball (1990) calls the 'discourse of derision', in which empirically and critically informed opinion is summarily rejected because it is just that. Governments have to be brought face to face with what Campbell (1981) calls 'dystopias': the undesirable consequences likely to follow from the adoption of utopian policies. As Gipps (1993) puts it:

> If we do not describe the possible dystopias we shall be left only with the politicians' utopias. If we do not insist on bringing research findings (which may be politically inconvenient) into the public arena, we shall contribute to the erosion of democracy. The 'discourse of derision' which results must be seen as an

inconvenient, if unpleasant, occupational hazard, but its power will be far greater if we allow it to silence us.

Developing the significance of science education

The agenda of challenges for schools is, to a greater or lesser extent, shared by many countries. Those concepts which are going to be important in the future of science must be identified and taught to students in such a way that understanding is achieved by most, if not all, of them. Valid conceptions of scientific enquiry must be identified and taught to students so that they both understand those conceptions and carry them out in practice, including a suitable emphasis on collaborative aspects. The interrelations between science, technology and society, particularly those concerned with the environment, must move to a central role in the science curriculum. Only in this way will science education be seen to be relevant to the personal development of individuals, and indeed to the development of science itself. The Science curriculum must more faithfully reflect what is known about the nature of science itself, and identify, as well as prepare students for, the role of science in major forms of employment. Lastly, much more attention is needed to these issues in the context of adult, continuing and higher education.

Developing the significance of research in science education

The above agenda for the development of science education implies a rapid and substantial expansion in research in the field. In some countries, a start seems to have been made. For the example, the National Science Foundation in the USA (NSF 1992) has proactively called for research proposals in high priority areas, which are to be carried out with those for whom the work is intended (teachers, business), and which are to be intended to be useful in specific ways. The illustrations given (NSF 1992) suggest that genuinely important issues will be addressed, e.g. the implications of the uneven distribution of resources between schools, the lack of particular specialisms in teachers, the curriculum impact of testing. However, such proactivity has dangers. Dunkin (1989), in introducing a symposium on the implications of governmental research funding policies for research on teacher education in Australia, Canada, England and Wales, and the USA, notes that:

> In several instances, funds that have formerly been available through application and open competition among researchers who had initiated and designed research on the basis of their academic judgement and expertise, were diverted to government departments which decided upon research priorities on the basis of their policy orientations. They then usually called for tenders from researchers to carry out the investigations. Timetables were set, specifications for reports issues, and ownership of the project and the reports vested in the

government… Such projects also faced the risk of being overtly concerned with short-term and specific issues, and of being non-cumulative.

(Dunkin 1989: 229)

The major issue here is that researchers must find ways to influence both the purposes for which, and the mechanisms by which, research priorities are set and contracts specified.

The notion of 'mind set' is, in Shavelson's (1988) view, the key to this exercise of influence. He says, to fellow researchers, that:

> We frame problems in ways consistent with the latest research and use approved methods. We are cautious in reporting and interpreting findings, findings that usually bear on the theory that originally motivated the enquiry. We may, somewhat gratuitously, suggest possible applications, but are hesitant to do so.

Other groups have other mind-sets. Weiss and Bucuvalas (1980) found that, for administrators:

> Research was judged to be useful to the extent that it: (*a*) was high in technical quality, (*b*) recommends actions that policy makers could do something about, (*c*) fit with the bureaucrat's prior knowledge, (*d*) challenged accepted truth, and (*e*) was relevant to the issue.

In a similar way, Gifford and Gabelko (1987) believe that:

> mind frames [of teachers] are goal driven. They seek information that fits with familiar teaching situations. They seek recommendations for actions that experience tells them will most likely help them realize their goals.

Work will more closely approximate to the mind-set of policy makers and practitioners if those groups are active members of a research project. Erickson (1991) has pointed to the value of collaborative research in producing well-targeted studies with high impact on practice. Such collaborative enquiries could readily fall into one of the following study types: a description of the nature and extent of a problem; a description of practice which addresses that problem; an account of the effectiveness of existing and innovatory practices; the setting out of options for future policies and practice (NSF 1992). Whilst such an approach would be admirable, it may not always be attainable. One has to ask, of the three parties to such a possible collaboration (researcher, teacher, policy maker): what will each get out of such a collaboration? It may well be that differences between the three parties, those of the context within which they normally work, the purposes of their work, the power structures of their respective organizations, the respective reward and penalty structures, preclude full collaboration. What one could then hope for would be effective communication throughout a project, with supportive negotiation at the three crucial phases of design, conduct and dissemination.

What emerges from the above discussion is the undesirability of only having any one type of relationship between research and practice in science education. The maximum benefit to both research and practice will accrue if different approaches are vigorously pursued. This implies that all must be properly funded.

References

Ball, S. (1990), *Politics and Policy Making in Education*, London: Routledge.

Campbell, D. (1981) 'Introduction: getting ready for the experimenting society', in L. Saxe and M. Fine *Social Experiments*, London: Sage.

Dunkin, M. (1989) 'An international symposium on the implications of governmental research funding policies for research on teaching and teacher education: an introduction', *Teaching and Teacher Education* 5(4): 249–50.

Erickson, G. (1991) 'Collaborative inquiry and the professional development of teachers', *Journal of Educational Thought* 25(3): 228–45.

Gifford, B. and Gabelko, N. (1987) 'Linking practice-sensitive researchers to research-sensitive practitioners', *Education and Urban Society* 19: 368–88.

Gilbert, J. K. (1992) 'The interface between science education and technology education', *International Journal of Science Education* 14(5): 563–78.

Gipps, C. (1993) 'The profession of educational research', *British Educational Research Journal* 19(1): 5–16.

Hurd, P. (1991) 'Issues in linking research to science teaching', *Science Education* 75(6): 723–32.

Kyle, W., Linn, M.,Bitner, B., Mitchener, C. and Perry, B. (1991) 'The role of research in science teaching: an NSTA theme paper', *Science Education* 75(4): 413–18.

Millar, R. and Driver, R. (1987) 'Beyond processes', *Studies in Science Education* 14: 33–62.

NSF (1992) *Research on Key Issues in Science and Engineering Education: Targeted Program Solicitation*, Washington, DC: National Science Foundation.

Rutherford, F. (1993) 'Project 2061 draws on research', *2061 Today* 3(1): 1–5.

Shavelson, R. (1988) 'Contributions of educational research to policy and practice: constructing, challenging, changing cognition', *Educational Researcher* 17(7): 4–22.

Weiss, C. and Bucuvalas, M. (1980) *Social Science Research and Decision Making*, New York: Columbia University Press.

19 A study of children's understanding of electricity in simple DC circuits

David Shipstone

Introduction

It has become clear in recent years that children, in learning science, may use conceptual models which, in many cases, differ from those which are essential to understanding and efficient learning. These 'alternative frameworks', a term coined by Driver and Easley (1978), are sometimes formed by children as a result of their everyday experiences and before formal teaching of the relevant subject matter, in which case they may be referred to as preconceptions. There is accumulating evidence that these alternative frameworks, whether they arise before or during instruction, may be very resistant to extinction by normal teaching methods (e.g. Viennot 1979).

A number of studies has investigated the preconceptions concerning current flow held by young children, usually within the age range 8 to 12 years (e.g. Tiberghien and Delacôte 1976; Osborne 1982a). Interest centred here on very simple circuits, often comprising no more than a battery, a few connecting wires and a bulb. Typically, these young children treated the lamp as a one-terminal device with current flowing to it rather than through it. Andersson and Karrqvist (1979) and Osborne (1981) extended these investigations to students of up to 17 years of age and found that, despite teaching, many of them were still using typical, pre-instructional models well into the period of formal instruction. Fredette and Lochhead (1980) discovered similar misconceptions amongst university entrants studying engineering.

The study described here examines the models of current flow which children use when dealing with slightly more complex circuits, extending to those which include resistors, either fixed or variable, and connected in series or parallel.

Methodology

A pencil-and-paper test was devised which consisted of ten sets of questions on the distribution of current and voltage, and the effects of resistance upon these, in circuits containing cells, lamps and resistors. Lamps were used to indicate current flow in these questions because the courses followed by the children had adopted

Table 19.1 The sample

Year	No. of boys	No. of girls	Total	Mean age (months)	SD (months)
1	12	12	24	148	3.2
2	21	24	45	161	3.9
3	30	18	48	172	3.8
4	59	10	69	184	3.8
6	36	10	46	210	6.5

Note
The study was carried out in the early 1980s. The 1st year in this study is equivalent to what is now known as Year 7.

that approach in their initial stages. The circuit symbols used were those with which the subjects were familiar.

The test was administered to whole classes drawn from the first four years and the first year sixth-forms of three 11–18 comprehensive schools.

Because the resulting sixth-form sample was rather small, physics students from the first year of a sixth-form college were also included. Two of the comprehensive schools served essentially residential areas. The sixth-form college and the remaining comprehensive school drew their pupils from quite wide and varied catchment areas. Details of the sample used are set out in Table 19.1.

In each of the first three years, the samples covered most of the ability range whilst the fourth-year pupils were all following physics courses leading to either the Certificate of Secondary Education (CSE) or to the Ordinary Level General Certificate of Education (GCE) examinations, both normally taken at age 16. The sixth-year pupils were all studying physics at the Advanced GCE level.

All of the pupils included in the final sample of 232 had studied electrical circuits in the year in which they were tested, the sixth-year pupils having completed their studies of direct current (DC) circuitry.

Children's models of current flow

These models, as applied to series circuits, were investigated by two questions about circuits containing only a battery and a series of identical lamps, one of the circuits being shown in Figure 19.1. The two questions will be treated as one for the purposes of this paper. From a list of statements about the directions of the current at various points in the circuit, and about the relative brightnesses of various pairs of lamps, the pupils were asked to identify those statements that were correct and to explain their conclusion about the relative brightnesses of L_1 and L_2. From their responses, at times supported by

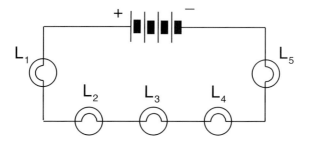

Figure 19.1 Circuit diagram for Question 1

evidence from elsewhere in the test, it was possible in most cases to deduce the current models used. Four models were distinguished as follows:

Model I   Current leaves the battery at both terminals and is used up within the circuit elements. Osborne (1981; 1982b) refers to this as the clashing currents model.

Model II   Current flows in one direction around the circuit, becoming gradually weakened as it goes so that later components receive less. Lamps furthest along the circuit in Figure 19.1 will be least bright.

Model III Current is shared between the components in a circuit. In Figure 19.1 where the lamps are identical, the current is shared equally so that they will all be of the same brightness. Here, too, the current is not regarded as being conserved.

Model IV   The scientific view, which is similar to Model II except that the current is the same throughout the circuit.

It was not possible in this study to distinguish Osborne's model A, in which no current returns to the battery, from other unidirectional models (Osborne 1981; 1982b). As its use was expected to be relatively rare, it was absorbed into Model II. A recent survey of New Zealand children described by Osborne (1983) revealed that his model A was used by less than 5 per cent of pupils over the age range studied here in situations where the cue of a complete circuit was provided.

The age distributions in the incidence of the models are set out graphically in Figure 19.2. In all cases, the plotted points give estimates of the percentages and the vertical bars indicate the extreme limits of uncertainty which resulted when those cases difficult to classify were all added to one or other of the relevant categories.

Uncertainties in classification arose in a number of ways; the most important are set out below.

1   Some students described observations rather than explaining them in terms of a model, e.g. 'Circuit is in series, all bulbs will be of same brightness.'
2   There were sometimes doubts about the meanings behind the terminology

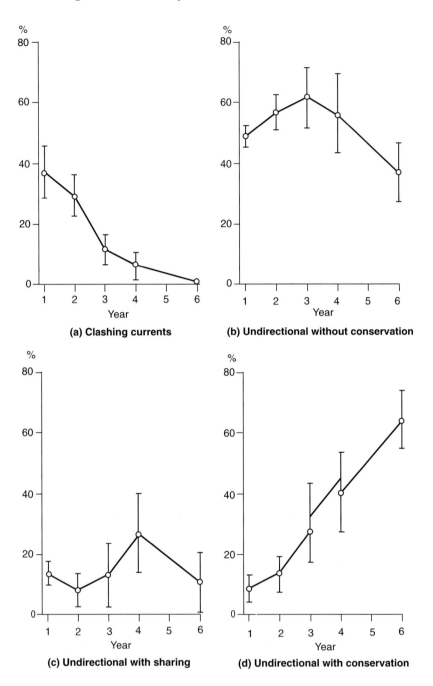

Figure 19.2 Age distributions in the choice of current models [N.B. Year one: mean age 12 years 4 months. Year six: mean age 17 years 6 months]

used, e.g. 'because the bulbs are in series which means they all obtain power from the same supply which is divided equally among all the bulbs giving them the same brightness.' This response, though it might reflect use of the correct model if the term power is being used correctly, might equally indicate use of Model III if 'power' equals 'current' for this child.

3   Some explanations simply would not fit any of the four models listed, e.g. [L_2 is dimmer than L_1] 'because there is the same amount of current going in but because there are three lamps on the bottom the current has to be shared between three.'

4   Some subjects appeared to be using different models in different questions.

Adherence to the 'clashing currents' model, Figure 19.2(a), decreased sharply with increasing age and so seemed to be readily challenged by teaching. The results presented here are remarkably similar to those found by Osborne (1983). Figure 19.2(b) gives the distribution of students using either of the Models II or III, in other words the proportion using Osborne's model C. The initial rise in this is brought about by a shift from the bidirectional Model I, in which current is not conserved, to a unidirectional model in which current is still not conserved. It is difficult to be certain what proportion of the decline in these models, coinciding with a switch to Model IV, results from teaching rather than from self-selection of courses by those pupils who are more able at physics. The initial decline in the proportion of subjects who described current as being shared out (Figure 19.2(c)), was not statistically significant. In year four (15-year-olds), however, there was a sharp rise in the number of clear statements of this model to a level which was significantly higher than in other year groups. It is difficult to see how this is conceptualized as a flow model, and this rise in year four may indicate that the sharing model has its origins in confusion between current and the energy-related quantities of power and voltage, both of which would be shared out equally between the lamps in Figure 19.1. Apart from one small second-year group (13-year-olds) these were the first pupils to have experienced any serious treatment of voltage. Figure 19.2(d) shows that there was a steady increase with age in the percentage of subjects who conserved current, though, when all uncertainties over classification are taken into account, at least 27 per cent of the sixth-year group definitely did not conserve.

Additional insights into the nature of Model II were available from the answers to Question 2, given in Figure 19.3. If the total resistance of a series circuit is increased then the current flowing will decrease. This is the case whatever the positions of the resistors are in the circuit. This question investigated children's understanding of these two rules. The question appears rather cumbersome but some children hold rather odd ideas in which the effect of increasing a resistor is not necessarily the inverse of the effect of decreasing it, and it was important that these were distinguished from correct responses.

The most interesting response types from the point of view of the current model used were those in which only a variable resistor situated 'before' the lamp was regarded as having any effect upon it while a variable resistor located 'after' the

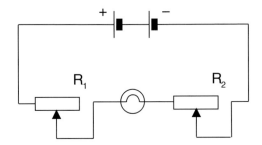

R₁ and R₂ are resistors which can be either increased or decreased.

(a) If R₁ is *decreased*, will the brightness of the lamp

INCREASE ☐   DECREASE ☐   or STAY THE SAME? ☐

(Please tick which)

Why do you say that?

(b) If R₂ is *increased*, will the brightness of the lamp

INCREASE ☐   DECREASE ☐   or STAY THE SAME? ☐

Why do you say that?

(c) If R₁ is *increased*, will the brightness of the lamp

INCREASE ☐   DECREASE ☐   or STAY THE SAME? ☐

Why do you say that?

(d) If R₂ is *decreased*, will the brightness of the lamp

INCREASE ☐   DECREASE ☐   or STAY THE SAME? ☐

Why do you say that?

Figure 19.3 Question 2: more space was provided for the written responses

lamp was thought to have no effect. For example, one sixth-form pupil said that the brightness of the lamp would stay the same if R₁ is decreased because

> R₁ is after the lamp (considering electron flow) hence it will not hinder the voltage;

but if R₂ is increased the brightness of the lamp would decrease because

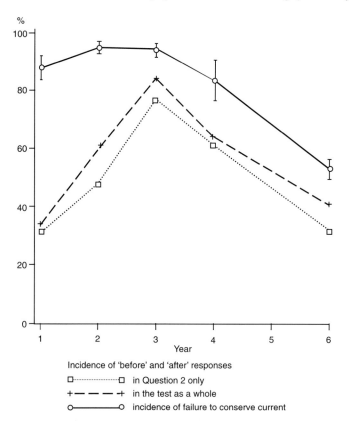

Figure 19.4 Incidence of 'before' and 'after' responses

R_2 is before the lamp therefore it will hinder the energy reaching the lamp (lower voltage) since electron flow is – to +.

The variation with age in the incidence of such responses is shown by the dotted line in Figure 19.4. Here, as in all subsequent analyses, pupils who had shown any indication whatever of reasoning in terms of a bidirectional current model were omitted from the sample. In Question 2, these would have given 'correct' responses because R_1 would always control the current flowing in one direction around the circuit while R_2 controlled the current flowing in the opposite direction. Actually, for a variety of reasons, this question did not detect all of those who reasoned in terms of 'before' and 'after', though it did identify the vast majority. The broken line in Figure 19.4 gives the percentages of each year group who worked in this way at some point in the test. Some of these additional cases had not answered the question completely and, amongst the remainder, were some who had avoided the error by switching the terms in which their explanations were couched from 'current' to 'voltage' or 'power' at critical points in the question.

The model of current flow which is implied by this 'before and after' error is one in which the current, as it progresses around the circuit, is influenced by each element that it encounters in turn. If a change is made at a particular point, then the current is influenced by the change when it reaches that point, but not before. In reality, if any change is made within a circuit, electromagnetic waves travel from the seat of the change in both directions around the circuit. A new steady state is rapidly established in which the voltages and currents in all parts of the circuit will have altered. The children are assuming that information about the change is transmitted only in the direction in which the current is flowing. This model is readily visualized, which is not the case with the accepted view of a circuit as an interacting system, and so has an appeal which is very readily appreciated. Other authors have referred to it as a time-dependent model of current flow (Riley *et al.* 1981). Here it will be given the shorter and more descriptive title of 'the sequence model', since a sequence of events is believed to occur as current flows around a circuit and spatial factors are at least as important as temporal factors in this model.

Clearly this misconception, which represents a fundamental misunderstanding of the behaviour of circuits, is of major importance because of its high incidence, particularly in the middle years of secondary education, and because of its persistence amongst those able pupils who have been studying electricity for about four years and to an advanced level. In fact, the opportunity arose recently to test a group of eighteen graduates at the beginning of their one-year course of training to become physics teachers. No less than seven of these (39 per cent), all of them physicists, still held the sequence model despite intensive study of physics in the preceding three years.

The nature of the model itself, together with the steady increase in its use over years one to three in secondary school, suggests that it is developed as children are introduced to more complex circuits during their formal instruction about electricity. There is evidence that it is the more able pupils who develop the sequence model most rapidly. Some in the first two years who did not apply the sequence model to Question 2 answered correctly, but many had no consistent way of answering the four parts of this question.

When, according to the sequence model, current reaches a resistor, the effect of that must be to alter the current strength, so that the current leaving the resistor differs from that entering. The familiar error of failing to conserve current is thus a logical consequence of the model. Riley *et al.* (1981) reached a similar conclusion in their discussion of localized reasoning in circuit problems. An association would therefore be expected between use of the sequence model and failure to conserve current in the situation depicted in Figure 19.1. The full-line graph of Figure 19.4 gives the percentages who, by implication, failed to conserve current through using the sequence model, or who had not conserved current in the first question, or both. The slight variations in these percentages over years one to four are not statistically significant.

Over the period from year three to year six, the holders of the sequence model formed a large proportion of those who failed to conserve. In year one, however, and to a lesser extent in year two, a large proportion did not hold the sequence model and yet failed to conserve. It is suggested that there are two sources of non-conservation of current, one appearing predominantly amongst the younger subjects and amounting to an intuitive source–consumer view of electricity in which current is used up as it flows around a circuit, the other associated with possession of the sequence model.

Knowledge that children hold the misconception that current is used up as it flows around a circuit is widespread amongst teachers, and it is striking that the problem is so persistent despite our awareness of it. Figure 19.4 suggests that our efforts may be hampered by the emergent use of the sequence model by pupils.

It is not, of course, being suggested that children consciously explore the logical consequences of the conceptual models that they hold. They do, however, use the sequence model readily in reasoning about circuit problems, and it would be very surprising if they did not employ it in seeking to understand as they are taught. The suggestion which is being made here is that use of this model in their learning prevents children assimilating, with understanding, the rule that current in a circuit is conserved.

Current in parallel circuits

Question 3 asked about the effect of increasing the variable resistor R upon the brightnesses of the lamps, L_1 and L_2, in the circuit of Figure 19.5. For each lamp, pupils were asked whether the brightness would increase, decrease or stay the same, and to explain their choices.

Most subjects who reached correct conclusions about the brightnesses of the lamps used the following argument, which still includes some localized reasoning. If R is increased, then more current will flow through L_2 since most current takes the easiest path. Consequently L_2 becomes brighter. However, increasing R will increase the total resistance of the circuit so L_1 carries less current and becomes dimmer.

When the sequence model is applied to this problem, though, the conclusion reached is that L_2 does not change, since the current through this lamp has already

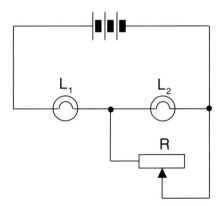

Figure 19.5 Circuit diagram for Question 3

divided from that to R before the change takes place. Again, information about the change in R is only carried forward in the direction of current flow, not backwards.

Investigation of the answers to this question was confined to students in years four and six where there was no doubt that the relevant subject matter had been covered. Through use of the algorithm 'most current takes the easiest path' many subjects explained the effect upon L_2 correctly whatever current model they held and the sixth-form sample relied heavily upon this algorithm. Nevertheless, the errors observed were substantially in agreement with expectations, particularly in year four where 72 per cent of errors made by those holding the sequence model (classified by Question 2) said that L_2 would not change, compared to 22 per cent for those not holding that model. These last reasoned that no current would flow through R anyway, e.g. 'because the current would take the easier route via L_2'.

Conclusions about L_1 by those subjects who reasoned in terms of conventional current flow, from positive to negative, were also as expected: the vast majority of those holding the sequence model concluded that L_1 would not change in brightness. In year four, 96 per cent of their errors were of this type and in year six, 100 per cent. Overall, 59 per cent of those who had used the sequence model in Question 2 definitely used that model again here.

Voltages in circuits

Children experience great difficulties in discriminating between current and voltage (e.g. Bullock 1979; Maichle 1981; von Rhöneck 1981) and Cohen *et al.* (1982) concluded that current is the primary concept used by students, while potential difference is regarded as a consequence of current flow and not as its cause. The study reported here also provides evidence that children learn about voltage (commonly introduced much later than current) in terms of what they understand, rightly or wrongly, about current. Question 4 asked about the effects of increasing the variable resistor R, in the circuit shown in Figure 19.6, upon the

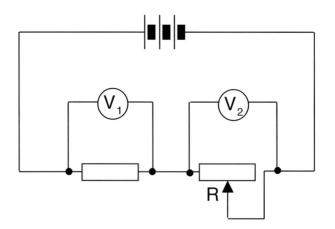

Figure 19.6 Circuit diagram for Question 4

readings of the voltmeters V_1 and V_2. Would they increase, decrease or remain the same?

In general, voltmeters have very high resistances compared with the components across which they are connected, so that they draw very little current from the circuit. The question may therefore be answered very simply, by saying that if R is increased the proportion of the total voltage which is dropped across R will increase. Consequently, the reading on V_2 increases while that on V_1 decreases. In explaining the behaviour of V_2, however, 75 per cent of year four pupils made no reference whatever to either voltage or potential difference, although all had covered the relevant subject matter in lessons. Most explanations were given in terms of current, electricity or power, despite the fact that the question was exclusively concerned with voltages. In addition, 31 per cent of the explanations which referred to voltage treated this as something which flows, e.g. the reading on V_2 will increase 'because more voltage is passing through the current in V_2'.

Where reasoning is in terms of current, application of the sequence model leads to the conclusion that V_2 will remain unchanged because the current entering V_2 has already divided from that entering R and so cannot be influenced by changes taking place within the other branch of the circuit. Also, for conventional current, V_1 will not change because R comes later in the circuit. None of the sixth-year sequence modelers concluded that V_1 would decrease, whereas 55 per cent of the others did so. This strongly suggests that all of those holding the sequence model had failed to assimilate the rules governing the distribution of voltages in circuits.

Implications for teaching

Evidence has been presented of the widespread use amongst pupils of an erroneous model of current flow. The extent to which use of that model persists amongst secondary school pupils has been described and a possible reason for that persistence has been suggested in the very concrete nature of this model compared with the more abstract and complex nature of the accepted model.

Several errors which arise when the sequence model is applied to simple circuits have also been described. It is probable, however, that the most important influence of the model is upon pupils' learning about electricity. As discussed earlier, since they use the model in reasoning when presented with simple problems, it is almost certain they will also use it when trying to understand what they are taught, and many electrical principles cannot be assimilated to this model.

One possible teaching approach to overcome the problem would be to encourage children to consider the models that they hold and to challenge the inadequate models experimentally. An application of this technique has been described recently by Osborne (1982b), who used it in an attempt to modify the incorrect models of current flow held by forty children, aged 8 to 12. No claim was made that the children's ideas were suddenly and permanently altered by the evidence, but all except five were able to see that the scientific model was confirmed by the experimental results. A small-scale study carried out at Nottingham which examined fifth-year pupils' reasoning about their models of current flow during individual interviews about circuits, strongly suggested that the sequence model could be successfully challenged (Shaw-Brown 1981). Osborne's experiment suggests that there may be no need to wait that long and there is a need now for experimental teaching of 12- to 13-year-old pupils, for example, where resistors are introduced into circuits as distinct elements at an early stage and in which children are encouraged to consider the models of current flow that they might apply to circuits such as that in Question 2.

At present, the tendency is to move on quickly from circuits with lamps in series to circuits with lamps in parallel, introducing another complication before the behaviour of series circuits has received adequate attention. Precisely what might amount to 'adequate attention' is a matter for experiment. Härtel (1982) has stressed the need to always treat the circuit as a complete system and has discussed an instructional sequence which provides this emphasis. Obviously, discussion of the mechanism by which information about a change in a circuit is transmitted 'backwards' as well as 'forwards' in the direction in which current is flowing must be in terms of an analogy, for younger pupils at least. It is extremely unlikely, in addition, that children will generalize readily from the simple series case to more complex circuits containing parallel elements, so that the discussion of processes will need to take place repeatedly if we are to encourage our pupils to treat circuits as fully interacting systems rather than as simple ones. Perhaps we unwittingly reinforce the sequence model as we talk to children. In describing a complex circuit such as that of Figure 19.5, we might say, for instance, 'The current flows out of the positive terminal of the battery here, passes through lamp L_1, then splits up at the junction with some going to lamp L_2 and the rest to the variable resistor R ...' A sequence of events is being described. Frequent discussions about the interactions taking place around circuits should help to overcome this problem also.

References

Andersson, B. and Karrqvist, C. (1979) *Elektriska Kretsar* (Electric Circuits), EKNA Report No. 2, Mölndal, Sweden: Göteborgs University.

Bullock, R. R. (1979) 'The pupil's conception of voltage in the middle years of the secondary school', unpublished Ph.D. thesis, University of Nottingham.

Cohen, R., Eylon, B. and Ganiel, U. (1982) 'Potential difference and current in simple electric circuits: a study of students' concepts', *American Journal of Physics* 51: 407–12.

Driver, R. and Easley, J. (1978) 'Pupils and paradigms: a review of the literature related to concept development in adolescent science students', *Studies in Science Education* 6: 61–84.

Fredette, N. and Lochhead, J. (1980) 'Students' conceptions of simple circuits', *The Physics Teacher* 18: 194–8.

Härtel, H. (1982) 'The electric circuit at a system: a new approach', *European Journal of Science Education* 4: 45–55.

Maichle, U. (1981) 'Representations of knowledge in basic electricity and its use for problem solving', paper presented at the conference *Problems Concerning Students' Representations of Physics and Chemistry Knowledge*, Ludwigsburg, FR Germany, September 1981.

Osborne, R. J. (1981) 'Children's ideas about electric current', *New Zealand Science Teacher* 29: 12–19.

Osborne, R. J. (1982a) *Investigating Children's Ideas about Electric Current using an Interview-about-instances Procedure*, Hamilton, New Zealand: SERU, University of Waikato.

Osborne, R. J. (1982b) 'Bridging the gap between teaching and learning', paper presented to the New Zealand Science Teachers' Association Conference, Hamilton, New Zealand.

Osborne, R. J. (1983) 'Towards modifying children's ideas about electric current', *Research in Science and Technological Education* 1: 73–82.

Riley, M. S., Bee, N. V. and Mokwa, J. J. (1981) 'Representations in early learning: the acquisition of problem-solving strategies in basic electricity/electronics', paper presented at the conference *Problems Concerning Students' Representations of Physics and Chemistry Knowledge*, Ludwigsburg, FR Germany.

Shaw-Brown, R. (1981) 'Models and pupils' understanding of electricity', unpublished M.Ed. assignment, University of Nottingham.

Tiberghien, A. and Delacôte, G. (1976) 'Manipulations, representations de circuits electrique simple chez les enfants de 6 à 12 ans', *Review Français de Pedagogie* 34: 32–44.

Viennot, L. (1979) 'Spontaneous reasoning in elementary dynamics', *European Journal of Science Education* 1: 205–21.

von Rhöneck, C. (1981) 'Student conceptions of the electric current before physics instruction', paper presented at the conference *Problems Concerning Students' Representations of Physics and Chemistry Knowledge*, Ludwigsburg, FR Germany.

20 Progression in children's understanding of a 'basic' particle theory

A longitudinal study

Philip Johnson

Introduction

Particle ideas are usually introduced at an early stage of secondary education to explain the three states and mixing (dissolving and diffusion). A model with sufficient detail to cover this territory is what is meant, here, by a 'basic particle theory'. It is not a model which necessarily needs to distinguish between *types* of particle (atoms, molecules and ions) and certainly does not need to consider atomic structure.

A considerable body of research into children's understanding of basic particle ideas exists (e.g. Benson *et al.* 1993; Ben-Zvi *et al.* 1986; Brook *et al.* 1984; Gabel 1993; Haidar and Abraham 1991; Lee *et al.* 1993; Novick and Nussbaum 1978; 1981; Sequeria and Leite 1990; Westbrook and Marek 1991: see Driver *et al.* 1994 and Pfundt and Duit 1994 for bibliographies). The picture that emerges from this work is one of children having a poor grasp of particle ideas. Indeed, even when prompted to think in terms of particles, a significant number of pupils in these studies (typically of the order of 25 per cent) responded only in macroscopic terms. For those that did talk of particles, common findings in relation to five important aspects of the particle theory are summarized below.

(a) *The relative spacing between the particles for the three states.*
Pupils' particle diagrams show the spacing for the liquid state as intermediate between solid and gas. And, furthermore, the relative spacing for the gas state is underestimated.

(b) *The intrinsic motion of the particles.*
Pupils show very little appreciation of the intrinsic motion of the particles. For example, not one student in Westbrook and Marek's (1991) study (which included one hundred undergraduates) thought to explain the diffusion of a dye throughout water in terms of the random movement of particles.

(c) *Ideas of forces/attractions between the particles.*
Very few pupils use ideas of forces/attractions/cohesion between particles, even for the solid state.

(d) *The 'space' between the particles.*
The idea of 'nothing' between the particles, especially for the gas state, appears

to cause considerable difficulties for pupils. Many seem to prefer to think of 'something', usually referred to as 'air', as being between the particles. What the pupils might mean by 'air' is open to doubt (Johnson and Gott 1996), but, whatever else, these pupils do not seem to have a particulate view of air as a material!

(e) *The nature of the particles themselves.*
    Many pupils attribute the macroscopic properties of the material sample to the individual particles.

   This paper reports findings from a study which explored the development of pupils' understanding of the particle theory. The challenge presented by the ideas is not denied, but it will be argued that many of our pupils' 'difficulties' might well be created by our teaching.

Methodology of this research

The results presented here are but part of a much wider exploration of the development of children's concept of a substance (Johnson 1996). Data were collected over a three-year period, in an English non-selective (comprehensive) secondary school, from a cohort of pupils as it moved from Year 7 to Year 9 (ages 11–14). The principal instrument was the periodic interviewing of a sample of pupils (n=33) chosen from the full achievement range and across all teaching groups. Four teaching units, directly concerned with the development of the concept of a substance, formed the background to the study. Figure 20.1 shows the relationship between the teaching units and the interviews.

   A 'basic' particle theory was introduced in Unit 2 as a means of accounting for the three states. The model, as presented, used 'particle' as a general term and included the idea of differing strengths of attraction between particles to account for differences in melting and boiling points between substances. The ideas were then revisited in Unit 3, in the contexts of evaporation, and of air as a mixture of substances in the gaseous state. Finally, Unit 4 applied basic particle ideas to dissolving, crystals, and, again, change of state (with an emphasis on energetic aspects), before introducing ideas of atoms, molecules and giant structures in relation to chemical change (results in this respect are beyond the remit of this paper). Interviews 1, 2, 4 and 5 included portions specifically directed at basic particle ideas and an outline of the tasks and questioning is given in Figure 20.2. It should be noted that a particle explanation of dissolving was not addressed until Unit 4 and did not include a 'gas' as a solute. Therefore, the dissolving tasks in Interviews 2 and 4 and the 'lemonade' task in Interview 5 were an opportunity for pupils to apply particle ideas to a new situation. Although results in relation to dissolving will not be reported here, these responses did help in the interpretation of what a pupil was saying when they talked of particles.

Academic year	Dates	'Activity'
6	June–July 1990	PRELIMINARY INTERVIEW
7	Sept.–Nov. 1990	UNIT 1 Properties of substances
7	Nov.–Dec. 1990	INTERVIEW 1
7	Feb.–April 1991	UNIT 2 Pure substances
7	June–July 1991	INTERVIEW 2
8	Nov.–Dec. 1991	INTERVIEW 3
8	Feb.–March 1992	UNIT 3 The earth as a resource
8	June–July 1992	INTERVIEW 4
9	Nov.–Dec. 1992	UNIT 4 Substances and change
9	Jan.–Feb. 1993	INTERVIEW 5
9	June–July 1993	'TEACHING' INTERVIEW

Figure 20.1 The timing of the interviews and teaching units

Interview 1

At the end of this interview the pupil was asked if he or she had:

- any ideas as to why substances can melt or boil;
- any ideas of what an iron nail might be made of, and what might be seen if it could be magnified a huge number of times;
- what, if anything, the terms atom and molecule meant to him or her.

Interview 2

(a) Sugar

The pupil was questioned about a single grain in the following stages.
What is the grain made of?
 – if particles were not mentioned, then the pupil was asked what he or she
   might see if the grain was magnified a huge numbers of times.
 – if still no mention, then a prompt for particles was given.
The pupil was then asked to draw a particle picture:

> 'Imagine you could look at the grain and see the particles we've talked
> about; could you draw some of what you'd see?'

On completion of the diagram, he or she was asked to label it and say where
the sugar is, and, as a follow up, to comment on what was between the particles as drawn.

(b) Water

This followed the same set of questions as for the sugar.

(c) Differences

The pupil was asked if there were any differences between sugar and water
that were difficult to show in a particle diagram, and the cause of any differences mentioned.

(d) Dissolving

The pupil was asked to predict what would happen if some sugar were to be
put into the water and stirred. After demonstrating this, the pupil was then
asked to draw a particle picture of the solution, and to say why he or she
thought such a thing happens.

(e) Particle picture of gas state

The pupil was shown a picture (of widely spaced dots) and asked what it
might represent.

   If necessary, the pupil was asked to think of it as being for a gas, and
methane in particular. All were then asked to say where the methane was in
the picture, and, as appropriate, to comment on what was between the
particles.

Interview 4

As parts (a) to (e) above (except the reasons in part (c) were not pursued due
to part (g) below), plus:

(f) Nature of particles

The pupil was asked about one particle from each of the sugar, water and
methane examples.

(g)   Three substances in different states
This was at the end of the whole interview. The pupil was asked to explain why three substances, on table in front of him or her, were each in a different state.

Interview 5

As parts (a) to (g) above with the difference in part (f) that:
 Carbon dioxide was used instead of methane, and the pupil was also asked about one particle from each of ice, water and 'water as a gas'. (The 'water as a gas' derived from an earlier section on boiling water.)

(h)   Not stirring
The pupil was asked if sugar would dissolve without stirring.

(i)   Lemonade
The top was unscrewed from a new, clear plastic, bottle of lemonade.
 After questioning to explore what the pupil thought had just happened, with a prompt if necessary, he or she was asked to explain how it is that carbon dioxide can be dissolved.

Figure 20.2 Interview tasks and questioning

The findings

Categories of response

The overwhelming response at Interview 1 (pre-instruction) was very much one of pupils having no real ideas about particles. Responses to the various tasks in Interviews 2, 4 and 5 were used to develop an *overall* picture of a pupil's particle thinking: four distinct particle models could be identified.

Model X   Continuous substance.
               Particle ideas have no meaning. Nothing that resembles the substance having particles of any description is drawn.
Model A   Particles *in* the continuous substance.
               Particles are drawn, but the substance is said to be between the particles. The particles are additional to the substance. There can be varying degrees of 'profile' for the particles (weak to strong) and of association with the substance (none to close).

Model B	Particles *are* the substance, but with *macroscopic* character.
	Particles are drawn and are said to be the substance. There is nothing between the particles. Individual particles are seen as being of the same quality as the macroscopic sample – literally small bits of it.
Model C	Particles *are* the substance, properties of state are *collective*.
	Particles are drawn and are said to be the substance. The properties of a state are seen as collective properties of the particles.

In terms of interpreting the responses, the pupils' meaning for 'particle' is crucial. By first focusing on *one* grain of sugar, and asking the pupils to draw *some* of what might be seen, possible confusion with the everyday meaning of the term (which would class a grain as a particle) was confronted. All the pupils who drew particle diagrams showed a number of particles grouped together in some way and commented that there would be a great many in the grain (or whatever). It seems they were talking about an idea of 'things' that were not directly visible. It is unlikely that the sheer numbers involved were appreciated, but here one must ask who really can; 'very small and lots of them' is sufficient for the working of the theory. Figure 20.3 gives some examples of Model A – this provided the greatest challenge to interpretation and was where the application to the dissolving task was most helpful (one example is given in Figure 20.3). The key point for Model A is that the particles were seen as 'something' separate from the substance. For this model and, of course, Model C, the 'substantive' nature of the particles themselves is beside the point and there was no attempt to interpret any images the pupils might have had in this respect. Model B is where pupils did have an image of the 'substantive' nature of the particle – it was the same as the sample of the substance itself. Pupil diagrams for Models B and C were relatively straightforward. Beyond establishing whether or not a pupil thought there were any differences between the particles of different substances or particles of the same substance in different states, the matter was not pursued in the questioning. The 'lemonade' (Interview 5) was perhaps the most challenging context for the pupils to apply particle ideas and some examples of Model C responses are given in Figure 20.4.

There were also cases of different models being used for substances in different states. Some pupils employed a mix of Models X and A, and others both A and B: labelled XA and AB, respectively. There were also pupils, in Interview 5, who used collective ideas for a substance changing state (i.e. no difference between one particle from ice, water and 'water as a gas') but assigned the macroscopic properties of the room temperature state to particles of different substances. These pupils have been put in an intermediate category, BC. Finally, a code of W was assigned where pupils' responses did not allow for a distinction between Models B and C. At Interview 2, this was for all pupils not at X or A, since the depth of the questioning at this early stage was not sufficient to make this resolution. Table 20.1 gives the numbers of pupils at each model category.

Pupil 12 (Interview 4)

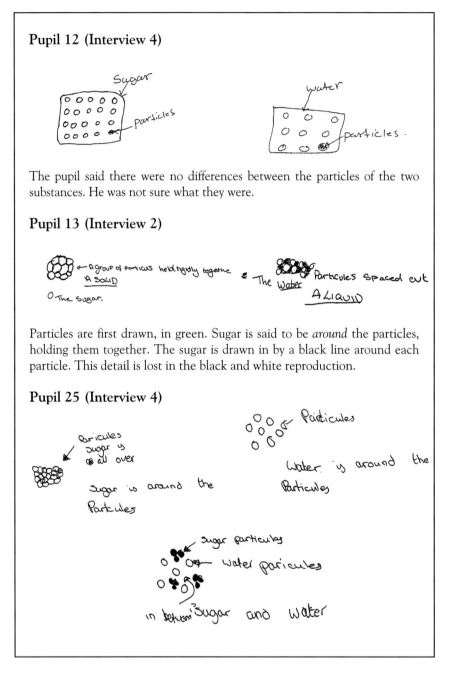

The pupil said there were no differences between the particles of the two substances. He was not sure what they were.

Pupil 13 (Interview 2)

Particles are first drawn, in green. Sugar is said to be *around* the particles, holding them together. The sugar is drawn in by a black line around each particle. This detail is lost in the black and white reproduction.

Pupil 25 (Interview 4)

Figure 20.3 Examples of Model A responses

Note
In the original drawings, different colours were used. Where necessary, particles have been 'filled' to maintain distinctions in the reproductions above.

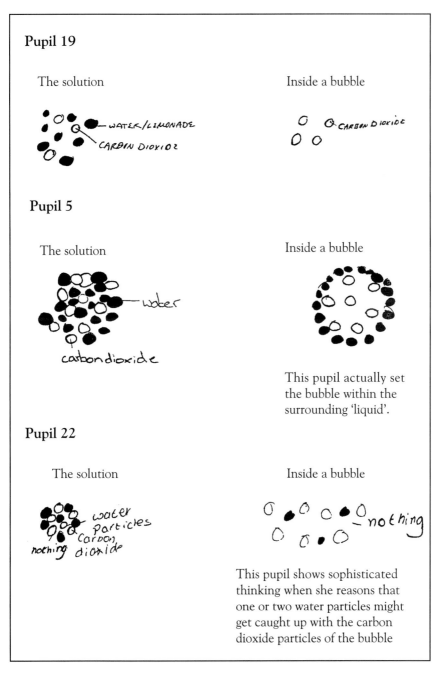

Figure 20.4 Examples of Model C responses to the lemonade task at Interview 5

Note
In the original drawings, different colours were used. Where necessary, particles have been 'filled' to maintain distinctions in the reproductions above.

Table 20.1 Results of the whole interview cohort

Model	Code	Interview 2	Interview 4	Interview 5
No idea of particles	X	1	0	0
Mixed	XA	2	0	0
Particles in the substance	A	9	5	4
Mixed	AW	3	3	1
Particles are the substance – macroscopic	B	—	11	9
Particles are the substance – undifferentiated	W	18	10	—
Particles are the substance – intermediate	BC	—	—	5
Particles are the substance – collective	C	—	4	15

Note
Cells with a — indicate where the questioning was not sufficient to access the model.

Changes between the categories for individual pupils

Figure 20.5 shows the changes between categories for individual pupils, from each starting category at Interview 2, over the interviews. For this purpose, the undifferentiated category of W has been grouped with category B. Responses in other aspects of the interviews (e.g. boiling water) suggest that very few, if any, of these pupils were at BC or C at Interview 2.

Using the idea of attractions between particles

There were four occasions where pupils were given a 'formal' opportunity to invoke ideas of attractions between particles to account for different states; the differences between particle diagrams of sugar and water in Interviews 2 and 4, and the 'three different substances in different states' in Interviews 4 and 5. In all, twenty-one pupils made some use of such thinking. There was a division between pupils who used ideas of attractions with the particle diagrams but not the three substances (n=7), and those who used them for both (at least once). The latter pupils seemed to appreciate the inherent nature of the attractions, i.e. the room temperature state was determined by the 'ability' the particles of a substance 'happen to have' to attract each other. However, it should be noted that five of these pupils were at Model B (the rest were at C), so still needing to think of the particles in macroscopic terms. On the other hand, those pupils who only used the ideas with the particle diagrams seemed to see the strength of attraction as something that was determined by the state; such reasoning does not account for the different states in the first place! This view is quite in keeping with Model A, where the substance

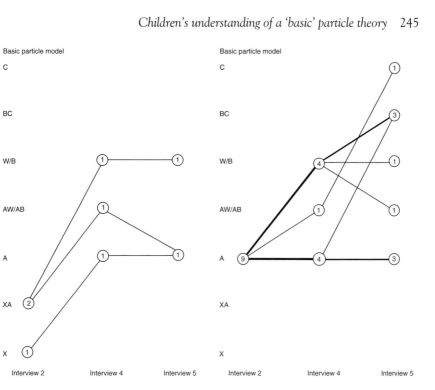

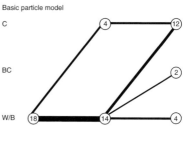

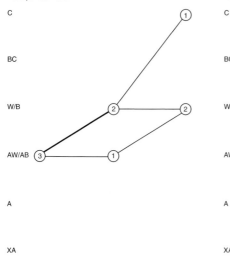

Figure 20.5 Changes in pupils' particle models

itself keeps the particles together; two pupils at Model A were in this group of pupils.

There were five pupils at Model C who did not use ideas of attraction at all. It was striking that four of these five focused very strongly, and exclusively, on the energy of the particles when discussing movement. This is in keeping with the properties of state being a collective property, but gives no account of why particles of different substances at the same temperature should be moving differently. In this sense a purely 'energetic' Model C is a more limited version.

The intrinsic motion of the particles

The intrinsic motion of particles in the gaseous state was less of a problem; after all, gases do have a habit of escaping on their own, if given the chance. However, for the liquid state, the kinetic aspect was seen more as *a potential to move*. While most conceded that the particles in a beaker of still water would be moving around, for many this would be only 'a bit', and seven pupils in Interview 5 said, quite definitely, that the particles would *not* be moving. These were not pupils struggling with the idea of particles, two were at Model C, one at BC and four at B. Furthermore, using the intrinsic motion of particles to account for observed behaviour did not come easily. Although most predicted that sugar would dissolve if left in water without stirring, not one of the pupils employed ideas of the intrinsic motion of the water particles to explain why the particles could mix up 'on their own'.

Dimensions and aspects of the development of pupils' understanding

Two distinct dimensions of development can be abstracted: continuous–particulate and macroscopic–collective. A change of X→A→B is to move along the first dimension. In Model A, the pupil still has an essentially continuous view of matter. However, as 'the particles' become associated with the substance and its behaviour, they can then be conceived as being similar to the substance, and, eventually, 'being the substance'. The pupils in the mixed category AB, indicate that it seems easier to move from A to B for the solid state, followed by the liquid and then the gaseous state. A change from B→C is to move along the second dimension. An extreme form of B would attribute *all* of the properties of a state to the individual particles and not in any way to their movement. The move to C requires relinquishing an image of the 'physical nature' of the particles as a prop for thinking; the properties of a state are explained by the collective behaviour only. Figure 20.5 shows a tendency for the pupils' thinking to develop first along the continuous–particulate dimension and then along the macroscopic–collective dimension. The complete 'basic particle theory' was taught from the start and revisited in each unit, but the pupils did not go straight to Model C. The ideas of attractions between particles and intrinsic motion appear to be aspects which can be incorporated to varying degrees along the way. However, it should be noted that the emphasis in Year 8 (Unit 3) was on the continuous–particle dimension and in Year 9 (Unit 4) it was on the macroscopic–collective dimension. In particular, in the light of the significant showing of Model A at Interview 2, Unit 3 sought to emphasize that the 'particles are the substance'. Teaching materials were re-worded to avoid any phrases such as 'the particles in a solid', which might encourage Model A. Nevertheless, there were examples of pupils progressing along these lines *in advance* of these emphases in instruction. Furthermore, there were many more pupils whose progression lagged *behind* these emphases. Therefore, although the *numbers* of pupils at each model could well be a function of the particular instruction, the results do seem to suggest that pupils' thinking develops in *one* of the dimensions, rather than *both* of the dimensions, at a time.

The time scale for the changes is also worth noting. Although many pupils remained in the same category for a pair of consecutive interviews, over the longer time span, the evidence is that most of the pupils *did* change in their thinking; and with a considerable number moving to Model C.

Implications for teaching and research

The idea of intrinsic motion would appear to be very demanding, but at the same time it can be viewed as just one *aspect* of the particle model and, in other respects, a number of pupils made good progress to a Model C. However, many of the tasks used in reported studies draw heavily upon this aspect, and, therefore, one has to ask if pupils are being denied the opportunity to show the extent to which they *do* understand the model. It may be that the research is presenting a gloomier picture than is the case. In conjunction with this, common ways of *introducing* the theory place great emphasis on precisely the aspect of intrinsic motion, i.e. Brownian motion and diffusion experiments. However, if the particle motion is interpreted by the pupils as an *ability* to move, this is entirely consistent with Model A. It follows that the particles for the solid state can only vibrate if they are stuck *in* a solid, can move around if *in* a liquid and can go where they like if *in* a gas. Renstrom (1988) and Andersson (1990) draw attention to text book illustrations which actually reinforce Model A. Perhaps even more misleading are phrases such as, 'the particles in a solid', which are so commonplace in the language of school science. Furthermore, many questions used to assess pupils' understanding of the particle theory can be answered quite 'correctly' using Model A. Therefore, while for some pupils Model A might be a necessary stage in the development of particle ideas, for others it may well be a direct result of inappropriate instruction: *there is nothing to make them think this is not the theory they are being taught!*

If not Model A, then talk of 'the smallest bit of a substance' would seem to be teaching Model B. De Vos and Verdonk (1987) comment that such thinking in our pupils may well have been encouraged and reinforced by teaching which introduces particles as the 'final result of some lengthy cleavage procedure' (1987: 693). In addition, Model B might well be reinforced by the classification of room temperature samples into 'solids', 'liquids' and 'gases'. This is a favourite activity of school science which might be furthering a notion that there are 'three *types* of substance' (Johnson 1996) and hence three *types* of particle – solid, liquid and gas. In terms of language, how often are pupils referred to the 'solid particles' (ditto, 'liquid' and 'gas' particles)?

Furthermore, if pupils are to progress to a Model C which can account for different substances at the same temperature being in different states, then ideas of 'inherent' attractions between particles must be addressed in general terms. One has to question how strongly this features in lower secondary science courses. Even when specifically included in a teaching scheme, Johnstone and Driver (1991) note, in practice, that teachers gave little time and attention to such ideas.

Finally, the timescale for developing a 'basic' particle model must be taken into account. Of course, this is but one longitudinal study and, given a different teaching background (and one that took note of the points made above), the pupils might have made quicker progress. However, in the absence of evidence to the contrary, it seems prudent to assume that it will take time for pupils to come to terms with the basic particle model. This might mean that the introduction of further ideas will need to be delayed. One has to question the wisdom of attempting to teach atomic structure before a pupil has developed a basic Model C. It is difficult to see what kind of sense this could make on top of either Models A or B!

Conclusions

It seems that pupils might well be in a situation of double jeopardy: teaching which leads with a very difficult aspect of the particle model at the same time as inadvertently promoting Models A or B and omitting a key aspect of Model C; coupled with researchers setting tasks which pick on ideas of intrinsic motion, usually for the state they find most mysterious. One must ask whether pupils have been given a fair chance to show what they could do and whether their poor understanding, so widely reported, is more a function of unfortunate circumstances than anything else. Certainly, it would seem this bears further exploration before the conclusion can be drawn that particle ideas are 'too difficult' (Fensham 1994). Furthermore, if Models A and B are stages (perhaps, necessary stages) of a progression towards the science view this puts such conceptions in a much more positive light than the 'alternative' label implies. This, however, is still no reason to teach such models as endpoints in themselves! (Given that pupils can progress, it might be argued that Model B is the best place to start – but this must be a conscious decision, as part of curriculum planning, not an accident.) Finally, though space precludes elaboration here, related aspects of the wider study gave evidence to suggest that particle ideas helped pupils to think of a 'gas' as being a substance and so opened the way to understanding chemical change (Johnson 2000; forthcoming). This makes a strong case for the need to retain and to improve our teaching of the particle theory. Given that present teaching might not be meeting the needs of pupils, it can be argued that the evidence presented in this paper suggests there is cause for optimism that this can be done.

References

Andersson, B. (1990) 'Pupils' conceptions of matter and its transformations (age 12–16)', *Studies in Science Education* 18: 53–85.

Benson, D., Wittrock, M. and Baur, M. (1993) 'Students' preconceptions of the nature of gases', *Journal of Research in Science Teaching* 30: 587–97.

Ben-Zvi, R., Eylon, B. and Silberstein, J. (1986) 'Is an atom of copper malleable?', *Journal of Chemical Education* 63: 64–6.

Brook, A., Briggs, H. and Driver, R. (1984) *Aspects of Secondary Students' Understanding of the Particulate Nature of Matter*, Leeds: Centre for Studies in Science and Mathematics Education, University of Leeds.

De Vos, W. and Verdonk, A. H. (1987) 'A new road to reactions: the substance and its molecules', *Journal of Chemical Education* 64: 692–4.

Driver, R., Squires, A., Rushworth, P. and Wood-Robinson, V. (1994) *Making Sense of Secondary Science – Research into Children's Ideas*, London: Routledge.

Fensham, P. (1994) 'Beginning to teach chemistry', in P. Fensham, R. Gunstone and R. White, *The Content of Science: A Constructivist Approach to its Teaching and Learning*, London: Falmer, pp. 14–28.

Gabel, D. (1993) 'Use of the particle nature of matter in developing conceptual understanding', *Journal of Chemical Education* 70: 193–4.

Haidar, A. H. and Abraham, M. R. (1991) 'A comparison of applied and theoretical knowledge of concepts based on the particle nature of matter', *Journal of Research in Science Teaching* 28: 919–38.

Johnson, P. M. (1996) 'What is a substance?', *Education in Chemistry* 33: 41–2.

Johnson, P.M. (2000). 'Children's understanding of substances, part 1: recognising chemical change', *International Journal of Science Education* 22(7): 719–37.

Johnson, P.M. (forthcoming) 'Children's understanding of substances, part 2: explaining chemical change', *International Journal of Science Education*.

Johnson, P. M. and Gott, R. (1996) 'Constructivism and evidence from children's ideas', *Science Education* 80: 561–77.

Johnston, K. and Driver, R. (1991) *A Case Study of Teaching and Learning about Particle Theory*, Leeds: Centre for Studies in Science and Mathematics Education, University of Leeds.

Lee, O., Eichinger, D., Anderson, C., Berkheimer, G. and Blakeslee, T. (1993) 'Changing middle school students' conceptions of matter and molecules', *Journal of Research in Science Teaching* 30: 249–70.

Novick, S. and Nussbaum, J. (1978) 'Junior high school pupil's understanding of the particulate nature of matter: an interview study', *Science Education* 62: 273–81.

Novick, S. and Nussbaum, J. (1981) 'Pupils' understanding of the particulate nature of matter: a cross-age study', *Science Education* 65: 187–96.

Pfundt, H. and Duit, R. (1994) *Bibliography: Students' Alternative Frameworks and Science Education*, fourth edition, Keil, Germany: Institute for Science Education.

Renstrom, L. (1988) 'Conceptions of matter: a phenomenographic approach', *Goteburg Studies in Educational Sciences* 69: 1–268.

Sequeira, M. and Leite, L. (1990) 'On relating macroscopic phenomena to microscopic particles at the junior high school level', in P. L. Lijnse, P. Licht, W. de Vos and A. J. Waarlo (eds), *Relating Macroscopic Phenomena to Microscopic Particles; A Central Problem in Secondary Science Education*, Centre for Science and Mathematics Education, University of Utrecht: CD-ß. Press, pp. 220–32.

Westbrook, S. L. and Marek, E. D. (1991) 'A cross-age study of student understanding of the concept of diffusion', *Journal of Research in Science Teaching* 28: 649–60.

21 Children's ideas about ecology

Theoretical background, design and methodology

John Leach, Rosalind Driver, Philip Scott and Colin Wood-Robinson

Background to the study

In 1989, the National Curriculum Council commissioned the Children's Learning in Science Research Group to carry out a research project to document, across the 5–16 age range, the development of children's conceptual understandings in science in order to inform revisions to the newly introduced National Curriculum. Some attention had already been given, in the UK research literature, to conceptual progression in the physical sciences across the 5–16 age range (e.g. Baxter 1989; Brook *et al.* 1989; Holding 1987) and it was thought that a study in the biological domain was necessary to provide a balanced research perspective in order to inform curriculum planning.

Although several studies have investigated children's understanding of photosynthesis at specific ages (reviewed by Wood-Robinson 1991), little work has been done to explore learners' understandings of matter cycling and energy flow. The present study was therefore designed to examine the ways in which children of different ages think about and explain situations which involve cycles of matter, flows of energy and the interdependency of organisms in ecosystems. The purpose of this introductory paper is to explain the rationale for the methodology used in the study, to outline how it was developed and to describe the tools used to probe children's understanding. The findings from the study are described in Leach *et al.* (1996a; 1996b).

Theoretical background

A fundamental issue for any study which sets out to monitor children's thinking in specific concept areas relates to the nature of the data which are collected. What, for example, are the assumptions being made about the status of the children's ideas which are collected and reviewed during the study? When reference is made to general trends in progression in children's thinking, how is progression in reasoning conceptualized? These are basic questions which have significance for both the research methodology and interpretation of data. The present study describes progression in thinking about natural phenomena in terms of three interrelated factors: students' knowledge of phenomena; the ontological commitments associated with that knowledge; and students' epistemological commitments.

Progression in learning is not only associated with students' knowledge of phenomena. It is often associated with changes in children's basic assumptions about the nature of the world, i.e. in their ontologies. Such ontological changes include, for example, moving from the idea that 'air is nothing' to believing that 'air is a substantive medium'; or coming to see that 'matter is conserved' rather than 'matter is used up'. Each of these examples represents shifts in students' fundamental assumptions about the nature of the world. In addition to developments in ontological commitments, learning science also involves changes in the assumptions children make about the nature of scientific knowledge: it involves epistemological changes. This becomes apparent when reviewing the nature of children's explanations at different ages. Young children, for example, tend to offer descriptions of phenomena rather than explanations: 'Why does the apple go rotten?' 'Because it is brown and soft'. As children get older, they are more likely to use causal explanations. Other epistemological changes may relate to the extent to which ideas are internally consistent or generalizable across a range of phenomena. The point which is being made here is that mapping progress in children's thinking with regard to particular phenomena involves more than just reporting the ideas and concepts used: progression is also characterized by developments in other aspects of children's reasoning.

A further issue for consideration relates to the question of what might prompt development in children's thinking. It is proposed that children's thinking about particular phenomena is influenced both by social factors (principally through language) and by experience with phenomena.

Social influences include everyday ways of talking about, and referring to, the phenomena under consideration. These everyday ways of knowing or 'life world knowledge' (Solomon 1987), are often taken for granted by both children and adults alike. They are views which are part of a common culture and, as such, they may, or may not, be in accord with the science perspective. One example of such an everyday way of knowing would be the notion that 'plants feed from the soil'. This is an idea which is counter to the science point of view, which is unsupported by any direct form of evidence (although there may be circumstantial evidence such as the use 'plant foods' which are added to the soil), and yet is firmly established as part of common knowledge. As social beings, children are enculturated into many such ways of knowing.

At the same time, experience of the natural world is likely to influence children's thinking, especially with regard to ecological phenomena. Children see for themselves nesting birds, grazing cattle, decaying fruit and the like, and these experiences are likely to affect their thinking and expectations about natural phenomena. Nevertheless, it is important to recognize that such 'experience' is always mediated by current social representations and, as such, it is difficult, in practice, to disentangle experiential and social influences.

Suffice it to say that when children are introduced, in school or elsewhere, to the science view of the concepts and phenomena which are of interest in this study, they start with an established personal history of listening, talking, experiencing and thinking about the matters under consideration. In this respect, progression in learning might be conceptualized as a dynamic and ongoing process involving additions, developments and changes to existing modes of thinking. Progression might be prompted by schooling or through more informal situations. In some instances, children will integrate the science concepts learned in school with existing knowledge structures. In other cases, science knowledge will build on existing structures but will tend to be held separately from everyday ways of knowing and will be drawn on as particular contexts demand. It is these developing, multiple ways of knowing which are probed in studies such as the one reported here. In designing the research methodology, the possible knowledge systems used by young people and the way that different research methods may elicit different types of understanding need to be taken into account.

Approaches to probing students' thinking

A wide range of methods for probing students' thinking in science has been developed in recent years (White and Gunstone 1992). Different methods are designed to access different aspects of students' reasoning.

Driver and Erickson (1983) have made the distinction between phenomenological and conceptually-based approaches. Phenomenological approaches to probing students' thinking involve presenting students with events or systems and asking them to make predictions and give explanations for the way things happen. No restraint is placed on the way the student responds as they talk about the phenomenon using conceptual categories of their own choice. The Piagetian clinical interview is the classical example of such an approach. Other phenomenologically-framed methodologies have been devised including 'interview-about-events' (Osborne and Gilbert 1980) and 'predict–observe–explain' techniques (Gunstone and White 1981). In all such approaches, it is the student's knowledge scheme relating to the phenomenon in question which is of interest. Moreover, it is the student who selects the language and representations to communicate that knowledge scheme.

Conceptually-based approaches to probing students' thinking focus on aspects of the students' propositional knowledge structure. Typically, words or propositions are presented and students are asked to perform specific tasks with them. Such approaches include word association techniques (Shavelson 1974), concept mapping (Novak and Gowin 1984), and defining the meaning of terms. Adeniyi (1985), for example, asked Nigerian students to define terms such as 'ecosystem', 'population', 'food chain', 'pyramid of numbers' and noted any differences between student and science definitions. Although this approach allows inferences to be made about the meaning that individuals ascribe to the language and ideas of science, it is not possible to make inferences about the way in which they construe phenomena in their own terms. For example, it is not a logical conclusion that a 13-year-old student from a Nigerian farming community, who cannot remember the meaning of the term 'ecosystem', has no ideas about the relationships between organisms.

The present study aims to document students' own reasoning about ecological phenomena without framing the terms in which responses are given. Hence a phenomenological approach has been used to probe students' thinking by presenting them with specific biological situations, illustrated through pictures, photographs and video.

Although the terms in which explanations are sought are not constrained explicitly, it is recognized that the social setting of interviews held in a school environment may influence the way students frame responses.

Conceptual analysis to define the study domain

Scientific explanations of the relationships between organisms in ecosystems are complex and draw on a number of key science concepts. In order to define the domain of the present study and to select appropriate phenomena for the probes, the specific science concepts and relationships of interest were first specified.

In broad terms, scientific explanations of organisms in ecosystems involve describing the needs of all organisms for matter and energy, and the mechanisms by which they get this matter and energy. Knowledge of the processes of photosynthesis, respiration, decay, competition and predation is applied to systems of living organisms and non-living entities in the environment to explain the relationship between organisms. In addition, other features such as the need for shelter, result in interdependency between organisms.

Six features of the relationship between organisms in ecosystems were identified. These were termed 'Key Ideas', and are summarized as follows:

- *Transfer of matter and energy between organisms*   The need of consumers for matter and energy from producers. The flow of organic matter in ecosystems, as summarized in food chains and webs. The interdependence of organisms in a food web and its importance to the stability of an ecosystem.
- *Exchange of matter and energy with the environment*   The need of organisms to exchange matter and energy with the environment in the form of gases, water, minerals and food. Energy exchanges with the environment, involving light and heat energy.
- *Habitat*   The relationship between the organism and its habitat including structure/function relationships.
- *Photosynthesis*   The process by which producers synthesize food materials using the sun's energy and matter from the environment. The importance of this energy conversion to the biosphere.
- *Respiration*   The process by which all organisms make energy in food available for use, and the associated dissipation of energy to the environment in the form of heat.
- *Decay*   The process of decay and its role in the cycling of organic and inorganic matter. The associated flow of energy to decomposers.

There are obviously relationships between the key ideas. For example, a scientific understanding of transfer of matter and energy between organisms and

Table 21.1 Mapping of probes onto key ideas

	Probes				
Key idea	Apple	Video	Community	Scene	Eat
Photosynthesis			*	*	*
Respiration			*	*	*
Decay	*	*			
Habitat			*	*	
Transfer of matter and energy between organisms			*	*	*
Exchange of matter and energy with the environment	*	*	*	*	*

exchange of matter and energy with the environment requires an understanding of the processes of photosynthesis, respiration and decay. In addition, the *context* in which phenomena are encountered is likely to affect the type of explanation given. For example, a biologist studying the ecology of a woodland habitat may focus on the *flow* of energy between organisms, whereas a biologist studying the ecology of one woodland species may focus on the *source* of energy for that species in a more restricted way.

The research probes

Rationale for the design of the research probes

Five diagnostic instruments or probes were designed to provide contexts through which children's thinking about each of the six key ideas could be investigated. (These probes, called 'Apple', 'Video', 'Community', 'Scene' and 'Eat' are described later in this paper.)

Biological situations were selected as contexts for the research probes in such a way as to provide coverage of all the key ideas. Individual probes provide opportunities to use more than one key idea and the overall pattern of coverage is summarized in Table 21.1.

Providing a context for the use of each key idea in more than one probe enabled some investigation of the extent to which children use different ideas in explaining what the scientist sees as being phenomena requiring a similar explanation (Engel Clough and Driver 1986).

As discussed earlier, the probes were framed in phenomenological terms, focusing observation and discussion on actual objects or events (such as a rotten apple) or on pictures of natural situations (such as photographs of woodland). Contexts were selected so as to be accessible to children right across the 5–16 age range in terms of both the content of the probes and the mode of presentation. All probes, with the exceptions of 'Video' and 'Community', were used with all ages. The probes were administered by interviews up to the age of 8 years and through a combination of interviews and paper-and-pencil tasks from age 8 upwards. The paper-and-pencil format provided the means to increase significantly the sample size in the older age groups. The validity of the written responses was investigated by comparing individual pupils' responses on interviews and paper-and-pencil tasks using the same probe.

The development of the research probes

All phases of the study, including the development of the probes, were carried out in association with a group of practising primary and secondary teachers. The development of probes involved a number of stages and is illustrated by considering one probe, 'Apple', in detail.

'Apple' was designed to probe children's ideas about cycling of matter in ecosystems and the role of decay in that process. Working with teachers, various examples of decay familiar to pupils in the 5–16 age range were identified. These included decaying leaf litter, wood and fruit. Photographs and artefacts for each of these examples were collected and presented to small samples of pupils across the age range, in order to determine which of these contexts were familiar to pupils. They were asked whether they had seen anything like these things before, and to describe what they noticed. From this piloting, it was decided that decaying fruit was more familiar to pupils than other examples, and this context was used for the development of the 'Apple' probe.

In the probe, pupils were presented with a photograph of a decaying apple lying under an apple tree. The photograph was enlarged to show detail of the apple to pupils, and younger pupils were also shown an actual decaying apple. Pupils were first asked to describe what they noticed about the apple and then to describe what they thought was making this happen. In this way, inferences could be made about the significant features of the phenomenon in the pupil's terms and the concepts drawn on by pupils to frame their descriptions and explanations.

During pilot studies, many pupils suggested that the apple would get smaller, and so a question was written into the probe to explore where pupils thought the 'stuff' from the apple might go.

In addition, many pupils used words with fairly specific scientific meanings such as 'germs', 'bacteria', 'rot', 'decay' and 'biodegrade'. Whenever these words were raised by pupils in the interviews, they were asked to explain to the interviewer what they meant. An outline interview schedule was devised, drawing both on the outcomes of the pilot trials and the conceptual analysis of the domain. Thus in the 'Apple' probe, some questions related to the nature and cause of decay and others to the fate of matter during the decaying process.

A similar process of piloting was undertaken with the other probes, identifying familiar contexts and using pupils' responses to identify common ways of reasoning. This information was used in designing interview protocols to probe commonly-noted forms of reasoning in a systematic way.

In certain parts of the probes, it was decided to use questions framed in scientific terms in order to find out whether pupils used different ideas when triggered by 'school science' language. These questions were always placed at the end of interviews, so as not to influence the ideas drawn on by pupils in phenomenologically-framed questions. Thus the final question on the 'Apple' probe presented pupils with a brief description of a germ theory of decay, and asked whether they had heard of ideas like this before. If they answered that they had, they were asked to tell the interviewer anything they knew about this.

The content validity of the probes was discussed with an ecologist, whose comments were incorporated into the design.

Probes relating to children's understanding of matter cycling

Two probes, 'Apple' and 'Video', were designed to elicit children's ideas about the process of decay, by presenting pupils with a pictorial or video example of decay, followed by questioning that allowed pupils to describe, in their own terms, what they noticed about the process.

'Apple' probe

The 'Apple' probe was used with pupils from age 5 to 16 as an interview task, and with pupils from age 8 to 16 as a pencil-and-paper task.

Pupils were presented with a colour photograph of an apple tree, as previously described. The questions asked are listed in Appendix 1 and focus on the appearance of the apple, possible explanations for any differences noted between the apple illustrated and 'normal' apples, and the fate of matter as the apple gets smaller (if this was mentioned).

Once these questions were completed (and collected up in the case of pencil-and-paper tasks), pupils were asked whether they had heard of a germ theory of decay, and to say or write down what they knew.

'Video' probe

This probe was administered to pupils from age 10 to 15 as a pencil-and-paper task.

The focus material was a sequence of time-lapse video photography of a bowl of fruit decaying over a period of months. Children were shown the sequence after some explanation of the process of time-lapse photography. They were then shown the video a second time at a slower speed, after which they were given their response sheets, and the questions were read through. The video sequence was then shown for a final time at the slower speed.

The questions asked pupils for explanations of the changes in the fruit, the time scale of the process and the fate of the fruit matter as the fruit gets smaller. Pupils were also asked to make predictions about possible further changes to the fruit.

Probes relating to children's ideas about the interdependence of organisms in ecosystems

Three probes, 'Community', 'Scene' and 'Eat', were designed to elicit children's ideas about the interdependency of organisms in ecosystems.

'Community' probe

The 'Community' probe was used as a pencil-and-paper task with children from age 8 to 16. Pupils were presented with a large, colour version of the illustration shown in Appendix 1 (Figure 21.1). They were first asked to select a group of six different organisms from those illustrated, using the criterion that they would be able to live together for a long period of time, getting everything they needed. The illustrated environment contained water and light in addition to the organisms selected by the pupils. Having selected a community of organisms, pupils were asked for each organism, 'What does it need' and 'Where does it get them from?' Finally, they were asked to consider the six organisms they had chosen and were asked 'Which do you think there might be most of?'. The words 'organism', 'animal' and 'plant' were avoided in the wording of the probe as pupils' meanings for these terms may differ from scientific meanings.

'Scene' probe

The 'Scene' probe was administered to pupils from age 5 to16 as an interview only. Pupils were presented with a large, colour photograph of a woodland scene, including a river and some grassland, and were given picture cards of forty organisms. They were asked to select from the illustrated organisms those most likely to be found in different places in the picture, including the canopy of a tree, in the river and on the grassy bank of the river. In each location, pupils were encouraged to choose as many organisms as they thought appropriate. Having identified a group of organisms for a specific location, the interviewer then selected a primary consumer, a secondary consumer and a producer, and pupils were asked about the needs of each organism and how those needs were met. They were also asked which organism would be most numerous and to explain their choice.

'Eat' probe

The 'Eat' probe was administered to pupils from age 8 to 16 as a pencil-and-paper task, and to pupils from age 5 to 16 as an interview. Pupils were presented with a line drawing of a large region including fields, mountains and woodland (see Appendix 1, Figure 21.2). They were told that the picture showed a place where plants and animals live together and get everything they need. Each organism in the picture was named. Attention was drawn to the food web for the community and some examples of using the food web were provided (e.g. where do mountain lions get their energy from?).

Pupils were then asked to predict the effects of changing the population of various species at different trophic levels in the food web. They were told that the population size of a primary consumer population was greater than that of a secondary consumer population that preyed on it, and were asked to explain the reason for this. Finally, they were asked about the sources of matter for growth of the plants and animals in the community.

The interpretation of arrows in food web diagrams has been found to be difficult for pupils (Schollum 1983). The purpose of the probe was not, however, to find out whether pupils can interpret food web diagrams, but rather to find out what reasoning is drawn on in thinking about populations of organisms. In administering this probe, help was given to pupils to ensure that they understood the feeding relationships represented in the food web. For the interviews with children aged 5–7, the food web diagram was considered to be inappropriate. Instead, the interviewer asked the child where they thought each organism might get energy from and then drew lines on the picture itself to represent this.

Administration of the probes and sampling

Two probes, 'Apple' and 'Eat', were administered as individual interviews and in paper-and-pencil formats. 'Scene' was administered only in interview format and 'Video' and 'Community' only in paper-and-pencil format. In the interviews, which were used with pupils aged 5–16, pupils were told that the purpose of the interview was to find out what they thought about an aspect of science which related to living things living together. The interviewer stressed at the beginning of the interview that he was interested in the subject's ideas, rather than in finding out what the 'right answers' were. All interviews were audio-taped for subsequent analysis, and subjects were told that these data would be treated anonymously.

Additional data were collected from children aged 8–16 in written form, using some of the probes. In most cases, a researcher was present in the classroom to introduce the task to pupils. Where a researcher was not available to introduce the task, the normal class teacher was given training in the administration of the probes. Silence was not requested while subjects completed the probes, and in practice, the atmosphere tended to be one of diligent hard work with some quiet exchanges between pupils rather than silent, examination-like conditions. The probes were read aloud for pupils, and pupils were encouraged to ask for help where they did not know what to do. Many pupils asked for help in *answering* the questions and the researcher and trained teachers dealt with these questions by asking pupils what *they* thought was the answer, and then encouraging them to write down their answer on the sheet.

Subjects were selected from four primary schools and four secondary schools, located in low- to middle-income areas near a large urban area in the north of England. The schools were identified as being typical of schools in the area and sampling of pupils within schools involved taking whole classes as far as was possible. Overall sample sizes and details of samples for each probe are shown in Tables 21.2 and 21.3.

Table 21.2 Details of sample

Age	Sample size	
	For interview sample	For pencil-and-paper sample
5–7	45	0
7–11	16	81
11–14	16	220
14–16	8	153

Table 21.3 Details of sample for each probe

Age	Probe				
	Apple	Video	Community	Scene	Eat
5–7	(30)	0	0	(30)	(14)
7–11	61 (16)	29	51	(16)	76 (16)
11–14	107 (16)	107	114	(16)	76 (16)
14–16	124 (16)	84	123	(8)	32 (8)

Note

Numbers in parentheses indicate the number of interviews carried out; other numbers indicate pencil-and-paper administration.

Analysis of the data

The data from the study comprised audio-taped interviews and pupils' written responses to the probes. The first stage of analysis involved the development of a coding scheme for each of the probes. This was achieved by reviewing pupils' responses at each age and identifying common ideas and modes of explanation. The coding schemes were thus developed from children's responses rather than being based, for example, on the normative science perspective. For each probe, a multiple-feature coding grid was devised to reflect the specific features in the responses, and this resulted in a string of codes for each student response.

Interviews and written responses were coded directly onto spreadsheets, probe by probe, by one researcher. A sample of the data was independently coded by the principal coder and another researcher, and an inter-rater reliability of above 90 per cent was achieved. Pupil responses to questions in each area were considered, and commonly-occurring patterns of response were identified. In some cases, it appeared that similar views underpinned a variety of responses from different pupils. For example, many pupils explained the decay of the apple with ideas such as the apple had 'died', it no longer received nourishment from the tree, or that it had got 'too old'. These ideas all seemed to involve a view of decay as a 'natural feature of apples' that required no further explanation. Such responses were therefore selected from the spreadsheets and reported together under a 'natural feature' category. In this way, broader reporting categories were generated from the initial codings.

The reliability of the probes was determined by comparison of interview and paper-and-pencil responses of individual pupils on the same probe between the ages of 7 and 16 (see Table 21.3). In practice, there was virtually no difference between the codes of students' responses to interview questions and written questions.

The data were examined for age-related patterns in types of explanation and the final stage of analysis involved a comparison of patterns of responses across different research probes.

Final comments

It is perhaps worth clarifying the claims which can and cannot be made about the findings of a study such as this. The first point to emphasize is that the study is of a cross-sectional design and, as such, it allows for the reporting of the frequencies with which different ideas and modes of explanation are used by children, in response to particular tasks, at different ages. The study cannot, however, provide details of how individual children's thinking progresses with time. To achieve this, a longitudinal design would be needed.

Furthermore, on the basis of studies such as this, any comment on the nature of progression and what drives it is pure speculation. Nevertheless, careful documentation of children's explanations can contribute to the ongoing debate about the nature of progression in learning by providing empirical evidence against which theories can be evaluated (Carey 1985). Information about the way children at different ages think about natural phenomena can be drawn on in curriculum design, so that teaching is planned to take account of children's current ways of thinking. It is hoped that the findings from this study, as reported in the forthcoming papers relating to children's ideas about the cycling of matter and of interdependency, will serve such functions.

Acknowledgements

We would like to thank Gustav Helldén, Kristianstad University College, Dick Konicek, University of Massachusetts at Amherst, and Bonnie Shapiro, University of Calgary, for their advice on the development of the probes used in this study. The research was funded by the National Curriculum Council for England and Wales.

References

Adeniyi, E. O. (1985) 'Misconceptions of selected ecological concepts held by some Nigerian students', *Journal of Biological Education* 19: 311–316.

Baxter, J. (1989) 'Children's understanding of familiar astronomical events', *International Journal of Science Education* 11: 502–13.

Brook, A., Driver, R. with Hind, D. (1989) *Progression in Science: The Development of Pupils' Understanding of Physical Characteristics of Air across the Age Range 5–16 Years*, Leeds: Centre for Studies in Science and Mathematics Education, University of Leeds.

Carey, S. (1985) *Conceptual Change in Childhood*, Cambridge, MA: MIT Press.

Driver, R. and Erickson, G. (1983) 'Theories-in-action: some theoretical and empirical issues in the study of students' conceptual frameworks in science', *Studies in Science Education* 10: 37–60.

Engel Clough, E. and Driver, R. (1986) 'A study of consistency in the use of students' conceptual frameworks across different task contexts', *Science Education* 70(4): 473–96.

Gunstone, R. F. and White, R. T. (1981) 'Understanding of gravity', *Science Education* 65: 291–99.

Holding, B. (1987) *Investigation of Schoolchildren's Understanding of the Process of Dissolving with Special Reference to the Conservation of Matter and the Development of Atomistic Ideas*, Leeds: School of Education, University of Leeds.

Leach, J., Driver, R., Scott, P. and Wood-Robinson, C. (1996a) 'Children's ideas about ecology 2: ideas found in children aged 5–16 about the cycling of matter', *International Journal of Science Education* 18(1): 19–34.

Leach, J., Driver, R., Scott, P. and Wood-Robinson, C. (1996b) 'Children's ideas about ecology 3: ideas found in children aged 5–16 about the interdependency of organisms', *International Journal of Science Education* 18(2): 129–42.

Novak, J. D. and Gowin, D. B. (1984) *Learning how to Learn*, Cambridge: Cambridge University Press.

Osborne, R. and Gilbert, J. (1980) 'A method for the investigation of concept understanding in science', *European Journal of Science Education* 2(3): 311–21.

Schollum, B. W. (1983) 'Arrows in science diagrams: help or hindrance for pupils?', *Research in Science Education* 1(3): 45–9.

Shavelson, R. J. (1974) 'Methods for examining representations of a subject-matter structure in a student's memory', *Journal of Research in Science Teaching*, 11: 231–49.

Solomon, J. (1987) 'Social influences on the construction of pupils' understanding of science', *Studies in Science Education* 14: 63–82.

White, R. T. and Gunstone, R. F. (1992) *Probing Understanding*, London: Falmer Press.

Wood-Robinson, C. (1991) 'Young people's ideas about plants', *Studies in Science Education* 19: 119–35.

Appendix 1   Questions used in the 'Apple' probe

- What do you notice about the apple?
- What do you think is making this happen? Write down what you think!
- Do you think that anything might happen to the other apples, left on the ground? Write down what you think!
- If nobody touches these apples after a whole year, what might happen? Write down what you think! Where might the 'stuff' that the apples are made of go to?

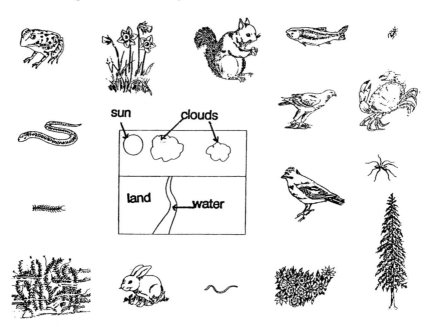

Figure 21.1 Diagram used in the 'Community' probe

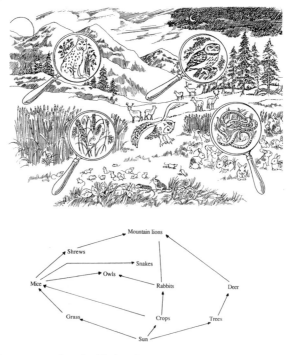

Figure 21.2 Diagrams used in the 'Eat' probe

22 Research, theories of learning, principles of teaching and classroom practice

Examples and issues

Richard White

Science education is not exempt from the general criticism that research has had little effect on classroom practice. It is significant that it is researchers, not teachers, who level this charge: teachers do not reject research, they ignore it.

Reasons for the apparent lack of influence of research on practice need examining, but it may be that the situation is not as bad as many fear. Schools and classroom methods do change (Cuban 1993). How much of that change is due to formal research, however, is difficult to determine, for, as Shavelson (1988) argues, research influences practice in subtle rather than simple ways. In examining that influence, we need to recognise that the relationship between research and practice is two-sided, with practice influencing research in return. Then there are two further partners, psychological theories of learning and principles of teaching, with further two-way relations (Figure 22.1). All six pairs of the relations in Figure 22.1 are complex.

The notion that research should have immediate and direct implications for practice appears to flow from an inappropriate model for the application of scientific discoveries. In this model, the scientist makes some breakthrough in the laboratory, which quickly appears as an invention in general use. Of course, the applications of science are hardly ever so simple and direct. There were many years between Oersted's discovery of the effect of electric current on a magnetic needle and the wide use of electric motors. The relations, as Gardner (1997) has described, between science and technology are complex. In any case, analogies between science and education overlook key differences between the physical sciences and the social. One of these is variability of context, another of individual differences, and another of personal purpose. As far as is known, one atom of iron is identical with another, but people differ. So, while we can be confident that iron expands with temperature at the same rate in the twentieth century as it did in the nineteenth, and the same in Europe as in Asia, we cannot be so certain that a teaching method that was successful in one society will be so in others. We cannot even be sure that it would have worked so well if one particular child had been present or absent from the class.

The most pessimistic conclusion is that contexts are so variable and ephemeral, and human beings so individual and wilful, that no relations between variables

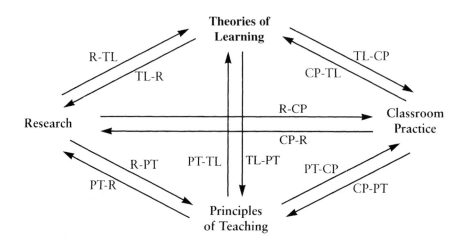

Figure 22.1 Relations between research, theories of learning, principles of teaching, and classroom practice

hold widely enough or stand for long enough to be useful. Therefore research is pointless. This extreme position is not tenable. If it were true, there would be none of the remarkable regularities of practice – the similarities between schools of different countries and between the ways most teachers teach, despite differences in culture and curriculum – which show that school administrators and teachers think about education in similar ways. They have similar theories for practice. Since this uniformity has arisen despite differences in context, we might also expect to find instances where research results, too, are robust and hold across contexts. We should then expect to find instances where research did, and does, influence practice, principles of teaching and theory.

An example of influential research is Piaget's studies of children's conceptions of the physical world, and of their abilities to conserve quantity and volume. Gradually, from his interviews with children, Piaget built a complex theory of operational thought, with subtle constructs such as accommodation and equilibration. This is an example of Relation R-TL in Figure 22.1. Eventually, simplified versions of this theory became known to large numbers of teachers and, presumably, affected how they thought about children's learning and so their practice in teaching (Relation TL-CP). Certainly, Piaget's theory influenced science curriculums in, for instance, the Australian Science Education Project (Ramsey and Dale 1971).

Another curriculum example is the relationship between Gagné's research on task analysis (Gagné 1962; Gagné and Paradise 1961) and his theory of learning hierarchies (Gagné 1965) (Relation R-TL) and the Intermediate Science Curriculum Study (1970) (Relation TL-CP).

Though it is less frequently heard of now, in the 1970s and 1980s many teachers knew of Bloom's research on mastery learning (Bloom 1968; 1971; Block 1971). University teachers applied its derivative, the Keller Plan, in science courses. Bloom based mastery learning on Carroll's (1963) theoretical analysis of why achievement generally followed the normal distribution curve. In this case, the causal direction was clearly one way, from psychological theory to research to practice.

A remarkable instance of the relations between research, learning theory, principles of teaching and practice is the effect that a few artificial psychological experiments had on science teaching in the 1960s. Bruner and colleagues studied people's ability to discover arbitrary rules applying to characteristics of cards that carried varying numbers of shapes of different colours (Bruner *et al.* 1956). The 'concept' that had to be discovered in trials where one card after another was presented, might be 'a green triangle when no red shape was present'. Bruner (1961) made a leap from this artificial context to advocate discovery methods in classrooms. While discovery had long been established as a principle of science teaching, Bruner's elaborations of his theory of learning stimulated many studies of discovery learning of science (Relation TL-R) (see Hermann 1969, for a review). Although the results of these studies were equivocal, discovery learning methods became popular in science teaching (TL-CP, R-CP), and became enshrined as principles of teaching (TL-PT). Perhaps they were more established as principles than practice, for Flanders' (1970) analyses of classroom behaviour showed that lessons remained more teacher-centred than the rhetoric of discovery implied or advocated.

The example of discovery learning illustrates significant features of the relations between learning theory, research, principles of teaching and practice. Bruner's research had an effect on science teaching partly because of his authority and eminence, but more so because it fitted in with a widely-held view that science progressed through discovery, and so it made sense that science learning should do the same. The research could also be summarized in the apparently simple principle that things learned through discovery were understood and remembered better than those one was told. Teachers were not aware of, and indeed might not have been interested in, Bruner's original research and the conflicting classroom studies that followed. If they had read these studies, they would still have had much to do before they could convert the procedures in them to their own teaching. What did affect teachers was the advocacy of discovery learning as a principle of teaching in their training, and the provision of discovery methods in curriculums such as the Earth Science Curriculum Project, the Biological Science Curriculum Study, and the Nuffield curriculums.

Although the examples provided by the work of Piaget and Bruner show that research has influenced practice, we should also consider whether that influence is sufficient and whether it can be enhanced. Reasons for lack of influence might be that there is insufficient research, that there is research but it is irrelevant to the classroom or unconvincing, that there is good relevant research but it needs replication across contexts before it should be applied, that there is useful and confirmed research but teachers do not know about it, that teachers know about research results but their conditions of work prevent them from applying them, and that teachers know about research and could apply it but tradition is against change in practice.

Is there no research?

Absence of research cannot be the reason for any perceived lack of influence it has on practice. The Educational Research Information Clearinghouse records over 80,000 journal articles on science education between the years 1966 and 1996, and the 1994 *Handbook of Research on Science Teaching and Learning* (Gabel 1994) runs to 600 pages, with several thousand references. Many studies are reported at the conferences of the European Science Education Research Association, the Australasian Science Education Research Association, the Association for Science Education, the National Association for Research on Science Teaching, Congreso Internacional Sobre Investigacion en la Didacta de las Ciencas, and others. Whatever else it is, science education research is active. There is a lot of it for teachers to ignore.

Is the research unconvincing and lacking in relevance?

Finn (1988) charged educational research with producing few useful findings. He claimed that many applications for research funds had marginal interest or value. Shavelson and Berliner (1988) rebutted Finn with the examples of work on effective schools, cooperative learning, and generalizability theory. Later, Kaestle (1993) added the examples of word problems in mathematics, the Head Start program, armed forces training, reading and studies from the Institute of Research on Teaching. For science, at least, there is much research on topics that are surely relevant: the laboratory, assessment, learning strategies, problem-solving, sex differences, abilities, attitudes, curricular evaluation, and motivation (White 1997). Although there is a lot of this research, Finn might still mount a case that it is unconvincing: the style of research, the way that it addresses these topics, may render it useless for the classroom. For why this is so, the relations involving psychological theories of learning and principles of teaching have to be considered.

From around 1910 to the 1960s, the almost unchallenged theory, or view, of learning was behaviourism. Behaviourism, and its principle of reinforcement, is a reasonable way of representing aspects of human learning, but it is too limited to meet the needs of teachers. Deese's book titled *The Psychology of Learning* (1958) exemplifies this limitation. Behaviourism omitted the subtleties of the content teachers wanted their students to understand, and the differences between students' purposes, beliefs, attitudes, physical states, and abilities. It also ignored another crucial element, that of the context in which learning occurred. Research on situated cognition (see Hennessy 1993, for a review) has shown how strongly context can affect learning. Above all, behaviourism ignored relations between people, between teacher and students and between students, which are the crucial elements in a teacher's work.

The limitations of behaviourism prevented research from being relevant (Eisner 1984; Glaser 1991). It inhibited researchers from looking into why students acted as they did. Its exclusion of context led researchers to seek relations between a very small number of variables while attempting to hold all other influences constant. The typical study of the 1960s and 1970s involved an artificial situation, in which two or more groups of students were taught by different methods and then tested. The methods were rarely rooted in theory. The teachers of these methods were often strangers to the students. Their usual teachers lent their classrooms and students to the researchers for a short time. The interventions were brief, and students' unfamiliarity with them was not a concern (except for the Hawthorne effect). The content was largely irrelevant, chosen for convenience, and often of neither interest nor value to the students, whom researchers referred to as 'sub-jects'. Most tests were short answer or multiple choice. Statistical tests determined whether the mean scores of the groups differed significantly (in statistical terms), which they might if the samples were large enough although the difference was educationally trivial. The variation of scores between students within each group was seen as a nuisance, frequently termed 'error' in analyses of variance, rather than as an important and interesting matter for study. Shulman (1987) summarizes these deficiencies:

> Critical features of teaching, such as the subject matter being taught, the class-room context, the physical and psychological characteristics of the students, or the accomplishment of purposes not readily assessed on standardized tests, are typically ignored in the quest for general principles of effective teaching.
> (Shulman 1987: 6)

It is perhaps ironic that the concentration on control of variables, and the conse-quent exclusion of attention to critical features of context, may have been respon-sible for the conflicting results that different researchers observed. Kennedy (1997) and Sroufe (1997) note that these conflicting results, and the subsequent argu-ments about their validity and the possible flaws in experimental methods, dimin-ished teachers' and administrators' confidence in the worth of research as a guide to practice.

A further shortcoming of research in the 1960s and 1970s, from teachers' point of view, was that the laboratory studies focused on individuals, whereas teachers work with groups of learners (Kennedy 1997). More subtle theories, that encom-passed variables such as the purposes, abilities and feeling of individuals, and included the social dynamics of groups, might have encouraged forms of research that led to principles of teaching that teachers would have found a useful guide in the many decisions that they have to make, both in the considered planning of lessons and moment by moment in the classroom. The relation between behaviourism and principles of teaching (TL-PT in Figure 22.1) was weak. The few principles that could be formed, such as the importance of intermittent reward for motivating students, were useful, but they did not guide enough of the decisions that teachers have to make. So, although behaviourism was taught in psychology courses in the training of teachers, with its ancillaries of behavioural objectives, programmed instruction and teaching machines, it had little effect on practice.

It was unfortunate that behaviourism was dominant when Education began to penetrate universities and when teacher training expanded after the Second World War, and that it led to research of such a kind. It formed attitudes to theory and research amongst teachers that, while no longer defensible, are now engrained.

Information processing and constructivist models of learning have supplanted behaviourism as the dominant theory. They encompass a much wider set of variables, including content, perception of context, abilities, prior knowledge, attitudes, and purposes.

The major theme of information processing and constructivism is that learning involves a sequence of mental operations that result in constructions of meaning for experiences, and the subsequent storage of those meanings. Further operations enable the recall or reconstruction of the meanings, and their use in coping with new situations. The operations begin with selection for attention of a fraction of the numerous events that surround the learner. The selection depends on what the learner knows and is interested in, his or her immediate purpose, and physical state. Another operation is translation of incoming physical stimuli into meanings. Translation, too, depends on what the learner knows, so that different learners may construct different meanings from the same information.

Most models of information processing postulate a short term memory store of limited capacity and a long term one that is effectively infinite. Processing of information from the short to the long term store involves an operation of linking of incoming to existing knowledge. The result is understanding, an outcome that represents the pattern of links and the various types of knowledge that are present.

The models account for differences in abilities to learn as variations in people's control over the separate operations. Hence they portray ability to learn as multi-dimensional. They opened the possibility that performance of the operations may be improved through training, which led to research on metacognition.

Information processing and constructivist theories present learning as essentially cognitive and individual. They can, however, be supplemented with postulates of affect and of social exchange. Koballa (1992) argues that persuasion theory has value for science teachers. Either alone or supplemented, these theories are more complex than behaviourism, and so more able to illuminate classroom practice.

The greater complexity of these theories is accompanied by a new style of research, characterized by longer interventions, an effort to ensure that they are a more natural part of schooling, less reliance on statistics, and a greater range of methods of collecting data – interviews and classroom observations as well as diverse tests such as concept maps (Novak and Gowin 1984), Prediction–Observation–Explanation, Venn diagrams, drawings and fortune lines (White and Gunstone 1992).

The revolution in style of research is integral with the revolution in theories of learning. Each influenced the other, and neither could have occurred alone. What remains to be considered is how much each influenced, and was influenced by, practice, and what principles of teaching followed. It may be that information processing and constructivism have yet to be condensed to a set of propositions that teachers can use, not only in curriculum and lesson planning decisions but also in the rapid sequence of actions they take in classrooms. This is an extension of Hargreaves' (1996) point that teachers lack a technical vocabulary with which they can think about, create, and share with each other, ideas about learning and teaching.

Should there be more replication of research?

Exact replications of studies in education are rare. Horton *et al.* (1993) estimate that fewer than 10 per cent of studies in science education are replicated. Different contexts make replication difficult, especially for large-scale and lengthy studies. When replication is attempted, these differences may produce different results. That, however, should not be a concern, for if principles are to emerge from research it is necessary to know whether they hold across contexts or whether they have to be qualified by context.

One clear example of replicated results is the discovery of alternative conceptions. Pfundt and Duit (1994) list thousands of reports on probes of students' understandings of natural phenomena and scientific principles, which provide evidence across topics and nations that students form their own beliefs and that these persist, despite teaching of opposing ideas. This evidence appears to have carried conviction, perhaps because the results are clear despite being counter-intuitive, and the studies can be repeated quickly by teachers with their own students.

Are teachers ignorant of research?

Oddly, there appears to be no study of teachers' knowledge of research, or of research's penetration of schools. It may be that teachers know more about research than they themselves recognize. Many attend meetings of the Association for Science Education, the National Science Teachers' Association, the Australasian Science Teachers' Association, and other organizations, where research is reported, and many subscribe to journals that carry research reports, such as *School Science and Mathematics,* the *Physics Teacher,* or the *Australian Science Teachers Journal.* Many enrol in higher degree programmes, where they not only hear about recent research but do some.

No doubt dissemination of research could be better, but the conferences, journals and further study that teachers undertake indicate that ignorance is not the major reason that research is ineffective, assuming it is.

Do conditions inhibit application of research?

Teachers might know about research but be unable to apply it because of the conditions in which they work. Any one of lack of time to plan, lack of equipment, large classes, isolation, inappropriate rooms, a mandated syllabus and a rigid examination system can prevent teachers from implementing a recommendation from research or theory, or new ideas of their own. Even when they do try something, conditions can inhibit them from telling others about the outcomes. So might custom. Lortie (1975) asserted that teachers are too dependent and subservient to engage in inquiry. They are not rewarded for it, and have no traditions that honour contributions to their craft. Isolation of the individual teacher means that even the outstanding among them leave no record and add nothing to knowledge about teaching.

Isolation also makes it difficult for ideas to get into the classroom from outside. 'For the past 150 years, educational reform efforts have tended to originate at the top of the system... and then work their way down through the hierarchy, usually petering out by the time they get to the classroom door.' (Labaree 1992: 130). Yet behind that door, as Labaree goes on to note, teachers have a surprising degree of autonomy. Conditions are one reason why they make so little use of that autonomy. Another is tradition. Teachers have brief pre-service training and receive little mentoring after graduation, so base their notions of teaching mainly on the thousands of hours they spent as pupils.

Is there a solution?

The greater complexity of information processing and constructivist theories and related research means that they should provide a much more useful support than behaviourism for the practice of teaching. Variations of those theories are now two to three decades old, and there is a huge body of related research in science education, yet concerns continue to be expressed about the weakness of the influence research has on practice. Is there not a way of cutting the Gordian knot of obstructions to the application of research? Several writers (e.g. Hargreaves 1996; Hurd 1991) suggest that there is, through the involvement of teachers in research, not as in the past, as targets or at best agents, but as true partners or principals. Kaestle (1993: 27) quotes from an interview with Senta Raizen: 'We need to make schools "learning communities" for teachers.'

Involvement does not mean domination. Gilbert (1994) cautions that, though practitioners should be active partners, for quality work projects must also have trained and experienced researchers. Of course, in time, a proportion of classroom teachers could acquire that training and research experience. This involvement will not, however, of itself lead to better practice. The function of teachers in research is to frame principles of teaching that other teachers can apply.

At least three examples demonstrate the effectiveness of teachers in research: the Cognitive Acceleration through Science Education (CASE) project (Adey and Shayer 1994), the Project for Enhancing Effective Learning (Baird and Mitchell 1986; Baird and Northfield 1992), and the Students' Intuitions and Science Instruction (SI)[2] project (Erickson 1991). In CASE, the teachers were not fully in partnership, but carried much responsibility. In PEEL, the teachers are the principals and the academics assist. In (SI)[2], the partnership was about even.

Cognitive Acceleration through Science Education

CASE has a strong theoretical base. Its principals, Adey and Shayer, combined Piaget's theory of development of operational thought with Vygotsky's notion of Zone of Proximal Development to devise thirty-two science activities. Each activity was intended to promote an aspect of operational thought, such as classifying, compound variables, and probability.

The activities were evaluated in a trial in ten schools. Science teachers used them in a quarter of their lessons with pupils originally in Year 7 or Year 8, for two years. Although the activities were pre-planned, the teachers controlled their presentation. At in-service meetings with the research principals, the teachers reported on difficulties and successes. Adey and Shayer ascribe much of the success of the programme to its in-service element. This is an important observation. Most research is simply reported, without any in-service follow-up activity. Research could have a much greater impact on practice if teachers had intensive and regular in-service meetings.

Adey and Shayer found that CASE had a positive effect on reasoning tasks and science achievement at the end of the programme. This advantage in achievement persisted, and was still evident a year later. Adey and Shayer even report an improvement, compared with a control group, in GCSE examinations one or two years later still in science, mathematics and English.

Project for Enhancing Effective Learning

PEEL began in 1985 in one secondary school on the outskirts of Melbourne. The dozen teachers and the two university staff who were involved shared the purpose of guiding the students to be more purposeful and reflective in their learning. The project differed from CASE, in that it covered English, history, commercial studies, geography, mathematics and physical education as well as Science, in having no predetermined methods, and in having no planned evaluation.

The main activity in PEEL was for the teachers to report, in a regular weekly meeting, on their experiences with procedures that were intended to encourage students to be responsible for their learning. The university academics suggested some procedures, but the teachers invented the majority. The teachers shared with their colleagues their successes and failures with the methods. This sharing led to amendments and further trials. The PEEL activity is similar to that described by Feldman (1996), which involved eight physics teachers engaging in action research. There is the same pattern of anecdote telling, trying out of ideas, and discussion by an interacting group of professionals. Feldman calls this enhanced normal practice. In normal practice, a reflective teacher considers the events of the day and changes methods accordingly. The enhancement comes from the discussion within the collaborative group, where the outside academics have a useful role. There is public and systematic critical inquiry.

PEEL expanded into other schools in Australia, then abroad – most notably in Sweden and Denmark, where, under the Scandinavian acronym PLAN (Projekt for Lärande under eget Ansvar), it is present in more than one hundred schools. The PEEL teachers have generated an offshoot, with yet another acronym, PAVOT – Perspectives And Voice Of the Teacher. PAVOT is a means of collecting and disseminating accounts of innovations and their outcomes.

PEEL, PAVOT and PLAN are development, the application of theory, rather than research, yet they have elements of research and have produced the sorts of insight that research is intended to feed back to theory. The projects raise important issues for research. The teachers' accounts differ markedly from the reports of the rigorous studies of the 1960s and 1970s, in which instructional treatments were predetermined and there were formal measures of outcomes. Instead, the accounts describe events and their effects on what the teacher and students did in reaction, and evaluation is mainly limited to subjective impressions of the participants.

Each single account can be dismissed as invalid and inconclusive, yet collectively they carry conviction. From the accounts, White (1992) derived a number of principles of teaching:

> *Vocabulary*   Knowledge of terms for processes of learning improves a student's rate of acquisition of learning strategies.

> *Innovation*   During innovation, things get worse before they get better. Teachers need time to develop and become skilled at new practices, and students need time to learn how to benefit from them.

> *Matching*   Teaching method and learning style must match for effective learning of content, but in order for new strategies of learning to develop they must not always match.

> *Minimum expenditure of energy, and variation*   People expend as little energy as they need to, and frequently-repeated actions become automatic. Hence variation in activity is essential for the maintenance of good learning.

> *Maximum opportunity*   The pace and style of each lesson must be chosen to give students the maximum opportunity to learn.

> *Support*   Support is essential for overt good learning behaviour, while criticism destroys it.

Another outcome of PEEL is a set of indicators of purposeful learning, termed Good Learning Behaviours. Examples are: Plans a general strategy before starting a task; Seeks links between activities and ideas; Independently seeks further information; Asks relevant questions; Offers ideas, new insights and explanations; Reacts to comments of other students. Audio-recordings and transcripts for lessons of traditional stamp in science contain about five identifiable instances of Good Learning Behaviours per 40-minute lesson, whereas by the fourth year of PEEL, Mitchell's lessons with 15-year-old students contained about ten times as many (White and Mitchell 1993).

Early on, the PEEL teachers found that any single method of teaching, no matter how good, if used alone soon became ineffective. Variety is essential to maintain Good Learning Behaviours and metacognition. Although versions of that principle have long been current, there have been few specifics on how to implement it. A major practical outcome of PEEL is the invention or adaptation of more than a hundred procedures for encouraging purposeful learning. Mitchell and Mitchell (1992) describe seventy-six.

Students' Intuitions and Science Instruction

A key tenet of information processing and constructivist theories is that prior knowledge is an important factor in learning, for it affects the operations of selection, translation, and linking. Students' Intuitions and Science Instruction is a study of how science lessons can incorporate students' prior knowledge.

Like PEEL and CASE, (SI)[2] is a partnership of teachers and academics. It involved three of each.

In the first year of the project, the teachers experimented with methods for identifying and making use of students' ideas. As in PEEL, the methods were not predetermined or rigid, but were altered to meet circumstances and through experience. Also as in PEEL, the academics did not provide direction but were useful reactants in discussions.

The group found that it took a year to learn how to explain to each other the insights and the frustrations for each experience. This learning required evolution of a common language: 'Now it seems clear that this time period of close to a year was necessary in order to negotiate among one another the unique personal meanings that underlie many of the terms that were used in these group meetings.' (Erickson 1991: 233). If this small group that met often took so long to understand what each other meant, it is not surprising that teachers do not grasp immediately the practical significance of the printed outcomes of a research study in which they had no part.

It is significant that the group had to develop, not simply import, the meanings for terms that then enabled them to relate theory, research, principles of teaching and practice. This raises problems for the dissemination of research outcomes. The problems should not, however, be insuperable. Proliferation of reflective accounts of teaching and learning, either by individuals or groups, as in PAVOT, should overcome them.

Erickson concludes that, although diversity of contexts and purposes militates against the formulation of a definitive set of principles, some general ones can be asserted. Among them is that collaboration is essential for the improvement of teaching and learning. Erickson notes that collaboration involves various pairings, and that it occurs at several levels of educational systems. At the classroom level, there has to be collaboration between student and student, teacher and student, teacher and teacher, and teacher and university academic; at the school level between teacher and administration; and at the district level between school and school, district and district, and district and university. These collaborations parallel other conclusions, which are supported by PEEL, that there must be mutual trust and openness, and a recognition that teaching and learning require a taking of risks that must be shared in collaborations. Risk needs to be balanced by support, so there must be personal and intellectual respect for learners; indeed, all partners in the collaborations must be seen as learners.

In projects like CASE, and even more so with PEEL and (SI)[2], the problems of application of research are largely absent, since the research is part of the normal operation of the classroom. The separation of research and practice has vanished. This is the implementation of Hargreaves' (1996) plea for reaching to become a research-based profession through the involvement of practitioners in research. We should recognize that this implementation required, and will continue to require, certain conditions to be met. Among the conditions are a subtle and elaborate theory of learning; an expansion of research methods, that admits as legitimate case studies and qualitative data from interviews and classroom observations; and support, from partnerships with university scholars, and from administrators who determine teachers' conditions of work, such as hours, class sizes, and the freedom to experiment. I take it as axiomatic that there will always be sufficient teachers with the ability, professional curiosity and commitment to do research and to make use of it, whenever these conditions are fulfilled.

References

Adey, P. and Shayer, M. (1994) *Really Raising Standards: Cognitive Intervention and Academic Achievement,* London: Routledge.

Baird, J. R. and Mitchell, I. J. (eds) (1986) *Improving the Quality of Teaching and Learning: An Australian Case Study – The PEEL Project,* Melbourne: Monash University.

Baird, J. R. and Northfield, J. R. (eds) (1992) *Learning from the PEEL Experience,* Melbourne: Monash University Faculty of Education.

Block, J. H. (ed.) (1971) *Mastery Learning: Theory and Practice,* New York: Holt, Rinehart and Winston.

Bloom, B. S. (1968) 'Learning for mastery', *Evaluation Comment,* Los Angeles: Center for the Study of Evaluation of Instructional Programs, UCLA.

Bloom, B. S. (1971) 'Mastery learning', in J. H. Block (ed.) *Mastery Learning: Theory and Practice,* New York: Holt, Rinehart and Winston.

Bruner, J. S. (1961) 'The act of discovery', *Harvard Educational Review* 31: 21–32.

Bruner, J. S., Goodnow, J. J. and Austin, G. A. (1956) *A Study of Thinking,* New York: John Wiley.

Carroll, J. B. (1963) 'A model of school learning', *Teachers College Record* 64: 723–33.

Cuban, L. (1993) *How Teachers Taught: Constancy and Change in American Classrooms 1890–1990* (second edition), New York: Teachers College Press.

Deese, J. E. (1958) *The Psychology of Learning* (second edition), New York: McGraw-Hill.

Eisner, E. W. (1984) 'Can educational research inform educational practice?', *Phi Delta Kappan* 65: 447–52.

Erickson, G. L. (1991) 'Collaborative inquiry and the professional development of science teachers', *Journal of Educational Thought* 25: 228–45.

Feldman, A. (1996) 'Enhancing the practice of physics teachers: mechanisms for the generation and sharing of knowledge and understanding in collaborative action research', *Journal of Research in Science Teaching* 33: 513–40.

Finn, C. E. (1988) 'What ails education research?', *Educational Researcher* 17(1): 5–8.

Flanders, N. A. (1970) *Analyzing Reaching Behaviour*, Reading, MA: Addison-Wesley.

Gabel, D. L. (ed.) (1994) *Handbook of Research on Science Teaching and Learning*, New York: Macmillan.

Gagné, R. M. (1962) 'The acquisition of knowledge', *Psychological Review* 69: 355–65.

Gagné, R. M. (1965) *The Conditions of Learning*, New York: Holt, Rinehart and Winston.

Gagné, R. M. and Paradise, N. E. (1961) 'Abilities and learning sets in knowledge acquisition', *Psychological Monographs* 75:14 (whole number 518).

Gardner, P. L. (1997) 'The roots of technology and science: a philosophical and historical view', *International Journal of Technology and Design Education* 7: 13–20.

Gilbert, J. K. (1994) 'On the significance of journals in science education: the case of *IJSE*', *International Journal of Science Education* 16: 375–84.

Glaser, R. (1991) 'The maturing of the relationship between the science of learning and cognition and educational practice', *Learning and Instruction* 1: 129–44.

Hargreaves, D. H. (1996) *Teaching as a Research-based Profession: Possibilities and Prospects*, Teacher Training Agency Annual Lecture.

Hennessy, S. (1993) 'Situated cognition and cognitive apprenticeship: implications for classroom learning', *Studies in Science Education* 22: 1–41.

Hermann, G. (1969) 'Learning by discovery: a critical review of studies', *Journal of Experimental Education* 38: 58–72.

Horton, P. B., McConney, A. A., Woods, A. L., Barry, K., Krout, H. L. and Doyle, B. K. (1993) 'A content analysis of research published in the *Journal of Research in Science Teaching* from 1985 through 1989', *Journal of Research in Science Teaching* 30: 857–69.

Hurd, P. D. (1991) 'Issues in linking research to science teaching', *Science Education* 75: 723–32.

Intermediate Science Curriculum Study (1970) *Probing the Natural World*, Morristown, NJ: Silver Burdett.

Kaestle, C. F. (1993) 'The awful reputation of educational research', *Educational Researcher*, 22(1): 23, 26–31.

Kennedy, M. M. (1997) 'The connection between research and practice', *Educational Researcher* 26(7): 4–12.

Koballa, T. R. (1992) 'Persuasion and attitude change in science education', *Journal of Research in Science Teaching* 29: 63–80.

Labaree, D. F. (1992) 'Power, knowledge, and the rationalization of teaching: a genealogy of the movement to professionalize teaching', *Harvard Educational Review* 62: 123–54.

Lortie, D. C. (1975) *School-teacher: a Sociological Study*, Chicago: University of Chicago Press.

Mitchell, J. and Mitchell, I. (1992) 'Some classroom procedures', in J. R. Baird and J. R. Northfield (eds) *Learning from the PEEL Experience*, Melbourne: Monash University Faculty of Education.

Novak, J. D. and Gowin, D. B. (1984) *Learning how to Learn*, Cambridge: Cambridge University Press.

Pfundt, H. and Duit, R. (1994) *Bibliography: Students' Alternative Frameworks and Science Education* (fourth edition), Kiel: Institute for Science Education, University of Kiel.

Ramsey, G. A. and Dale, L. G. (1971) 'The Australian Science Education Project: its rationale', *Australian Science Teachers Journal* 17(3): 51–7.

Shavelson, R. J. (1988) 'Contributions of educational research to policy and practice: constructing, challenging, changing cognition', *Educational Researcher* 17(7): 4–11.

Shavelson, R. J. and Berliner, D. C. (1988) 'Erosion of the education research infrastructure: a reply to Finn', *Educational Researcher* 17(1): 9–12.

Shulman, L. S. (1987) 'Knowledge and teaching: foundations of the new reform', *Harvard Educational Review* 57: 1–22.

Sroufe, G. E. (1997) 'Improving the "awful reputation" of education research', *Educational Researcher* 26(7): 26–8.

White, R. T. (1992) 'Raising the quality of learning: principles from long-term action research' in F. K. Oser, A. Dick, and J.-L. Party (eds) *Effective and Responsible Teaching: The New Synthesis*, San Francisco: Jossey-Bass.

White, R. T. (1997) 'The revolution in research on science teaching', Manuscript submitted for publication.

White, R. T. and Gunstone, R. F. (1992) *Probing Understanding*, London: Falmer.

White, R. T. and Mitchell, I. J. (1993) 'The promotion of good learning behaviours', paper given at the conference of the European Association for Research on Learning and Instruction, Aix-en-Provence.

Index